Database Systems:
Design and Management

Database Systems: Design and Management

Camila Thompson

MURPHY & MOORE
www.murphy-moorepublishing.com

Database Systems: Design and Management
Camila Thompson
ISBN: 978-1-63987-151-3 (Hardback)

MURPHY & MOORE

Published by Murphy & Moore Publishing,
1 Rockefeller Plaza,
New York City, NY 10020, USA

Cataloging-in-Publication Data

Database systems : design and management / Camila Thompson.
    p. cm.
Includes bibliographical references and index.
ISBN 978-1-63987-151-3
1. Databases. 2. Database design. 3. Database management. I. Thompson, Camila.
QA76.9.D32 D38 2022
005.74--dc23

For more information regarding Murphy & Moore Publishing and its products, please visit the publisher's website www.murphy-moorepublishing.com

TABLE OF CONTENTS

Permissions

Index

PREFACE

This book is a culmination of my many years of practice in this field. I attribute the success of this book to my support group. I would like to thank my parents who have showered me with unconditional love and support and my peers and professors for their constant guidance.

A database refers to systematic collection of data which is stored and can be accessed electronically. The software system that allows users to create, define and maintain this database is known as database management system. It collectively defines database, database model and database management system. It is used to manage internal operations of organizations and determine online interactions with suppliers and customers. They are categorized on the basis of the database model they support, the types of systems they run on, the language used to access it and on their internal engineering. The different types of databases are in-memory database, cloud database, deductive database, document-oriented database, federated database system, active database and data warehouses. Database systems are used in areas such as flight reservation systems, content management systems, library systems and computerized parts inventory systems. The topics covered in this extensive book deal with the core concepts related to database systems. Such selected concepts that redefine this discipline have been presented herein. The book is appropriate for those seeking detailed information in this area.

The details of chapters are provided below for a progressive learning:

Chapter – Introduction

An organized collection of data that can be stored and accessed from computer is referred to as a database. Some of its aspects are database language, graph database, NoSQL database, NewSQL database, etc. This chapter has been carefully written to provide an easy understanding of database.

Chapter – Concepts and Elements

Transaction log, database trigger, database index, database schema, database cursor, database partition, java and open database connectivity, query optimization, etc. are a few concepts and elements that fall under the domain of database systems. The topics elaborated in this chapter will help in gaining a better perspective of various elements and concepts of database systems.

Chapter – Database Models

A type of data model that determines the logical structure of a database is called a database model. It includes network model, object oriented data model, object relation model, associative model, generic data model, semantic data model, etc. All the aspects related to these database models have been carefully analyzed in this chapter.

Chapter – Database Management Systems

Database management system is a software that stores and retrieves users' data for managing it by taking appropriate security measures. A few of its types are hierarchical database, network database, relational database, object-oriented database, document database, etc. This chapter discusses database management system in detail.

Chapter – Relational Database Management Systems

Relational database is a set of a database structured to recognize relations between stored items of information. The program that creates, updates and administers a relational database is termed as relational database management system. This chapter closely examines the related concepts of relational database management system to provide an extensive understanding of the subject.

Camila Thompson

Introduction

1

- **Data**
- **Database**
- **Cloud Database**
- **Database Security**
- **Database Design**
- **Database Languages**
- **Database Query Languages**
- **Structure Query Language**

- **Unified Modeling Language**
- **Object-oriented Database**
- **Document-oriented Database**
- **Graph Database**
- **NoSQL Database**
- **NewSQL Database**

An organized collection of data that can be stored and accessed from computer is referred to as a database. Some of its aspects are database language, graph database, NoSQL database, NewSQL database, etc. This chapter has been carefully written to provide an easy understanding of database.

Data

Computer data is information processed or stored by a computer. This information may be in the form of text documents, images, audio clips, software programs, or other types of data. Computer data may be processed by the computer's CPU and is stored in files and folders on the computer's hard disk.

At its most rudimentary level, computer data is a bunch of ones and zeros, known as binary data. Because all computer data is in binary format, it can be created, processed, saved, and stored digitally. This allows data to be transferred from one computer to another using a network connection or various media devices. It also does not deteriorate over time or lose quality after being used multiple times.

Database

Database, also called electronic databases is a collection of data, or information that is specially organized for rapid search and retrieval by a computer. Databases are structured to facilitate the storage, retrieval, modification, and deletion of data in conjunction with various data-processing operations. A database management system (DBMS) extracts information from the database in response to queries.

A database is stored as a file or a set of files on magnetic disk or tape, optical disk, or some other secondary storage device. The information in these files may be broken down into records, each of which consists of one or more fields. Fields are the basic units of data storage, and each field typically contains information pertaining to one aspect or attribute of the entity described by the database. Records are also organized into tables that include information about relationships between its various fields. Although database is applied loosely to any collection of information in computer files, a database in the strict sense provides cross-referencing capabilities. Using keywords and various sorting commands, users can rapidly search, rearrange, group, and select the fields in many records to retrieve or create reports on particular aggregates of data.

Database records and files must be organized to allow retrieval of the information. Queries are the main way users retrieve database information. The power of a DBMS comes from its ability to define new relationships from the basic ones given by the tables and to use them to get responses to queries. Typically, the user provides a string of characters, and the computer searches the database for a corresponding sequence and provides the source materials in which those characters appear; a user can request, for example, all records in which the contents of the field for a person's last name is the word Smith.

The many users of a large database must be able to manipulate the information within it quickly at any given time. Moreover, large business and other organizations tend to build up many independent files containing related and even overlapping data, and their data-processing activities often require the linking of data from several files. Several different types of DBMS have been developed to support these requirements: flat, hierarchical, network, relational, and object-oriented.

Early systems were arranged sequentially (i.e., alphabetically, numerically, or chronologically); the development of direct-access storage devices made possible random access to data via indexes. In flat databases, records are organized according to a simple list of entities; many simple databases for personal computers are flat in structure.

The records in hierarchical databases are organized in a treelike structure, with each level of records branching off into a set of smaller categories. Unlike hierarchical databases, which provide single links between sets of records at different levels, network databases create multiple linkages between sets by placing links, or pointers, to one set of records in another; the speed and versatility of network databases have led to their wide use within businesses and in e-commerce. Relational databases are used where associations between files or records cannot be expressed by links; a simple flat list becomes one row of a table, or "relation", and multiple relations can be mathematically associated to yield desired information. Various iterations of SQL (Structured Query Language) are widely employed in DBMS for relational databases. Object-oriented databases store and manipulate more complex data structures, called "objects", which are organized into hierarchical classes that may inherit properties from classes higher in the chain; this database structure is the most flexible and adaptable.

The information in many databases consists of natural-language texts of documents; number-oriented databases primarily contain information such as statistics, tables, financial data, and raw scientific and technical data. Small databases can be maintained on personal-computer systems and may be used by individuals at home. These and larger databases have become increasingly important in business life, in part because they are now commonly designed to be integrated with other office software, including spreadsheet programs.

Typical commercial database applications include airline reservations, production management functions, medical records in hospitals, and legal records of insurance companies. The largest databases are usually maintained by governmental agencies, business organizations, and universities. These databases may contain texts of such materials as abstracts, reports, legal statutes, wire services, newspapers and journals, encyclopaedias, and catalogs of various kinds. Reference databases contain bibliographies or indexes that serve as guides to the location of information in books, periodicals, and other published literature. Thousands of these publicly accessible databases now exist, covering topics ranging from law, medicine, and engineering to news and current events, games, classified advertisements, and instructional courses.

Increasingly, formerly separate databases are being combined electronically into larger collections known as data warehouses. Businesses and government agencies then employ "data mining" software to analyze multiple aspects of the data for various patterns. For example, a government agency might flag for human investigation a company or individual that purchased a suspicious quantity of certain equipment or materials, even though the purchases were spread around the country or through various subsidiaries.

Data within the most common types of databases in operation today is typically modeled in rows and columns in a series of tables to make processing and data querying efficient. The data can then be easily accessed, managed, modified, updated, controlled, and organized. Most databases use structured query language (SQL) for writing and querying data.

What is Structured Query Language?

SQL is a programming language used by nearly all relational databases to query, manipulate, and define data, and to provide access control. SQL was first developed at IBM in the 1970s with Oracle as a major contributor, which led to implementation of the SQL ANSI standard, SQL has spurred many extensions from companies such as IBM, Oracle, and Microsoft. Although SQL is still widely used today, new programming languages are beginning to appear.

Evolution of the Database

Databases have evolved dramatically since their inception in the early 1960s. Navigational databases such as the hierarchical database (which relied on a tree-like model and allowed only a one-to-many relationship), and the network database (a more flexible model that allowed multiple relationships), were the original systems used to store and manipulate data. Although simple, these early systems were inflexible. In the 1980s, relational databases became popular, followed by object-oriented databases in the 1990s. More recently, NoSQL databases came about as a response to the growth of the internet and the need for faster speed and processing of unstructured data. Today, cloud databases and self-driving databases are breaking new ground when it comes to how data is collected, stored, managed, and utilized.

What is the Difference Between a Database and a Spreadsheet?

Databases and spreadsheets (such as Microsoft Excel) are both convenient ways to store information. The primary differences between the two are:

- How the data is stored and manipulated?

- Who can access the data?

- How much data can be stored?

Spreadsheets were originally designed for one user, and their characteristics reflect that. They're great for a single user or small number of users who don't need to do a lot of incredibly complicated data manipulation. Databases, on the other hand, are designed to hold much larger collections of organized information—massive amounts, sometimes. Databases allow multiple users at the same time to quickly and securely access and query the data using highly complex logic and language.

Types of Databases

The best database for a specific organization depends on how the organization intends to use the data. There are many different types of databases:

- Relational databases: Relational databases became dominant in the 1980s. Items in a relational database are organized as a set of tables with columns and rows. Relational database technology provides the most efficient and flexible way to access structured information.

- Object-oriented databases: Information in an object-oriented database is represented in the form of objects, as in object-oriented programming.

- Distributed databases: A distributed database consists of two or more files located in different sites. The database may be stored on multiple computers, located in the same physical location, or scattered over different networks.

- Data warehouses: A central repository for data, a data warehouse is a type of database specifically designed for fast query and analysis.

- NoSQL databases: A NoSQL, or nonrelational database, allows unstructured and semistructured data to be stored and manipulated (in contrast to a relational database, which defines how all data inserted into the database must be composed). NoSQL databases grew popular as web applications became more common and more complex.

- Graph databases: A graph database stores data in terms of entities and the relationships between entities.

- OLTP databases: An OLTP database is a speedy, analytic database designed for large numbers of transactions performed by multiple users.

These are only a few of the several dozen types of databases in use today. Other, less common databases are tailored to very specific scientific, financial, or other functions. In addition to the different database types, changes in technology development approaches and dramatic advances such as the cloud and automation are propelling databases in entirely new directions. Some of the latest databases include:

- Open source databases: An open source database system is one whose source code is open source; such databases could be SQL or NoSQL databases.

- Cloud databases: A cloud database is a collection of data, either structured or unstructured, that resides on a private, public, or hybrid cloud computing platform. There are two types of cloud database models: traditional and database as a service (DBaaS). With DBaaS, administrative tasks and maintenance are performed by a service provider.

- Multimodel database: Multimodel databases combine different types of database models into a single, integrated back end. This means they can accommodate various data types.

- Document/JSON database: Designed for storing, retrieving, and managing document-oriented information, document databases are a modern way to store data in JSON format rather than rows and columns.

- Self-driving databases: The newest and most groundbreaking type of database, self-driving databases (also known as autonomous databases) are cloud-based and use machine learning to automate database tuning, security, backups, updates, and other routine management tasks traditionally performed by database administrators.

Depending upon the usage requirements, there are following types of databases available in the market:

- Centralised database.
- Distributed database.
- Personal database.
- End-user database.
- Commercial database.
- NoSQL database.
- Operational database.
- Relational database.
- Cloud database.
- Object-oriented database.
- Graph database.

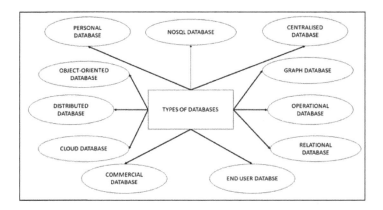

Centralised Database

The information (data) is stored at a centralized location and the users from different locations can access this data. This type of database contains application procedures that help the users to access the data even from a remote location.

Various kinds of authentication procedures are applied for the verification and validation of end users, likewise, a registration number is provided by the application procedures which keeps a track and record of data usage. The local area office handles this thing.

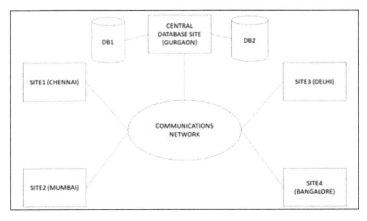

Distributed Database

Just opposite of the centralized database concept, the distributed database has contributions from the common database as well as the information captured by local computers also. The data is not at one place and is distributed at various sites of an organization. These sites are connected to each other with the help of communication links which helps them to access the distributed data easily.

You can imagine a distributed database as a one in which various portions of a database are stored in multiple different locations (physical) along with the application procedures which are replicated and distributed among various points in a network.

There are two kinds of distributed database, viz. homogenous and heterogeneous. The databases which have same underlying hardware and run over same operating systems and application procedures are known as homogeneous DDB, for eg. All physical locations in a DDB. Whereas, the operating systems, underlying hardware as well as application procedures can be different at various sites of a DDB which is known as heterogeneous DDB.

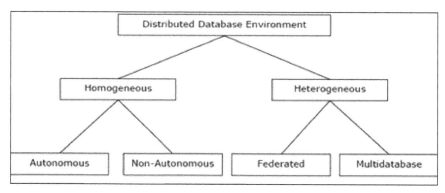

Personal Database

Data is collected and stored on personal computers which is small and easily manageable. The data is generally used by the same department of an organization and is accessed by a small group of people.

End User Database

The end user is usually not concerned about the transaction or operations done at various levels and is only aware of the product which may be a software or an application. Therefore, this is a shared database which is specifically designed for the end user, just like different levels' managers. Summary of whole information is collected in this database.

Commercial Database

These are the paid versions of the huge databases designed uniquely for the users who want to access the information for help. These databases are subject specific, and one cannot afford to maintain such a huge information. Access to such databases is provided through commercial links.

NoSQL Database

These are used for large sets of distributed data. There are some big data performance issues which are effectively handled by relational databases, such kind of issues are easily managed by NoSQL databases. There are very efficient in analyzing large size unstructured data that may be stored at multiple virtual servers of the cloud.

Operational Database

Information related to operations of an enterprise is stored inside this database. Functional lines like marketing, employee relations, customer service etc. require such kind of databases.

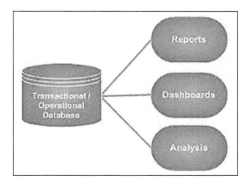

Relational Databases

These databases are categorized by a set of tables where data gets fit into a pre-defined category. The table consists of rows and columns where the column has an entry for data for a specific category and rows contains instance for that data defined according to the category. The Structured Query Language (SQL) is the standard user and application program interface for a relational database.

There are various simple operations that can be applied over the table which makes these databases easier to extend, join two databases with a common relation and modify all existing applications.

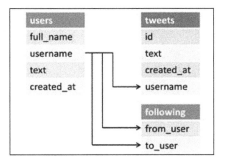

Object-oriented Databases

An object-oriented database is a collection of object-oriented programming and relational database. There are various items which are created using object-oriented programming languages like C++, Java which can be stored in relational databases, but object-oriented databases are well-suited for those items.

An object-oriented database is organized around objects rather than actions, and data rather than logic. For example, a multimedia record in a relational database can be a definable data object, as opposed to an alphanumeric value.

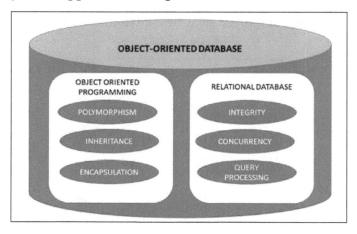

Graph Databases

The graph is a collection of nodes and edges where each node is used to represent an entity and each edge describes the relationship between entities. A graph-oriented database, or graph database, is a type of NoSQL database that uses graph theory to store, map and query relationships.

Graph databases are basically used for analyzing interconnections. For example, companies might use a graph database to mine data about customers from social media.

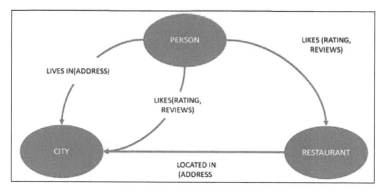

Cloud Database

A cloud database is a database service built and accessed through a cloud platform. It serves many of the same functions as a traditional database with the added flexibility of cloud computing. Users install software on a cloud infrastructure to implement the database.

Key features:

- A database service built and accessed through a cloud platform.

- Enables enterprise users to host databases without buying dedicated hardware.

- Can be managed by the user or offered as a service and managed by a provider.

- Can support relational databases (including MySQL and PostgreSQL) and NoSQL databases (including MongoDB and Apache CouchDB).

- Accessed through a web interface or vendor-provided API.

Why use Cloud Databases?

- Ease of access: Users can access cloud databases from virtually anywhere, using a vendor's API or web interface.

- Scalability: Cloud databases can expand their storage capacities on run-time to accommodate changing needs. Organizations only pay for what they use.

- Disaster recovery: In the event of a natural disaster, equipment failure or power outage, data is kept secure through backups on remote servers.

Considerations for Cloud Databases

- Control options: Users can opt for a virtual machine image managed like a traditional database or a provider's database as a service (DBaaS).

- Database technology: SQL databases are difficult to scale but very common. NoSQL databases scale more easily but do not work with some applications.

- Security: Most cloud database providers encrypt data and provide other security measures; organizations should research their options.

- Maintenance: When using a virtual machine image, one should ensure that IT staffers can maintain the underlying infrastructure.

Database Security

Data is a valuable entity that must have to be firmly handled and managed as with any economic resource. So some part or all of the commercial data may have tactical importance to their respective organization and hence must have to be kept protected and confidential. There is a range of computer-based controls that are offered as countermeasures to these threats.

Database security is the technique that protects and secures the database against intentional or accidental threats. Security concerns will be relevant not only to the data resides in an organization's database: the breaking of security may harm other parts of the system, which may ultimately affect the database structure. Consequently, database security includes hardware parts, software parts, human resources, and data. To efficiently do the uses of security needs appropriate controls, which are distinct in a specific mission and purpose for the system. The requirement for getting proper security while often having been neglected or overlooked in the past days; is now more and more thoroughly checked by the different organizations.

We consider database security about the following situations:

- Theft and fraudulent.

- Loss of confidentiality or secrecy.

- Loss of data privacy.

- Loss of data integrity.

- Loss of availability of data.

These listed circumstances mostly signify the areas in which the organization should focus on reducing the risk that is the chance of incurring loss or damage to data within a database. In some conditions, these areas are directly related such that an activity that leads to a loss in one area may also lead to a loss in another since all of the data within an organization are interconnected.

What is a Threat?

Any situation or event, whether intentionally or incidentally, can cause damage, which can reflect an adverse effect on the database structure and, consequently, the organization. A threat may occur by a situation or event involving a person or the action or situations that are probably to bring harm to an organization and its database.

The degree that an organization undergoes as a result of a threat's following which depends upon some aspects, such as the existence of countermeasures and contingency plans. Let us take an example where you have a hardware failure that occurs corrupting secondary storage; all processing activity must cease until the problem is resolved.

Computer-based Controls

The different forms of countermeasure to threats on computer systems range from physical controls to managerial procedures. In spite of the range of computer-based controls that are preexisting, it is worth noting that, usually, the security of a DBMS is merely as good as that of the operating system, due to the close association among them.

Most of the computer-based database security are listed below:

- Access authorization.
- Access controls.
- Views.
- Backup and recovery of data.
- Data integrity.
- Encryption of data.
- RAID technology.

What is Access Control?

The usual way of supplying access controls to a database system is dependent on the granting and revoking of privileges within the database. A privilege allows a user to create or access some database object or to run some specific DBMS utilities. Privileges are granted users to achieve the tasks required for those jobs.

The database provides various types of access controls:

- Discretionary Access Control (DAC).
- Mandatory Access Control (MAC).

Backup and Recovery

Every Database Management System should offer backup facilities to help with the recovery of a database after a failure. It is always suitable to make backup copies of the database and log files at the regular period and for ensuring that the copies are in a secure location. In the event of a failure that renders the database unusable, the backup copy and the details captured in the log file are used to restore the database to the latest possible consistent state.

Database Design

Database design is a collection of processes that facilitate the designing, development, implementation and maintenance of enterprise data management systems. Properly designed database are easy to maintain, improves data consistency and are cost effective in terms of disk storage space. The database designer decides how the data elements correlate and what data must be stored.

The main objectives of database designing are to produce logical and physical designs models of the proposed database system.

The logical model concentrates on the data requirements and the data to be stored independent of physical considerations. It does not concern itself with how the data will be stored or where it will be stored physically.

The physical data design model involves translating the logical design of the database onto physical media using hardware resources and software systems such as database management systems (DBMS).

Why Database Design is Important?

It helps produce database systems:

- That meets the requirements of the users.

- Have high performance.

Database designing is crucial to high performance database system.

Database Development Life Cycle

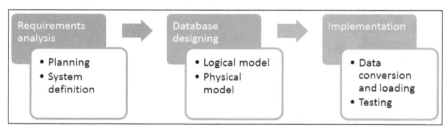

The database development life cycle has a number of stages that are followed when developing database systems.

The steps in the development life cycle do not necessary have to be followed religiously in a sequential manner.

On small database systems, the database system development life cycle is usually very simple and does not involve a lot of steps.

Requirements Analysis

- Planning: This stages concerns with planning of entire Database Development Life Cycle. It takes into consideration the Information Systems strategy of the organization.

- System definition: This stage defines the scope and boundaries of the proposed database system.

Database Designing

- Logical model: This stage is concerned with developing a database model based on requirements. The entire design is on paper without any physical implementations or specific DBMS considerations.

- Physical model: This stage implements the logical model of the database taking into account the DBMS and physical implementation factors.

Implementation

- Data conversion and loading: This stage is concerned with importing and converting data from the old system into the new database.

- Testing: This stage is concerned with the identification of errors in the newly implemented system.It checks the database against requirement specifications.

Database Languages

Database languages are used to read, update and store data in a database. There are several such languages that can be used for this purpose; one of them is SQL (Structured Query Language).

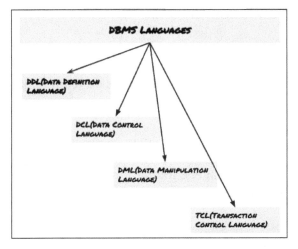

Data Definition Language

DDL is used for specifying the database schema. It is used for creating tables, schema, indexes, constraints etc. in database. The operations that we can perform on database using DDL:

- To create the database instance – CREATE.

- To alter the structure of database – ALTER.

- To drop database instances – DROP.

- To delete tables in a database instance – TRUNCATE.

- To rename database instances – RENAME.

- To drop objects from database such as tables – DROP.

- To Comment – COMMENT.

All of these commands either defines or update the database schema that's why they come under Data Definition language.

Data Manipulation Language

DML is used for accessing and manipulating data in a database. The following operations on database come under DML:

- To read records from tables – SELECT.

- To insert records into the tables – INSERT.

- Update the data in tables – UPDATE.

- Delete all the records from the table – DELETE.

Data Control Language

DCL is used for granting and revoking user access on a database:

- To grant access to user – GRANT.

- To revoke access from user – REVOKE.

In practical data definition language, data manipulation language and data control languages are not separate language, rather they are the parts of a single database language such as SQL.

Transaction Control Language

The changes in the database that we made using DML commands are either performed or rollbacked using TCL:

- To persist the changes made by DML commands in database – COMMIT.

- To rollback the changes made to the database – ROLLBACK.

Database Query Languages

Database query languages allow the creation of database tables, read/write access to those tables, and many other functions. Database query languages have at least two subsets of commands: Data Definition Language (DDL) and Data Manipulation Language (DML). DDL is used to create, modify, and delete tables. DML is use to query and update data stored in the tables.

The most popular relational database query language is SQL (Structured Query Language), created by IBM in 1974. Many types of SQL exist, including MySQL, PostgreSQL, PL/SQL (Procedural Language/SQL, used by Oracle), T-SQL and ANSI SQL (used by Microsoft SQL), and many others.

Common SQL commands include:

- CREATE: create a table.

- SELECT: select a record.

- DELETE: delete a record (or a whole table).

- INSERT: insert a record.

- UPDATE: change a record.

Tables are created with the CREATE command, which uses Data Definition Language to describe the format of the table that is being created. An example of a Data Manipulation Language command is SELECT, which is used to search and choose data from a table. The following SELECT command could be used to create the database view:

```
SELECT * FROM Employees WHERE Title = "Detective"
```

This means: show any ("*") records where the Title is "Detective".

A query language provides a way to ask a question. The question is posed to a system that processes the query and replies with an answer. That answer can come in many forms—a Yes or No (ASK), a table (SELECT), or, as we just saw, a set of triples (CONSTRUCT). It is reasonable to wonder, where does this information go? For a Yes/No answer or a table, one can easily imagine a user interface like a web page that displays that information in some form. But one could also imagine integrating the information into another application—putting a table into Excel or injecting it into a database.

In some sense, it isn't the job of the query language to specify this. The query language just provides a formalism to describe the meaning of a query, i.e., it specifies what answers a particular query will return, given the data. Most query languages are accompanied with (often proprietary) scripting languages that provide ways to specify what happens to the results of the queries. Sophisticated RDF query systems provide workbenches where users are afforded a variety of options for what to do with constructed triples:

- Insert the constructed triples back into the original data source that the query was run against.

- Store the constructed triples as a separate graph, for processing further triples.

- Store the constructed triples into a new dataset (in another database) for publication.

- Serialize the results in some standard form, and save them to a file.

Any of these options could be appropriate, depending on a user's future plans for the data. These options are similar to information storage options available in other query systems.

In a web service context, there is another option for what to do with the constructed triples. The "P" in SPARQL stands for "protocol". Since SPARQL was designed as a query language for the Web, it includes a protocol for publishing the results of a query to the web. The protocol can deal with binary results (from Yes/No ASK queries), tabular results (from SELECT queries), and, of course, triples (from CONSTRUCT queries). This means that the output of a SPARQL query could be used on the Web as input for another query (since a SPARQL query retrieves information from a set of triples, and CONSTRUCT provides a set of triples). A server for the SPARQL protocol is called a SPARQL Endpoint—it is a service that accepts SPARQL queries, and returns results, according to the details of the protocol. Many SPARQL Endpoints are available today, providing information about a variety of subjects.

A SPARQL endpoint is the most web-friendly way to provide access to RDF data. The endpoint is identified with a URL and provides flexible access to its data set. It is common to speak of "wrapping" some data set with a SPARQL endpoint—that is, providing a service that responds to the SPARQL protocol, providing access to that data set.

Structure Query Language

Structure Query Language (SQL) is a database query language used for storing and managing data in Relational DBMS. SQL was the first commercial language introduced for E.F Codd's Relational model of database. Today almost all RDBMS (MySql, Oracle, Infomix, Sybase, MS Access) use SQL as the standard database query language. SQL is used to perform all types of data operations in RDBMS.

SQL Command

SQL defines following ways to manipulate data stored in an RDBMS.

DDL: Data Definition Language

This includes changes to the structure of the table like creation of table, altering table, deleting a table etc.

All DDL commands are auto-committed. That means it saves all the changes permanently in the database.

Command	Description
create	to create new table or database
alter	for alteration
truncate	delete data from table
drop	to drop a table
rename	to rename a table

DML: Data Manipulation Language

DML commands are used for manipulating the data stored in the table and not the table itself.

DML commands are not auto-committed. It means changes are not permanent to database, they can be rolled back.

Command	Description
insert	to insert a new row
update	to update existing row
delete	to delete a row
merge	merging two rows or two tables

TCL: Transaction Control Language

These commands are to keep a check on other commands and their affect on the database. These commands can annul changes made by other commands by rolling the data back to its original state. It can also make any temporary change permanent.

Command	Description
commit	to permanently save

rollback	to undo change
savepoint	to save temporarily

DCL: Data Control Language

Data control language is the commands to grant and take back authority from any database user.

Command	Description
grant	grant permission of right
revoke	take back permission

DQL: Data Query Language

Data query language is used to fetch data from tables based on conditions that we can easily apply.

Command	Description
select	retrieve records from one or more table

Unified Modeling Language

Unified Modeling Language (UML) is a general purpose modelling language. The main aim of UML is to define a standard way to visualize the way a system has been designed. It is quite similar to blueprints used in other fields of engineering.

UML is not a programming language, it is rather a visual language. We use UML diagrams to portray the behavior and structure of a system. UML helps software engineers, businessmen and system architects with modelling, design and analysis. The Object Management Group (OMG) adopted Unified Modelling Language as a standard in 1997. Its been managed by OMG ever since. International Organization for Standardization (ISO) published UML as an approved standard in 2005. UML has been revised over the years and is reviewed periodically.

- Complex applications need collaboration and planning from multiple teams and hence require a clear and concise way to communicate amongst them.

- Businessmen do not understand code. So UML becomes essential to communicate with non programmers essential requirements, functionalities and processes of the system.

- A lot of time is saved down the line when teams are able to visualize processes, user interactions and static structure of the system.

UML is linked with object oriented design and analysis. UML makes the use of elements and forms associations between them to form diagrams.

Diagrams in UML can be broadly classified as:

- Structural Diagrams: Capture static aspects or structure of a system. Structural Diagrams include. Component Diagrams, Object Diagrams, Class Diagrams and Deployment Diagrams.

- Behavior Diagrams: Capture dynamic aspects or behavior of the system. Behavior diagrams include. Use Case Diagrams, State Diagrams, Activity Diagrams and Interaction Diagrams.

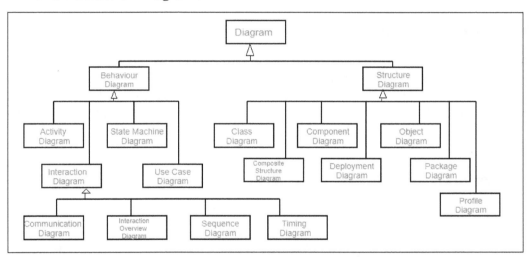

Object Oriented Concepts used in UML

- Class: A class defines the blue print i.e. structure and functions of an object.

- Objects: Objects help us to decompose large systems and help us to modularize our system. Modularity helps to divide our system into understandable components so that we can build our system piece by piece. An object is the fundamental unit (building block) of a system which is used to depict an entity.

- Inheritance: Inheritance is a mechanism by which child classes inherit the properties of their parent classes.

- Abstraction: Mechanism by which implementation details are hidden from user.

- Encapsulation: Binding data together and protecting it from the outer world is referred to as encapsulation.

- Polymorphism: Mechanism by which functions or entities are able to exist in different forms.

Additions in UML 2.0

- Software developments methodologies like agile have been incorporated and scope of original UML specification has been broadened.

- Originally UML specified 9 diagrams. UML 2.x has increased the number of diagrams from 9 to 13. The four diagrams that were added are: timing diagram, communication diagram, interaction overview diagram and composite structure diagram. UML 2.x renamed statechart diagrams to state machine diagrams.

- UML 2.x added the ability to decompose software system into components and sub-components.

Structural UML Diagrams

- Class Diagram: The most widely use UML diagram is the class diagram. It is the building block of all object oriented software systems. We use class diagrams to depict the static structure of a system by showing system's classes,their methods and attributes. Class diagrams also help us identify relationship between different classes or objects.

- Composite Structure Diagram: We use composite structure diagrams to represent the internal structure of a class and its interaction points with other parts of the system. A composite structure diagram represents relationship between parts and their configuration which determine how the classifier (class, a component, or a deployment node) behaves. They represent internal structure of a structured classifier making the use of parts, ports, and connectors. We can also model collaborations using composite structure diagrams. They are similar to class diagrams except they represent individual parts in detail as compared to the entire class.

- Object Diagram: An Object Diagram can be referred to as a screenshot of the instances in a system and the relationship that exists between them. Since object diagrams depict behaviour when objects have been instantiated, we are able to study the behaviour of the system at a particular instant. An object diagram is similar to a class diagram except it shows the instances of classes in the system. We depict actual classifiers and their relationships making the use of class diagrams. On the other hand, an Object Diagram represents specific instances of classes and relationships between them at a point of time.

- Component Diagram: Component diagrams are used to represent the how the physical components in a system have been organized. We use them for modelling implementation details. Component Diagrams depict the structural relationship between software system elements and help us in understanding if functional requirements have been covered by planned development. Component Diagrams become essential to use when we design and build complex systems. Interfaces are used by components of the system to communicate with each other.

- Deployment Diagram: Deployment Diagrams are used to represent system hardware and its software. It tells us what hardware components exist and what software components run on them. We illustrate system architecture as distribution of software artifacts over distributed targets. An artifact is the information that is generated by system software. They are primarily used when a software is being used, distributed or deployed over multiple machines with different configurations.

- Package Diagram: We use Package Diagrams to depict how packages and their elements have been organized. A package diagram simply shows us the dependencies between different packages and internal composition of packages. Packages help us to organise UML diagrams into meaningful groups and make the diagram easy to understand. They are primarily used to organise class and use case diagrams.

Behavior Diagrams

- State Machine Diagrams: A state diagram is used to represent the condition of the system or part of the system at finite instances of time. It's a behavioral diagram and it represents the behavior using finite state transitions. State diagrams are also referred to as State machines and State-chart Diagrams. These terms are often used interchangeably. So simply, a state diagram is used to model the dynamic behavior of a class in response to time and changing external stimuli.

- Activity Diagrams: We use Activity Diagrams to illustrate the flow of control in a system. We can also use an activity diagram to refer to the steps involved in the execution of a use case. We model sequential and concurrent activities using activity diagrams. So, we basically depict workflows visually using an activity diagram. An activity diagram focuses on condition of flow and the sequence in which it happens. We describe or depict what causes a particular event using an activity diagram.

- Use Case Diagrams: Use Case Diagrams are used to depict the functionality of a system or a part of a system. They are widely used to illustrate the functional requirements of the system and its interaction with external agents(actors). A use case is basically a diagram representing different scenarios where the system can be used. A use case diagram gives us a high level view of what the system or a part of the system does without going into implementation details.

- Sequence Diagram: A sequence diagram simply depicts interaction between objects in a sequential order i.e. the order in which these interactions take place.We can also use the terms event diagrams or event scenarios to refer to a sequence diagram. Sequence diagrams describe how and in what order the objects in a system function. These diagrams are widely used by businessmen and software developers to document and understand requirements for new and existing systems.

- Communication Diagram: A Communication Diagram(known as Collaboration Diagram in UML 1.x) is used to show sequenced messages exchanged between objects. A communication diagram focuses primarily on objects and their relationships. We can represent similar information using Sequence diagrams,however, communication diagrams represent objects and links in a free form.

- Timing Diagram: Timing Diagram are a special form of Sequence diagrams which are used to depict the behavior of objects over a time frame. We use them to show time and duration constraints which govern changes in states and behavior of objects.

- Interaction Overview Diagram: An Interaction Overview Diagram models a sequence of actions and helps us simplify complex interactions into simpler occurrences. It is a mixture of activity and sequence diagrams.

Logical Database Design with Unified Modeling Language

UML modeling is based on object-oriented programming principals. UML defines a standard set of modeling diagrams for all stages of developing a software system.

The basic difference between the entity-relationship model and the UML model is that, instead of designing entities as this information illustrates, you model objects. Conceptually, UML diagrams are like the blueprints for the design of a software development project.

Some examples of UML diagrams are listed below:

Class

Identify high-level entities, known as classes. A *class* describes a set of objects that have the same attributes. A class diagram shows the relationships between classes.

Use Case

Presents a high-level view of a system from the user's perspective. A *use case* diagram defines the interactions between users and applications or between applications. These diagrams graphically depict system behavior. You can work with use-case diagrams to capture system requirements, learn how the system works, and specify system behavior.

Activity

Models the workflow of a business process, typically by defining rules for the sequence of activities in the process. For example, an accounting company can use activity diagrams to model financial transactions.

Interaction

Shows the required sequence of interactions between objects. Interaction diagrams can include sequence diagrams and collaboration diagrams.

- Sequence diagrams show object interactions in a time-based sequence that establishes the roles of objects and helps determine class responsibilities and interfaces.

- Collaboration diagrams show associations between objects that define the sequence of messages that implement an operation or a transaction.

Component

Shows the dependency relationships between components, such as main programs, and subprograms.

Many available tools from the WebSphere and Rational product families ease the task of creating a UML model. Developers can graphically represent the architecture of a database and how it interacts with applications using the following UML modeling tools:

- WebSphere Business Integration Workbench, which provides a UML modeler for creating standard UML diagrams.

- A WebSphere Studio Application Developer plug-in for modeling Java and web services applications and for mapping the UML model to the entity-relationship model.

- Rational Rose Data Modeler, which provides a modeling environment that connects database designers who use entity-relationship modeling with developers of OO applications.

- Rational Rapid Developer, an end-to-end modeler and code generator that provides an environment for rapid design, integration, construction, and deployment of web, wireless, and portal-based business applications.

- IBM Rational Data Architect (RDA) has rich functionality that gives data professionals the ability to design a relational or federated database, and perform impact analysis across models.

Similarities exist between components of the entity-relationship model and UML diagrams. For example, the class structure corresponds closely to the entity structure.

Using the modeling tool Rational Rose Data Modeler, developers use a specific type of diagram for each type of development model:

- Business models: Use case diagram, activity diagram, sequence diagram.

- Logical data models or application models: Class diagram.

- Physical data models: Data model diagram.

The logical data model provides an overall view of the captured business requirements as they pertain to data entities. The data model diagram graphically represents the physical data model. The physical data model uses the logical data model's captured requirements, and applies them to specific DBMS languages. Physical data models also capture the lower-level detail of a DBMS database.

Database designers can customize the data model diagram from other UML diagrams, which enables them to work with concepts and terminology, such as columns, tables, and relationships, with which they are already familiar. Developers can also transform a logical data model into to a physical data model.

Because the data model diagram includes diagrams for modeling an entire system, it enables database designers, application developers, and other development team members to share and track business requirements throughout the development process. For example, database designers can capture information, such as constraints, triggers, and indexes directly on the UML diagram. Developers can also transfer between object and data models and use basic transformation types such as many-to-many relationships.

Object-oriented Database

An object-oriented database is a collection of object-oriented programming and relational database. There are various items which are created using object-oriented programming languages like C++, Java which can be stored in relational databases, but object-oriented databases are well-suited for those items. An object-oriented database is organized around objects rather than actions, and data rather than logic. For example, a multimedia record in a relational database can be a definable data object, as opposed to an alphanumeric value.

Object database management systems (ODBMSs) are based on objects in object-oriented programing (OOP). In OOP, an entity is represented as an object and objects are stored in memory. Objects have members such as fields, properties, and methods. Objects also have a life cycle that includes the creation of an object, use of an object, and deletion of an object. OOP has key characteristics, encapsulation, inheritance, and polymorphism. Today, there are many popular OOP languages such as C++, Java, C#, Ruby, Python, JavaScript, and Perl.

The idea of object databases was originated in 1985 and today has become common for various common OOP languages, such as C++, Java, C#, Smalltalk, and LISP. Common examples are Smalltalk is used in GemStone, LISP is used in Gbase, and COP is used in Vbase.

Object databases are commonly used in applications that require high performance, calculations, and faster results. Some of the common applications that use object databases are real-time systems, architectural & engineering for 3D modeling, telecommunications, and scientific products, molecular science, and astronomy.

Advantages of Object Databases

ODBMS provide persistent storage to objects. Imagine creating objects in your program and saving them as it is in a database and reading back from the database.

In a typical relational database, the program data is stored in rows and columns. To store and read that data and convert it into program objects in memory requires reading data, loading data into objects, and storing it in memory. Imagine creating a class in your program and saving it as it is in a database, reading back and start using it again.

Object databases bring permanent persistent to objects. Objects can be stored in persistent storage forever.

In typical RDBMS, there is a layer of object-relational mapping that maps database schemas with objects in code. Reading and mapping an object database data to the objects is direct without any API or OR tool. Hence faster data access and better performance.

Some object database can be used in multiple languages. For example, Gemstone database supports C++, Smalltalk and Java programming languages.

Drawbacks of Object Databases

- Object databases are not as popular as RDBMS. It is difficult to find object DB developers.

- Not many programming language support object databases.

- RDBMS have SQL as a standard query language. Object databases do not have a standard.

- Object databases are difficult to learn for non-programmers.

Cache

InterSystems's Caché is a high-performance object database. Caché database engine is a set of services including data storage, concurrency management, transactions, and process management. You can think of the Caché engine as a powerful database toolkit.

Caché is also a full-featured relational database. All the data within a Caché database is available as true relational tables and can be queried and modified using standard SQL via ODBC, JDBC, or object methods. Caché is one of the fastest, most reliable, and most scalable relational databases.

Cache offers the following features:

- The ability to model data as objects (each with an automatically created and synchronized native relational representation) while eliminating both the impedance mismatch between databases and object-oriented application environments as well as reducing the complexity of relational modelling.

- A simpler, object-based concurrency model.

- User-defined data types.

- The ability to take advantage of methods and inheritance, including polymorphism, within the database engine.

- Object-extensions for SQL to handle object identity and relationships.

- The ability to intermix SQL and object-based access within a single application, using each for what they are best suited.

- Control over the physical layout and clustering used to store data in order to ensure the maximum performance for applications.

Cache offers a broad set of tools, which include:

- ObjectScript, the language in which most of Caché is written.

- Native implementations of SQL, MultiValue, and Basic.

- A well-developed, built-in security model.

- A suite of technologies and tools that provide rapid development for database and web applications.

- Native, object-based XML and web services support.

- Device support (such as files, TCP/IP, printers).

- Automatic interoperability via Java, JDBC, ActiveX,.NET, C++, ODBC, XML, SOAP, Perl, Python, and more.

- Support for common Internet protocols: POP3, SMTP, MIME, FTP, and so on.

- A reusable user portal for your end users.

- Support for analyzing unstructured data.

- Support for Business Intelligence (BI).

- Built-in testing facilities.

Concept Base

ConceptBase.cc is a multi-user deductive database system with an object-oriented (data, class, metaclass, meta-metaclass, etc.) makes it a powerful tool for metamodeling and engineering of customized modeling languages. The system is accompanied by a highly configurable graphical user interface that builds upon the logic-based features of the ConceptBase.cc server.

ConceptBase.cc is developed by the ConceptBase Team at University of Skövde (HIS) and the University of Aachen (RWTH). ConceptBase.cc is available for Linux, Windows, and Mac OS-X. There is also a pre-configured virtual appliance that contains the executable system plus its sources plus the tools to compile them. The system is distributed under a FreeBSD-style license.

Db4o

b4o is the world's leading open-source object database for Java and.NET. Leverage fast native object persistence, ACID transactions, query-by-example, S.O.D.A object query API, automatic class schema evolution, small size.

ObjectDB

ObjectDB is a powerful Object-Oriented Database Management System (ODBMS). It is compact, reliable, easy to use and extremely fast. ObjectDB provides all the standard database management services (storage and retrieval, transactions, lock management, query processing, etc.) but in a way that makes development easier and applications faster.

- ObjectDB Database Key Features.

- 100% pure Java Object-Oriented Database Management System (ODBMS).

- No proprietary API - managed only by standard Java APIs (JPA 2 / JDO 2).

- Extremely fast - faster than any other JPA / JDO product.

- Suitable for database files ranging from kilobytes to terabytes.

- Supports both Client-Server mode and Embedded mode.

- Single JAR with no external dependencies.

- The database is stored as a single file.

- Advanced querying and indexing capabilities.

- Effective in heavy loaded multi-user environments.

- Can easily be embedded in applications of any type and size.

- Tested with Tomcat, Jetty, GlassFish, JBoss, and Spring.

Object Database++

Object Database++ (ODBPP) is an embeddable object-oriented database designed for server applications that require minimal external maintenance. It is written in C++ as a real-time ISAM level database with the ability to auto recover from system crashes while maintaining database integrity.

Objectivity/DB

Objectivity/DB is a scalable, high performance, distributed Object Database (ODBMS). It is extremely good at handling complex data, where there are many types of connections between objects and many variants.

Objectivity/DB runs on 32 or 64-bit processors running Linux, Mac OS X, UNIX (Oracle Solaris) or Windows.

There are C++, C#, Java and Python APIs.

All platform and language combinations are interoperable. For example, objects stored by a program using C++ on Linux can be read by a C# program on Windows and a Java program on Mac OS X.

Objectivity/DB generally runs on POSIX filesystems, but there are plugins that can be modified for other storage infrastructure.

Objectivity/DB client programs can be configured to run on a standalone laptop, networked workgroups, large clusters or in grids or clouds with no changes to the application code.

ObjectStore

ObjectStore is an enterprise object-oriented database management system for C++ and Java.

ObjectStore delivers multi-fold performance improvement by eliminating the middleware requirement to map and convert application objects into flat relational rows by directly persisting objects within an application into an object store.

ObjectStore eliminates need to flatten complex data for consumption in your application logic reducing the overhead of using a translation layer that converts complex objects into flat objects, dramatically improving performance and often entirely eliminating the need to manage a relational database system.

ObjectStore is OO storage that directly integrates with Java or C++ applications and treats memory and persistent storage as one – improving the performance of application logic while fully maintaining ACID compliance against the transactional and distributed load.

Versant Object-oriented Database

Versant Object-Oriented Database is an object database that supports native object persistence and used to build complex and high-performance data management systems.

Key Benefits:

- Real-time analytical performance.

- Big Data management.

- Cut development time by up to 40%.

- Significantly lower total ownership cost.

- High availability.

WakandaDB

WakandaDB is an object database and provides a native REST API to access interconnected DataClasses defined in Server-Side JavaScript. WakandaDB is the server within Wakanda which includes a dedicated, but not mandatory, Ajax Framework, and a dedicated IDE.

Object-relational Databases

Object-relational database (ORD), or object-relational database management systems (ORDBMS) are databases that support both objects and relational database features. OR databases are relational database management systems with the support of an object-oriented database model. That means, the entities are represented as objects and classes and OOP features such as inheritance are supported in database schemas and in the query language.

PostgreSQL is the most popular pure ORDBMS. Some popular databases including Microsoft SQL Server, Oracle, and IBM DB2 also support objects and can be considered as ORDBMS.

Document-oriented Database

A document-oriented database is a specific kind of database that works on the principle of dealing with 'documents' rather than strictly defined tables of information.

The document-oriented database plays an important role is aggregating data from documents and getting them into a searchable, organized form.

A document-oriented database, as a particular kind of NoSQL database, is able to 'parse' data from documents that store that data under certain 'keys,' with sophisticated support for retrieval.

For example, suppose one document has two names, one address, and a list of ages of a home's occupants. A second document might have four names, two addresses, and no age information. A document-oriented database will take the data in both and store them according to type, able to handle non-fixed length data sets.

Different document-oriented database products are available, some of them with free Apache licensing and other with proprietary licensing.

A document-oriented database or a NoSQL document store is a modern way to store data in JSON format rather than simple rows and columns. It allows you to express data in its natural form the way it's meant to be.

For the past 40 years, relational databases have dominated the database industry. Relational databases organize data in tables of rows and columns and generate relationships between them. These relationships are considered to be the logical connections between the tables and are defined on the basis of the data itself.

However relational databases were unable to cope up with the challenges stated below:

- Agile software development requires adaptable processes and quicker shipment of software. This means the underlying database should enable this methodology. In contrast, rows and columns are inherently rigid data structure. One column addition impacts the whole table.

- With relational databases, a change in the data model means a developer requests changes from a database administrator. This people-intensive process can take too long for emerging and growing companies that rely on speedy deployment.

- Lastly, data expressed in rows and columns is an unnatural way to store information. The reason being, a row in an RDBMS is just a flat data structure, with data divided into columns, whereas, data schemas are much more complex therefore demand more flexibility.

NoSQL Document-oriented Database

With such problems faced by data intensive and fast moving organizations, new technology solutions were demanded and the answer is NoSQL Document Databases. In contrast to rows and columns, NoSQL databases keep data in documents. These documents follow a minimum of standard format rules (so that the database can understand it for post processing). The format used could be JSON, XML, YAML etc. The JSON format is the format of choice for NoSQL databases, and for good reason. A JSON document is simply more compact and more readable.

JSON (JavaScript Object Notation) is a data representation format formulated by the JavaScript programming language. But because of its textual nature it is also used by all other programming languages.

JSON in NoSQL: A Flexible, Fluid and Rich Data Model

The beauty of JSON lies in its ease of use, by both humans and computers. The JSON format has three basic foundations:

- Key value pairs or attributes: Every value in JSON is stored in a key value pair. These pairs are sometimes referred to as attributes. The keys are simple strings and the values could be of any type e.g. int, float, double, boolean etc.

- Embedding JSON objects: Other than primitive types, values in a key value pair can also be other JSON objects allowing you to create a hierarchy of JSON Objects. Placing JSON objects inside another JSON object is called an "embedded data model" in document databases.

- Arrays: Arrays are a natural programming idiom in all programming languages and data structures, so why not store data the way it is expressed? The JSON format also supports storing arrays as values against a key.

```
                    Customer Document

"customer" =
{
    "id": "Customer:1",
    "firstName": "John",
    "lastName": "Wick",
    "age: 25,
    "address": {
            "country": "US",
            "city": "New York",
            "state": "NY"
            "street": "21 2nd Street",
        },
    "hobbies": { Football, Hiking },
    "phoneNumbers": [
        {
            "type": "Home",
            "number": "212 555-1234"
        },
        {
            "type": "Office",
            "number": "616 565-6789"
        }
    ]
}
```

Here you can see that the JSON document holds primitive types as values as well as other JSON objects and array types. What's interesting is that values can also host arrays of JSON objects. Thus JSON documents allow you to create a hierarchy of embedded JSON objects to an unlimited level. It's completely up to the user what shape he or she wants to give to the data stored in a NoSQL document database.

RDBMS vs. NoSQL Document Databases

With such great advantages of the JSON data format, let's re-visit the challenges relational databases face and how a document database overcomes them.

Accomodates Agile Software Development

Agile Software Development is a process built on principles which follow adaptive and evolutionary processes. Therefore, it is essential that all of the platforms taking part in the software process are responsive to the application changes required. NoSQL document databases are purpose built for this.

JSON documents are stored in a collection, a term identical to tables (that store rows and columns). At the time of inception of a collection there is no need to define the attributes. Thus if there is a need to change the schema, simply add new JSON documents following the new schema without affecting existing data.

Accomodates Faster Deployment Cycles

Document databases also eliminate the need for specific database modeling teams since the data schema is directly generated by the application. Therefore, document databases promote application driven data models. The.NET API of NosDB automatically generates the corresponding JSON schema with respect to the provided.NET objects. Thus it also eliminates the need for specific ORM libraries, making your applications lightweight.

Accomodates Rich Data Structures

In relational databases, you create relations between different tables and then perform JOIN queries repeatedly to obtain the same piece of information again and again. It would be faster to group these pieces of data together since they are repeatedly accessed together. JSON documents allow you to embed related documents allowing easy fetching of data in one single call. Therefore, storing data in the JSON format is truly a natural way to store information unlike the flat data structure of rows and columns.

Graph Database

A database designed to treat the relationships between data as equally important to the data itself. It is intended to hold data without constricting it to a pre-defined model.

Instead, the data is stored like we first draw it out – showing how each individual entity connects with or is related to others.

Why Graph Databases?

There are no isolated pieces of information, but rich, connected domains all around us. Only a database that natively embraces relationships is able to store, process, and query connections efficiently. While other databases compute relationships at query time through expensive JOIN operations, a graph database stores connections alongside the data in the model.

Accessing nodes and relationships in a native graph database is an efficient, constant-time operation and allows you to quickly traverse millions of connections per second per core.

Independent of the total size of your dataset, graph databases excel at managing highly-connected data and complex queries. With only a pattern and a set of starting points, graph databases explore the neighboring data around those initial starting points — collecting and aggregating information from millions of nodes and relationships — and leaving any data outside the search perimeter untouched.

The Property Graph Model

As with most technologies, there are few different approaches to what makes up the key components of a graph database. One such approach is the property graph model, where data is organized as nodes, relationships, and properties (data stored on the nodes or relationships).

Nodes are the entities in the graph. They can hold any number of attributes (key-value pairs) called properties. Nodes can be tagged with labels, representing their different roles in your domain. Node labels may also serve to attach metadata (such as index or constraint information) to certain nodes.

Relationships provide directed, named, semantically-relevant connections between two node entities (e.g. Employee WORKS_FOR Company). A relationship always has a direction, a type, a start node, and an end node. Like nodes, relationships can also have properties. In most cases, relationships have quantitative properties, such as weights, costs, distances, ratings, time intervals, or strengths. Due to the efficient way relationships are stored, two nodes can share any number or type of relationships without sacrificing performance. Although they are stored in a specific direction, relationships can always be navigated efficiently in either direction.

Building Blocks of the Property Graph Model

Neo4j

Neo4j is an open-source, NoSQL, native graph database that provides an ACID-compliant transactional backend for your applications. Initial development began in 2003, but it has been publicly available since 2007. The source code, written in Java and Scala, is available for free on GitHub or as a user-friendly desktop application download. Neo4j has both a Community Edition and Enterprise Edition of the database. The Enterprise Edition includes all that Community Edition has to offer, plus extra enterprise requirements such as backups, clustering, and failover abilities.

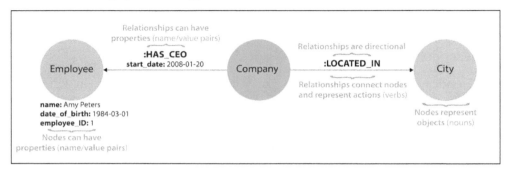

Neo4j is referred to as a native graph database because it efficiently implements the property graph model down to the storage level. This means that the data is stored exactly as you whiteboard it, and the database uses pointers to navigate and traverse the graph. In contrast to graph processing or in-memory libraries, Neo4j also provides full database characteristics, including ACID transaction compliance, cluster support, and runtime failover – making it suitable to use graphs for data in production scenarios.

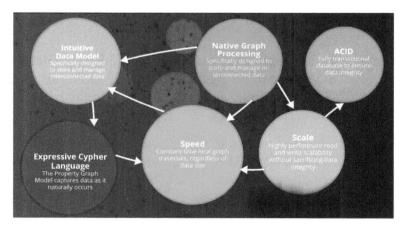

Some of the following particular features make Neo4j very popular among developers, architects, and DBAs:

- Cypher, a declarative query language similar to SQL, but optimized for graphs. Now used by other databases like SAP HANA Graph and Redis graph via the openCypher project.

- Constant time traversals in big graphs for both depth and breadth due to efficient representation of nodes and relationships. Enables scale-up to billions of nodes on moderate hardware.

- Flexible property graph schema that can adapt over time, making it possible to materialize and add new relationships later to shortcut and speed up the domain data when the business needs change.

- Drivers for popular programming languages, including Java, JavaScript,.NET, Python, and many more.

NoSQL Database

A NoSQL originally referring to non SQL or non relational is a database that provides a mechanism for storage and retrieval of data. This data is modeled in means other than the tabular relations used in relational databases. Such databases came into existence in the late 1960s, but did not obtain the NoSQL moniker until a surge of popularity in the early twenty-first century. NoSQL databases are used in real-time web applications and big data and their use are increasing over time. NoSQL systems are also sometimes called Not only SQL to emphasize the fact that they may support SQL-like query languages.

A NoSQL database includes simplicity of design, simpler horizontal scaling to clusters of machines and finer control over availability. The data structures used by NoSQL databases are different from those used by default in relational databases which makes some operations faster in NoSQL. The suitability of a given NoSQL database depends on the problem it should solve. Data structures used by NoSQL databases are sometimes also viewed as more flexible than relational database tables.

Many NoSQL stores compromise consistency in favor of availability, speed and partition tolerance. Barriers to the greater adoption of NoSQL stores include the use of low-level query languages, lack of standardized interfaces, and huge previous investments in existing relational databases. Most NoSQL stores lack true ACID(Atomicity, Consistency, Isolation, Durability) transactions but a few databases, such as MarkLogic, Aerospike, FairCom c-treeACE, Google Spanner (though technically a NewSQL database), Symas LMDB, and OrientDB have made them central to their designs.

Most NoSQL databases offer a concept of eventual consistency in which database changes are propagated to all nodes so queries for data might not return updated data immediately or might result in reading data that is not accurate which is a problem known as stale reads. Also some NoSQL systems may exhibit lost writes and other forms of data loss. Some NoSQL systems provide concepts such as write-ahead logging to avoid data loss. For distributed transaction processing across multiple databases, data consistency is an even bigger challenge. This is difficult for both NoSQL and relational databases.

Even current relational databases do not allow referential integrity constraints to span databases. There are few systems that maintain both X/Open XA standards and ACID transactions for distributed transaction processing.

Advantages of NoSQL

There are many advantages of working with NoSQL databases such as MongoDB and Cassandra. The main advantages are high scalability and high availability:

- High scalability: NoSQL database use sharding for horizontal scaling. Partitioning of data and placing it on multiple machines in such a way that the order of the data is preserved is sharding. Vertical scaling means adding more resources to the existing machine whereas horizontal scaling means adding more machines to handle the data. Vertical scaling is not that easy to implement but horizontal scaling is easy to implement. Examples of horizontal scaling databases are MongoDB, Cassandra etc. NoSQL can handle huge amount of data because of scalability, as the data grows NoSQL scale itself to handle that data in efficient manner.

- High availability: Auto replication feature in NoSQL databases makes it highly available because in case of any failure data replicates itself to the previous consistent state.

Disadvantages of NoSQL

NoSQL has the following disadvantages:

- Narrow focus: NoSQL databases have very narrow focus as it is mainly designed for storage but it provides very little functionality. Relational databases are a better choice in the field of Transaction Management than NoSQL.

- Open-source: NoSQL is open-source database. There is no reliable standard for NoSQL yet. In other words two database systems are likely to be unequal.

- Management challenge: The purpose of big data tools is to make management of a large amount of data as simple as possible. But it is not so easy. Data management in NoSQL is much more complex than a relational database. NoSQL, in particular, has a reputation for being challenging to install and even more hectic to manage on a daily basis.

- GUI is not available: GUI mode tools to access the database is not flexibly available in the market.

- Backup: Backup is a great weak point for some NoSQL databases like MongoDB. MongoDB has no approach for the backup of data in a consistent manner.

- Large document size: Some database systems like MongoDB and CouchDB store data in JSON format. Which means that documents are quite large (Big-Data, network bandwidth, speed), and having descriptive key names actually hurts, since they increase the document size.

Types of NoSQL Database

Types of NoSQL databases and the name of the databases system that falls in that category are:

- MongoDB falls in the category of NoSQL document based database.

- Key value store: Memcached, Redis, Coherence.

- Tabular: Hbase, Big Table, Accumulo.

- Document based: MongoDB, CouchDB, Cloudant.

When should NoSQL be Used

- When huge amount of data need to be stored and retrieved.

- The relationship between the data you store is not that important.

- The data changing over time and is not structured.

- Support of Constraints and Joins is not required at database level.

- The data is growing continuously and you need to scale the database regular to handle the data.

NewSQL Database

NewSQL is a type of database language that incorporates and builds on the concepts and principles of Structured Query Language (SQL) and NoSQL languages. By combining the reliability of SQL with the speed and performance of NoSQL, NewSQL provides improved functionality and services.

Conceived in 2011 to address challenges faced by traditional SQL-based systems, NewSQL was designed for online transaction processing (OLTP) systems, while complying with atomicity, consistency, isolation and durability (ACID). NewSQL architecture natively supports applications that have a large number of transactions, are repetitive in their processes and utilize a small subset of data retrieving processes.

VoltDB is a NewSQL database system that provides speed up to 50 times faster than SQL and more than eight times faster than NoSQL.

NewSQL promises to combine benefits from RDBMS (strong consistency) with benefits from NoSQL (scalability); it mainly achieves this through new architecture patterns and efficient SQL storage engines.

Most current NewSQL databases are based on Google's Spanner database and the theories in academic papers such as Calvin: Fast Distributed Transactions for Partitioned Database Systems from Yale. Spanner is Google's scalable, multi-version, globally-distributed, and synchronously-replicated database. It was the first system to distribute data at global scale and support externally-consistent distributed transactions.

TiDB, CockroachDB, FaunaDB, Vitess are a few of the leading NewSQL databases. Each database implementation has its own take on how to ensure strong consistency with scalable architecture.

TiDB

TiDB is an open source database that supports distributed HTAP (Hybrid Transactional and Analytical Processing) and is compatible with MySQL. PingCap is the company which backs TiDB. The initial version was released in Oct 2017 and its current stable version is 2.1.9.

TiDBs salient features are:

- Hybrid: TiDB supports both analytical processing (OLAP) and transaction processing (OLTP) workloads. This means there is no need to do ETL from application transaction database to analytical database. TiDB's storage layer TiKV is accessed by TiDB clusters for OLTP and by natively supported TiSpark for OLAP.

- Cloud Native: TiDB is designed to operate in the cloud (public, private, and hybrid) and its storage layer TiKV has been accepted as a sandbox project by the Cloud Native Computing Foundation.

- MySQL Compatible: Applications can treat TiDB as a MySQL server and connect using its existing client libraries without any change from the application side.

- Less ETL: Since TiDB operates as both OLTP and OLAP, there's no need to do ETL from OLTP to OLAP.

CockroachDB

CockroachDB is a distributed SQL open source database built on a transactional and strongly-consistent key-value store. It scales horizontally; survives disk, machine, rack, and even datacenter failures with minimal disruption and manual intervention; supports strongly-consistent ACID transactions; and provides a familiar SQL API for structuring, manipulating, and querying data.

Cockroach Labs is the company backing CockroachDB. The initial version was released in Sept 2015 and its current stable version is 19.1.1.

CockroachDB's salient features are:

- SQL Compatible: Though CockroachDB has distributed, strongly-consistent, transactional key-value store underneath, its external API is standard SQL compatible.

- Multiple-Active Availability: CockroachDB's availability model is termed as "multi-active availability". Multi-active availability provides benefits of reading and writing every node in a cluster without conflicts. Multiple replicas run identical services, and traffic is routed to all of them. If any replica fails, the others simply handle the traffic that would've been routed to it.

- Online Schema Changes: CockroachDB provides a built-in online schema changes feature; a simple way to update a table schema without imposing any negative consequences on an application. Changes to table schema happen while the database is running. Schema change runs as a background process without holding locks on the underlying table data.This allows application queries to execute normally without any effect on read/write.

FaunaDB

FaunaDB is a modern distributed operational database for cloud and container-centric environments. It is the world's first commercial database that is inspired by Calvin, a strictly serializable transaction protocol for multi-region environments.

Fauna is the company backing FaunaDB and they have on-prem, cloud, and serverless offerings of FaunaDB.

FaunaDB's salient features are:

- Active-Active: FaunaDB supports a masterless, multi-cloud, active-active architecture which helps applications with 100% DB uptime.

- Multiple Models: FaunaDB can manage multiple data models such as relational, graph, and document.

- Data Temporality: FaunaDB provides a snapshot-based storage engine that retains historical data for a configurable period and permits correction of data errors in snapshots.

- Horizontal Scalability: FaunaDB supports horizontal scalability allowing you to add and remove nodes without interrupting application service within the same site or across global data centers.

Vitess

Vitess is an open source database clustering system for horizontal scaling of MySQL through generalized sharding.

Vitess was born out of YouTube's scaling needs and currently supports its backend. PlanetScale is the company backing the open source project. The current stable version of Vitess is 3.0.

Vitess' salient features are:

- Scalable MySQL: This brings in all the features of SQL (JOINs, indexing, aggregation, etc) with all the benefits of NoSQL.

- Lightweight Connections: Compared to MySQL connection size, Vitess makes very lightweight connections allowing it to scale easily.

- Topology Service: Topology Service is a metadata store (ETCD or Zookeeper) that contains information about running servers, the sharding scheme, and the replication graph. Because of Topology Service, the cluster view is always up-to-date and consistent for different clients.

References

- What-is-database, database: oracle.com, Retrieved 09 January, 2020

- What-is-cloud-database, cloud: ibm.com, Retrieved 11 June, 2020

- Query-languages, computer-science: sciencedirect.com, Retrieved 09 January, 2020

- Unified-modeling-language-uml-introduction: geeksforgeeks.org, Retrieved 06 March, 2020

- What-are-object-oriented-databases-and-their-advantages2: c-sharpcorner.com, Retrieved 15 June, 2020

- Document-oriented-database-30329: techopedia.com, Retrieved 11 April, 2020

Concepts and Elements 2

- **Table**
- **Column**
- **Row**
- **View**
- **Procedures and Functions**
- **Database Transaction**
- **Transaction Log**
- **Database Trigger**
- **Database Index**
- **Database Schema**
- **Stored Procedure**
- **Database Cursor**
- **Database Partition**
- **Data Dictionary**
- **Java Database Connectivity**
- **Open Database Connectivity**
- **Query Plan**

Transaction log, database trigger, database index, database schema, database cursor, database partition, java and open database connectivity, query optimization, etc. are a few concepts and elements that fall under the domain of database systems. The topics elaborated in this chapter will help in gaining a better perspective of various elements and concepts of database systems.

Table

A table is a collection of rows having one or more columns. A row is an instance of a row type. Every row of the same table has the same row type. The value of the n-th field of every row in a table is the value of the n-th column of that row in the table. The row is the smallest unit of data that can be inserted into a table and deleted from a table.

The number of rows in a table is its cardinality. A table whose cardinality is 0 (zero) is said to be empty.

Following image are pictorial presentation of a table and different components of it:

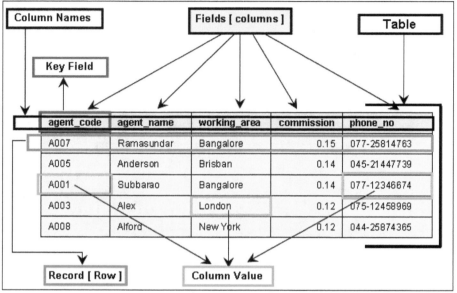

A column name can be used in more than one tables and to maintain the integrity of data and reduce redundancy. This is called a relation.

Elements of a Table

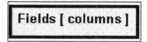

The information of a table stored in some heads, those are fields or columns. Columns show vertically in a table.

Each field or column has an individual name. A table cannot contain the same name of two different columns.

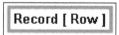

All the columns in a table make a row. Each row contains all the information of individual topics.

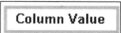

The value of each field makes a row is the column value.

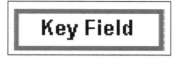

Each table should contain a field which can create a link with another one or more table is the key field of a table.

A table is a collection of related data held in a table format within a database. It consists of columns, and rows.

In relational databases, and flat file databases, a *table* is a set of data elements (values) using a model of vertical columns (identifiable by name) and horizontal rows, the cell being the unit where a row and column intersect. A table has a specified number of columns, but can have any number of rows. Each row is identified by one or more values appearing in a particular column subset. A specific choice of columns which uniquely identify rows is called the primary key.

"Table" is another term for "relation"; although there is the difference in that a table is usually a multiset (bag) of rows where a relation is a set and does not allow duplicates. Besides the actual data rows, tables generally have associated with them some metadata, such as constraints on the table or on the values within particular columns.

The data in a table does not have to be physically stored in the database. Views also function as relational tables, but their data are calculated at query time. External tables (in Informix or Oracle, for example) can also be thought of as views.

Tables versus Relations

In terms of the relational model of databases, a table can be considered a convenient representation of a relation, but the two are not strictly equivalent. For instance, a SQL table can potentially contain duplicate rows, whereas a true relation cannot contain duplicate rows that we call as tuples. Similarly, representation as a table implies a particular ordering to the rows and columns, whereas a relation is explicitly unordered. However, the database system does not guarantee any ordering of the rows unless an ORDER BY clause is specified in the SELECT statement that queries the table.

An equally valid representation of a relation is as an *n*-dimensional chart, where *n* is the number of attributes (a table's columns). For example, a relation with two attributes and three values can be represented as a table with two columns and three rows, or as a two-dimensional graph with three points. The table and graph representations are only equivalent if the ordering of rows is not significant, and the table has no duplicate rows.

Comparisons

Hierarchical Databases

In non-relational systems, hierarchical databases, the distant counterpart of a table is a structured file, representing the rows of a table in each row of the file and each column in a row. This structure implies that a row can have repeating information, generally in the child data segments. Data are stored in sequence of physical records.

Spreadsheets

Unlike a spreadsheet, the datatype of a column is ordinarily defined by the schema describing the table. Some SQL systems, such as SQLite, are less strict about column datatype definitions.

Column

In a relational database, a column is a set of data values of a particular simple type, one value for each row of the database. A column may contain text values, numbers, or even pointers to files in the operating system. Some relational database systems allow columns to contain more complex data types; whole documents, images or even video clips are examples. A column can also be called an attribute.

An example of output columns from a Postgres database.

Each row would provide a data value for each column and would then be understood as a single structured data value. For example, a database that represents company contact information might have the following columns: ID, Company Name, Address Line 1, Address Line 2, City, and Postal Code. More formally, each row can be interpreted as a relvar, composed of a set of tuples, with each tuple consisting of the relevant column and its value, for example, the tuple ('Address 1', '12345 West Example Street').

Field

The word 'field' is normally used interchangeably with 'column'. However, database perfectionists tend to favor using 'field' to signify a specific cell of a given row. This is to enable accuracy in communicating with other developers. Columns (really column names) being referred to as field names (common for each row/record in the table). Then a field refers to a single storage location in a specific record (like a cell) to store one value (the field value). The terms record and field come from the more practical field of database usage and traditional DBMS system usage (This was linked into business like terms used in manual databases e.g. filing cabinet storage with records for each customer). The terms row and column come from the more theoretical study of relational theory.

Row

In the context of a relational database, a row—also called a tuple—represents a single, implicitly structured data item in a table. In simple terms, a database table can be thought of as consisting of *rows* and columns. Each row in a table represents a set of related data, and every row in the table has the same structure.

For example, in a table that represents companies, each row would represent a single company. Columns might represent things like company name, company street address, whether the company is publicly held, its VAT number, etc.. In a table that represents *the association* of employees with departments, each row would associate one employee with one department.

The implicit structure of a row, and the meaning of the data values in a row, requires that the row be understood as providing a succession of data values, one in each column of the table. The row is then interpreted as a relvar composed of a set of tuples, with each tuple consisting of the two items: the name of the relevant column and the value this row provides for that column.

Each column expects a data value of a particular type. For example, one column might require a unique identifier, another might require text representing a person's name, another might require an integer representing hourly pay in cents.

	Column 1	Column 2
Row 1	Row 1, Column 1	Row 1, Column 2
Row 2	Row 2, Column 1	Row 2, Column 2
Row 3	Row 3, Column 1	Row 3, Column 2

View

In a database, a view is the result set of a *stored* query on the data, which the database users can query just as they would in a persistent database collection object. This pre-established query command is kept in the database dictionary. Unlike ordinary base tables in a relational database, a view does not form part of the physical schema: as a result set, it is a virtual table computed or collated dynamically from data in the database when access to that view is requested. Changes applied to the data in a relevant underlying table are reflected in the data shown in subsequent invocations of the view. In some NoSQL databases, views are the only way to query data.

Views can provide advantages over tables:

- Views can represent a subset of the data contained in a table. Consequently, a view can limit the degree of exposure of the underlying tables to the outer world: a given user may have permission to query the view, while denied access to the rest of the base table.

- Views can join and simplify multiple tables into a single virtual table.

- Views can act as aggregated tables, where the database engine aggregates data (sum, average, etc.) and presents the calculated results as part of the data.

- Views can hide the complexity of data. For example, a view could appear as Sales2000 or Sales2001, transparently partitioning the actual underlying table.

- Views take very little space to store; the database contains only the definition of a view, not a copy of all the data that it presents.

- Depending on the SQL engine used, views can provide extra security.

Just as a function (in programming) can provide abstraction, so can a database view. In another parallel with functions, database users can manipulate nested views, thus one view can aggregate data from other views. Without the use of views, the normalization of databases above second normal form would become much more difficult. Views can make it easier to create lossless join decomposition.

Just as rows in a base table lack any defined ordering, rows available through a view do not appear with any default sorting. A view is a relational table, and the relational model defines a table as a set of rows. Since sets are not ordered — by definition — neither are the rows of a view. Therefore, an ORDER BY clause in the view definition is meaningless; the SQL standard does not allow an ORDER BY clause in the subquery of a CREATE VIEW command, just as it is refused in a CREATE TABLE statement. However, sorted data can be obtained from a view, in the same way as any other table

— as part of a query statement on that view. Nevertheless, some DBMS (such as Oracle Database) do not abide by this SQL standard restriction.

Read-only vs. Updatable Views

Database practitioners can define views as read-only or updatable. If the database system can determine the reverse mapping from the view schema to the schema of the underlying base tables, then the view is updatable. INSERT, UPDATE, and DELETE operations can be performed on updatable views. Read-only views do not support such operations because the DBMS cannot map the changes to the underlying base tables. A view update is done by key preservation.

Some systems support the definition of INSTEAD OF triggers on views. This technique allows the definition of other logic for execution in place of an insert, update, or delete operation on the views. Thus database systems can implement data modifications based on read-only views. However, an INSTEAD OF trigger does not change the read-only or updatable property of the view itself.

Materialized Views

Various database management systems have extended the views from read-only subsets of data, particularly materialized views: pre-executed, non-virtual views commonly used in data warehousing. They give a static snapshot of the data and may include data from remote sources. The accuracy of a materialized view depends on the frequency of trigger mechanisms behind its updates.

Materialized views were introduced by Oracle Database, while IBM DB2 provides so-called "materialized query tables" (MQTs) for the same purpose. Microsoft SQL Server introduced in its 2000 version indexed views which only store a separate index from the table, but not the entire data. PostgreSQL implemented materialized views in its 9.3 release.

Equivalence

A view is equivalent to its source query. When queries are run against views, the query is modified. For example, if there exists a view named accounts_view with the content as follows:

```
accounts_view:

------------

SELECT name,

       money_received,

       money_sent,
```

```
      (money_received - money_sent) AS balance,

      address,

          . . .

  FROM table_customers c

  JOIN accounts_table a

    ON a.customer_id = c.customer_id
```

then the application could run a simple query such as:

```
Simple query

------------

SELECT name,

       balance

  FROM accounts_view
```

The RDBMS then takes the simple query, replaces the equivalent view, then sends the following to the query optimizer:

```
Preprocessed query:

-------------------

SELECT name,

       balance

  FROM (SELECT name,

               money_received,

               money_sent,

               (money_received - money_sent) AS

balance,

               address,

                   . . .

        FROM table_customers c JOIN accounts_table

a

               ON a.customer_id = c.customer_id

  )
```

The optimizer then removes unnecessary fields and complexity (for example: it is not necessary to read the address, since the parent invocation does not make use of it) and then sends the query to the SQL engine for processing.

Procedures and Functions

"A procedures or function is a group or set of SQL and PL/SQL statements that perform a specific task». A function and procedure is a named PL/SQL Block which is similar. The major difference between a procedure and a function is, a function must always return a value, but a procedure may or may not return a value.

Procedures

A procudure is a named PL/SQL block which performs one or more specific task. This is similar to a procedure in other programming languages. A procedure has a header and a body. The header consists of the name of the procedure and the parameters or variables passed to the procedure. The body consists or declaration section, execution section and exception section similar to a general PL/SQL Block. A procedure is similar to an anonymous PL/SQL Block but it is named for repeated usage. We can pass parameters to procedures in three ways:

Parameters	Description
IN type	These types of parameters are used to send values to stored procedures.
OUT type	These types of parameters are used to get values from stored procedures. This is similar to a return type in functions.
IN OUT type	These types of parameters are used to send values and get values from stored procedures.

A procedure may or may not return any value.

Syntax

```
CREATE [OR REPLACE] PROCEDURE procedure_name (<Argument> {IN, OUT,
IN OUT}

  <Datatype>, …)

IS

    Declaration section<variable, constant> ;

    BEGIN

    Execution section
```

```
EXCEPTION

      Exception section

END
```

IS - marks the beginning of the body of the procedure and is similar to DECLARE in anonymous PL/SQL Blocks. The code between IS and BEGIN forms the Declaration section. The syntax within the brackets [ ] indicate they are optional. By using CREATE OR REPLACE together the procedure is created if no other procedure with the same name exists or the existing procedure is replaced with the current code.

How to Execute a Procedure?

There are two ways to execute a procedure:

- From the SQL prompt: EXECUTE [or EXEC] procedure_name,

- Within another procedure – simply use the procedure name: procedure_name;

Example:

Create table named emp have two column id and salary with number datatype:

```
CREATE OR REPLACE PROCEDURE p1(id IN NUMBER, sal IN NUMBER)

AS

BEGIN

      INSERT INTO emp VALUES(id, sal);

      DBMD_OUTPUT.PUT_LINE('VALUE INSERTED.');

END;

/
```

Output

Run SQL Command Line:

```
SQL>set serveroutput on

SQL>start D://pr.sql

Procedure created.

SQL>exec p1(5,4);

VALUE INSERTED.

PL/SQL procudere successfully completed.
```

```
SQL>select * from emp;

    ID      SALARY

  -----    --------

    2        5000
```

Functions

A function is a named PL/SQL Block which is similar to a procedure. The major difference between a procedure and a function is, a function must always return a value, but a procedure may or may not return a value.

Syntax

```
CREATE [OR REPLACE] FUNCTION function_name [parameters]

RETURN return_datatype;   {IS, AS}

Declaration_section <variable,constant> ;

BEGIN

    Execution_section

    Return return_variable;

EXCEPTION

    exception section

     Return return_variable;

END;
```

Return Type

The header section defines the return type of the function. The return datatype can be any of the oracle datatype like varchar, number etc. The execution and exception section both should return a value which is of the datatype defined in the header section.

How to Execute a Function?

A function can be executed in the following ways:

- As a part of a SELECT statement: SELECT emp_details_func FROM dual,

- In a PL/SQL Statements like: dbms_output.put_line(emp_details_func).

This line displays the value returned by the function.

Example:

```
create or replace function getsal (no IN number) return number
is
    sal number(5);
begin
    select salary into sal from emp where id=no;
    return sal;
end;
/
```

Output

Run SQL Command Line

```
SQL>select * from emp;
    ID      SALARY
  -----   --------
    2       5000
SQL>start D://fun.sql
Function created.
SQL>select getsal(2) from dual;
GETSAL(2)
---------
    5000
```

In the example we are retrieving the 'salary' of employee with id 2 to variable 'sal'. The return type of the function is number.

Destroying Procedure and Function

Syntax

```
DROP PROCEDURE/FUNCTION PROCEDURE/FUNCTION_NAME;
```

Procedures VS Functions:

- A function MUST return a value,

- A procedure cannot return a value,

- Procedures and functions can both return data in OUT and IN OUT parameters,

- The return statement in a function returns control to the calling program and returns the results of the function,

- The return statement of a procedure returns control to the calling program and cannot return a value,

- Functions can be called from SQL, procedure cannot,

- Functions are considered expressions, procedure are not.

Database Transaction

A database transaction symbolizes a unit of work performed within a database management system (or similar system) against a database, and treated in a coherent and reliable way independent of other transactions. A transaction generally represents any change in a database. Transactions in a database environment have two main purposes:

- To provide reliable units of work that allow correct recovery from failures and keep a database consistent even in cases of system failure, when execution stops (completely or partially) and many operations upon a database remain uncompleted, with unclear status,

- To provide isolation between programs accessing a database concurrently. If this isolation is not provided, the programs' outcomes are possibly erroneous.

In a database management system, a transaction is a single unit of logic or work, sometimes made up of multiple operations. Any logical calculation done in a consistent mode in a database is known as a transaction. One example is a transfer from one bank account to another: the complete transaction requires subtracting the amount to be transferred from one account and adding that same amount to the other.

A database transaction, by definition, must be atomic (it must either complete in its entirety or have no effect whatsoever), consistent (it must conform to existing constraints in the database), isolated (it must not affect other transactions) and durable (it must get written to persistent storage). Database practitioners often refer to these properties of database transactions using the acronym ACID.

Databases and other data stores which treat the integrity of data as paramount often include the ability to handle transactions to maintain the integrity of data. A single transaction consists of one or more independent units of work, each reading and/or writing information to a database or other data store. When this happens it is often important to ensure that all such processing leaves the database or data store in a consistent state.

Examples from double-entry accounting systems often illustrate the concept of transactions. In double-entry accounting every debit requires the recording of an associated credit. If one writes a check for $100 to buy groceries, a transactional double-entry accounting system must record the following two entries to cover the single transaction:

- Debit $100 to Groceries Expense Account,

- Credit $100 to Checking Account.

A transactional system would make both entries pass or both entries would fail. By treating the recording of multiple entries as an atomic transactional unit of work the system maintains the integrity of the data recorded. In other words, nobody ends up with a situation in which a debit is recorded but no associated credit is recorded, or vice versa.

Transactional Databases

A transactional database is a DBMS that provides the ACID properties for a bracketed set of database operations (begin-commit). All the write operations within a transaction have an all-or-nothing effect, that is, either the transaction succeeds and all writes take effect, or otherwise, the database is brought to a state that does not include any of the writes of the transaction. Transactions also ensure that the effect of concurrent transactions satisfies certain guarantees, known as isolation level. The highest isolation level is serializability, which guarantees that the effect of concurrent transactions is equivalent to their serial (i.e. sequential) execution.

Most modern relational database management systems fall into the category of databases that support transactions. NoSQL data stores prioritize scalability along with supporting transactions in order to guarantee data consistency in the event of concurrent updates and accesses.

In a database system, a transaction might consist of one or more data-manipulation statements and queries, each reading and/or writing information in the database. Users of database systems consider consistency and integrity of data as highly important. A simple transaction is usually issued to the database system in a language like SQL wrapped in a transaction, using a pattern similar to the following:

- Begin the transaction,

- Execute a set of data manipulations and/or queries,

- If no error occurs, then commit the transaction,

- If an error occurs, then roll back the transaction.

A transaction commit operation persists all the results of data manipulations within the scope of the transaction to the database. A transaction rollback operation does not persist the partial results of data manipulations within the scope of the transaction to the database. In no case can a partial transaction be committed to the database since that would leave the database in an inconsistent state.

Internally, multi-user databases store and process transactions, often by using a transaction ID or XID.

There are multiple varying ways for transactions to be implemented other than the simple way documented above. Nested transactions, for example, are transactions which contain statements within them that start new transactions (i.e. sub-transactions). *Multi-level transactions* are a variant of nested transactions where the sub-transactions take place at different levels of a layered system architecture (e.g., with one operation at the database-engine level, one operation at the operating-system level). Another type of transaction is the compensating transaction.

In SQL

Transactions are available in most SQL database implementations, though with varying levels of robustness. For example, MySQL began supporting transactions from early version 3.23, but the InnoDB storage engine was not default before version 5.5. The earlier available storage engine, MyISAM does not support transactions.

A transaction is typically started using the command BEGIN (although the SQL standard specifies START TRANSACTION). When the system processes a COMMIT statement, the transaction ends with successful completion. A ROLLBACK statement can also end the transaction, undoing any work performed since BEGIN. If autocommit was disabled with the start of a transaction, autocommit will also be re-enabled with the end of the transaction.

One can set the isolation level for individual transactional operations as well as globally. At the highest level (READ COMMITTED), the result of any operation performed after a transaction has started will remain invisible to other database users until the transaction has ended. At the lowest level (READ UNCOMMITTED), which may occasionally be used to ensure high concurrency, such changes will be immediately visible.

Object Databases

Relational databases are traditionally composed of tables with fixed-size fields and records. Object databases comprise variable-sized blobs, possibly serializable or incorporating a mime-type. The fundamental similarities between Relational and Object databases are the start and the commit or rollback.

After starting a transaction, database records or objects are locked, either read-only or read-write. Reads and writes can then occur. Once the transaction is fully defined, changes are committed or rolled back atomically, such that at the end of the transaction there is no inconsistency.

Distributed Transactions

Database systems implement distributed transactions as transactions accessing data over multiple nodes. A distributed transaction enforces the ACID properties over multiple nodes, and might include systems such as databases, storage managers, file systems, messaging systems, and other data managers. In a distributed transaction there is typically an entity coordinating all the process to ensure that all parts of the transaction are applied to all relevant systems.

Transactional Filesystems

The Namesys Reiser4 filesystem for Linux supports transactions, and as of Microsoft Windows Vista, the Microsoft NTFS filesystem supports distributed transactions across networks. There is occurring research into more data coherent filesystems, such as the Warp Transactional Filesystem (WTF).

Transaction Log

In the field of databases in computer science, a transaction log (also transaction journal, database log, binary log or audit trail) is a history of actions executed by a database management system used to guarantee ACID properties over crashes or hardware failures. Physically, a log is a file listing changes to the database, stored in a stable storage format.

If, after a start, the database is found in an inconsistent state or not been shut down properly, the database management system reviews the database logs for uncommitted transactions and rolls back the changes made by these transactions. Additionally, all transactions that are already committed but whose changes were not yet materialized in the database are re-applied. Both are done to ensure atomicity and durability of transactions.

This term is not to be confused with other, human-readable logs that a database management system usually provides.

In database management systems, a journal is the record of data altered by a given process.

Anatomy of a General Database Log

A database log record is made up of:

- Log Sequence Number (LSN): A unique ID for a log record. With LSNs, logs can be recovered in constant time. Most LSNs are assigned in monotonically increasing order, which is useful in recovery algorithms, like ARIES,

- Prev LSN: A link to their last log record. This implies database logs are constructed in linked list form,

- Transaction ID number: A reference to the database transaction generating the log record,

- Type: Describes the type of database log record,

- Information about the actual changes that triggered the log record to be written.

Types of Database Log Records

All log records include the general log attributes above, and also other attributes depending on their type (which is recorded in the *Type* attribute, as above).

- Update Log Record notes an update (change) to the database. It includes this extra information:

  ◦ PageID: A reference to the Page ID of the modified page,

  ◦ Length and Offset: Length in bytes and offset of the page are usually included,

  ◦ Before and After Images: Includes the value of the bytes of page before and after the page change. Some databases may have logs which include one or both images.

- Compensation Log Record notes the rollback of a particular change to the database. Each corresponds with exactly one other Update Log Record (although the corresponding update log record is not typically stored in the Compensation Log Record). It includes this extra information:

  ◦ undoNextLSN: This field contains the LSN of the next log record that is to be undone for transaction that wrote the last Update Log.

- Commit Record notes a decision to commit a transaction,

- Abort Record notes a decision to abort and hence roll back a transaction,

- Checkpoint Record notes that a checkpoint has been made. These are used to speed up recovery. They record information that eliminates the need to read a long way into the log's past. This varies according to checkpoint algorithm. If all dirty pages are flushed while creating the checkpoint (as in PostgreSQL), it might contain:

  ◦ redoLSN: This is a reference to the first log record that corresponds to a dirty page. i.e. the first update that wasn't flushed at checkpoint time. This is where redo must begin on recovery,

- ○ undoLSN: This is a reference to the oldest log record of the oldest in-progress transaction. This is the oldest log record needed to undo all in-progress transactions.

- Completion Record notes that all work has been done for this particular transaction. (It has been fully committed or aborted).

Database Trigger

A database trigger is procedural code that is automatically executed in response to certain events on a particular table or view in a database. The trigger is mostly used for maintaining the integrity of the information on the database. For example, when a new record (representing a new worker) is added to the employees table, new records should also be created in the tables of the taxes, vacations and salaries. Triggers can also be used to log historical data, for example to keep track of employees' previous salaries.

Triggers in DBMS

Oracle

Below follows a series of descriptions of how some popular DBMS support triggers.

In addition to triggers that fire (and execute PL/SQL code) when data is modified, Oracle 10g supports triggers that fire when schema-level objects (that is, tables) are modified and when user logon or logoff events occur.

Schema-level Triggers

- After Creation,
- Before Alter,
- After Alter,
- Before Drop,
- After Drop,
- Before Insert.

The four main types of triggers are:

- Row-level trigger: This gets executed before or after *any column value of a row* changes,

- Column-level trigger: This gets executed before or after the *specified column* changes,

- For each row type: This trigger gets executed once for each row of the result set affected by an insert/update/delete,

- For each statement type: This trigger gets executed only once for the entire result set, but also fires each time the statement is executed.

System-level Triggers

From Oracle 8i, database events - logons, logoffs, startups - can fire Oracle triggers.

Microsoft SQL Server

A full list is available on MSDN.

Performing conditional actions in triggers (or testing data following modification) is done through accessing the temporary *Inserted* and *Deleted* tables.

PostgreSQL

Introduced support for triggers in 1997. The following functionality in SQL:2003 was previously not implemented in PostgreSQL:

- SQL allows triggers to fire on updates to specific columns; As of version 9.0 of PostgreSQL this feature is also implemented in PostgreSQL.

- The standard allows the execution of a number of SQL statements other than SELECT, INSERT, UPDATE, such as CREATE TABLE as the triggered action. This can be done through creating a stored procedure or function to call CREATE TABLE.

Synopsis:

```
CREATE TRIGGER name { BEFORE | AFTER } { event [ OR... ] }

    ON TABLE [ FOR [ EACH ] { ROW | STATEMENT } ]

    EXECUTE PROCEDURE funcname ( arguments )
```

Firebird

Firebird supports multiple row-level, BEFORE or AFTER, INSERT, UPDATE, DELETE (or any combination of thereof) triggers per table, where they are always "in addition to" the default table changes, and the order of the triggers relative to each other can be specified where it would otherwise be ambiguous (POSITION clause.) Triggers may also exist on views, where they are always "instead of" triggers, replacing the default updatable view logic. (Before version 2.1, triggers on views deemed updatable would run in addition to the default logic.)

Firebird does not raise mutating table exceptions (like Oracle), and triggers will by default both nest and recurse as required (SQL Server allows nesting but not recursion, by default.) Firebird's triggers use NEW and OLD context variables (not Inserted and Deleted tables,) and provide UPDATING, INSERTING, and DELETING flags to indicate the current usage of the trigger.

```
{CREATE | RECREATE | CREATE OR ALTER} TRIGGER name FOR {table name |
view name}

 [ACTIVE | INACTIVE]

 {BEFORE | AFTER}

 {INSERT [OR UPDATE] [OR DELETE] | UPDATE [OR INSERT] [OR DELETE] |
DELETE [OR UPDATE] [OR INSERT] }

 [POSITION n] AS

BEGIN

 . . . .

END
```

As of version 2.1, Firebird additionally supports the following database-level triggers:

- CONNECT (exceptions raised here prevent the connection from completing),

- DISCONNECT,

- TRANSACTION START,

- TRANSACTION COMMIT (exceptions raised here prevent the transaction from committing, or preparing if a two-phase commit is involved),

- TRANSACTION ROLLBACK.

Database-level triggers can help enforce multi-table constraints, or emulate materialized views. If an exception is raised in a TRANSACTION COMMIT trigger, the changes made by the trigger so far are rolled back and the client application is notified, but the transaction remains active as if COMMIT had never been requested; the client application can continue to make changes and re-request COMMIT.

Syntax for database triggers:

```
{CREATE | RECREATE | CREATE OR ALTER} TRIGGER name

 [ACTIVE | INACTIVE] ON
```

```
{CONNECT | DISCONNECT | TRANSACTION START | TRANSACTION COMMIT |
TRANSACTION ROLLBACK}

[POSITION n] AS

BEGIN

.....

END
```

IBM DB2 LUW

IBM DB2 for distributed systems known as DB2 for LUW (LUW means Linux Unix Windows) supports three trigger types: Before trigger, After trigger and Instead of trigger. Both statement level and row level triggers are supported. If there are more triggers for same operation on table then firing order is determined by trigger creation data. Since version 9.7 IBM DB2 supports autonomous transactions.

Before trigger is for checking data and deciding if operation should be permitted. If exception is thrown from before trigger then operation is aborted and no data are changed. In DB2 before triggers are read only — you can't modify data in before triggers. After triggers are designed for post processing after requested change was performed. After triggers can write data into tables and unlike some other databases you can write into any table including table on which trigger operates. Instead of triggers are for making views writeable.

Triggers are usually programmed in SQL PL language.

SQLite

```
CREATE [TEMP | TEMPORARY] TRIGGER [IF NOT EXISTS] [database_name.]
trigger_name

[BEFORE | AFTER | INSTEAD OF] {DELETE | INSERT | UPDATE [OF column_name
[, column_name]...]}

ON {table_name | view_name}

   [FOR EACH ROW] [WHEN condition is mandatory ]

BEGIN

   ...

END
```

SQLite only supports row-level triggers, not statement-level triggers.

Updateable views, which are not supported in SQLite, can be emulated with INSTEAD OF triggers.

XML Databases

An example of implementation of triggers in non-relational database can be Sedna, that provides support for triggers based on XQuery. Triggers in Sedna were designed to be analogous to SQL:2003 triggers, but natively base on XML query and update languages (XPath, XQuery and XML update language).

A trigger in Sedna is set on any nodes of an XML document stored in database. When these nodes are updated, the trigger automatically executes XQuery queries and updates specified in its body. For example, the following trigger cancels person node deletion if there are any open auctions referenced by this person:

```
CREATE TRIGGER "trigger3"

    BEFORE DELETE

    ON doc("auction")/site//person

    FOR EACH NODE

    DO

    {

        if(exists($WHERE//open_auction/bidder/personref/@person=$OLD/@id))

        then ( )

        else $OLD;

    }
```

Row and Statement Level Triggers

To understand how trigger behavior works, you need to be aware of the two main types of triggers; these are Row and Statement level triggers. The distinction between the two is how many times the code within the trigger is executed, and at what time.

Suppose you have a trigger that is made to be called on an UPDATE to a certain table. Row level triggers would execute once for each row that is affected by the UPDATE. It is important to keep in mind if no rows are affected by the UPDATE command, the trigger will not execute any code within the trigger. Statement level triggers will be called once regardless of how many rows are affected by the UPDATE. Here it is important to note that even if the UPDATE command didn't affect any rows, the code within the trigger will still be executed once.

Using the BEFORE and AFTER options determine when the trigger is called. Suppose you have a trigger that is called on an INSERT to a certain table. If your trigger is using the BEFORE option, the code within the trigger will be executed before the INSERT into the table occurs. A common use of the BEFORE trigger is to verify the input values of the INSERT, or modify the values accordingly. Now let's say we have a trigger that uses AFTER instead. The code within the trigger is executed after the INSERT happens to the table. An example use of this trigger is creating an audit history of who has made inserts into the database, keeping track of the changes made. When using these options you need to keep a few things in mind. The BEFORE option does not allow you to modify tables, that is why input validation is a practical use. Using AFTER triggers allows you to modify tables such as inserting into an audit history table.

When creating a trigger to determine if it is statement or row level simply include the FOR EACH ROW clause for a row level, or omit the clause for a statement level. Be cautious of using additional INSERT/UPDATE/DELETE commands within your trigger, because trigger recursion is possible, causing unwanted behavior. In the examples below each trigger is modifying a different table, by looking at what is being modified you can see some common applications of when different trigger types are used.

Here is an Oracle syntax example of a row level trigger that is called AFTER an update FOR EACH ROW affected. This trigger is called on an update to a phone book database. When the trigger is called it adds an entry into a separate table named phone_book_audit. Also take note of triggers being able to take advantage of schema objects like sequences, in this example audit_id_sequence.nexVal is used to generate unique primary keys in the phone_book_audit table.

```
CREATE OR REPLACE TRIGGER phone_book_audit

  AFTER UPDATE ON phone_book FOR EACH ROW

BEGIN

  INSERT INTO phone_book_audit

      (audit_id,audit_change,  audit_l_name,  audit_f_name,  audit_old_
phone_number,  audit_new_phone_number,  audit_date)

    VALUES

        (audit_id_sequence.nextVal,'Update',:OLD.last_name,:OLD.first_
name,:OLD.phone_number,:NEW.phone_number, SYSDATE);

END;
```

Now calling an UPDATE on the phone_book table for people with the last name 'Jones'.

```
UPDATE phone_book SET phone_number = '111-111-1111' WHERE last_name =
'Jones';
```

G Notice that the phone_number_audit table is now populated with two entries. This is due to the database having two entries with the last name of 'Jones'. Since the update modified two separate row values, the created trigger was called twice; once after each modification.

After-statement-level Trigger

An Oracle syntax statement trigger that is called after an UPDATE to the phone_book table. When the trigger gets called it makes an insert into phone_book_edit_history table.

```
CREATE OR REPLACE TRIGGER phone_book_history

  AFTER UPDATE ON phone_book

BEGIN

  INSERT INTO phone_book_edit_history

    (audit_history_id, username, modification, edit_date)

    VALUES

    (audit_history_id_sequence.nextVal, USER,'Update', SYSDATE);

END;
```

Now lets do exactly the same update as the above example, however this time we have a statement level trigger.

```
UPDATE phone_book SET phone_number = '111-111-1111' WHERE last_name = 'Jones';
```

Audit_History_ID	Username	Modification	Edit_Date
1	HAUSCHBC	Update	02-MAY-14

You can see that the trigger was only called once, even though the update did change two rows.

Before-each-row-level Trigger

In this example we have a BEFORE EACH ROW trigger that modifies the INSERT using a WHEN conditional. If the last name is larger than 10 letters, using the SUBSTR function we change the last_name column value to an abbreviation.

```
CREATE OR REPLACE TRIGGER phone_book_insert

  BEFORE INSERT ON phone_book FOR EACH ROW

  WHEN (LENGTH(new.last_name) > 10)

BEGIN

  :new.last_name:= SUBSTR(:new.last_name,0,1);

END;
```

Now lets perform an INSERT of someone with a large name.

```
INSERT INTO phone_book VALUES

(6, 'VeryVeryLongLastName', 'Erin', 'Minneapolis', 'MN', '989 Universi-
ty Drive', '123-222-4456', 55408, TO_DATE('11/21/1991', 'MM/DD/YYYY'));
```

Person_ ID	Last_ Name	First_ Name	City	State_Ab-breviation	Address	Phone_Num-ber	Zip_code	DOB
6	V	Erin	Minne-apolis	MN	989 Uni-versity Drive	123-222-4456	55408	21-NOV-91

You can see that the trigger worked, modifying the value of the INSERT before it was executed.

Before-statement-level Trigger

Using a BEFORE statement trigger is particularly useful when enforcing database restrictions. For this example I am going to enforce a restriction upon someone named "SOMEUSER" on the table phone_book.

```
CREATE OR REPLACE TRIGGER hauschbc

    BEFORE INSERT ON SOMEUSER.phone_book

BEGIN

    RAISE_APPLICATION_ERROR (

        num => -20050,

        msg => 'Error message goes here.');

END;
```

Now when "SOMEUSER" is logged in after attempting any INSERT this error message will show:

```
SQL Error: ORA-20050: Error message goes here.
```

Custom errors such as this one has a restriction on what the num variable can be defined as. Because of the numerous other pre-defined errors this variable must be in the range of -20000 to -20999.

Database Index

A database index is a data structure that improves the speed of data retrieval operations on a database table at the cost of additional writes and storage space to maintain the index data structure. Indexes are used to quickly locate data without having to search every row in a database table every time a database table is accessed. Indexes can be created using one or more columns of a database table, providing the basis for both rapid random lookups and efficient access of ordered records.

An index is a copy of selected columns of data from a table, called a *database key* or simply *key*, that can be searched very efficiently that also includes a low-level disk block address or direct link to the complete row of data it was copied from. Some databases extend the power of indexing by letting developers create indexes on functions or expressions. For example, an index could be created on upper(last_name), which would only store the upper-case versions of the last_name field in the index. Another option sometimes supported is the use of partial indices, where index entries are created only for those records that satisfy some conditional expression. A further aspect of flexibility is to permit indexing on user-defined functions, as well as expressions formed from an assortment of built-in functions.

Usage

Support for Fast Lookup

Most database software includes indexing technology that enables sub-linear time lookup to improve performance, as linear search is inefficient for large databases.

Suppose a database contains N data items and one must be retrieved based on the value of one of the fields. A simple implementation retrieves and examines each item according to the test. If there is only one matching item, this can stop when it finds that single item, but if there are multiple matches, it must test everything. This means that the number of operations in the worst case is O(N) or linear time. Since databases may contain many objects, and since lookup is a common operation, it is often desirable to improve performance.

An index is any data structure that improves the performance of lookup. There are many different data structures used for this purpose. There are complex design trade-offs involving lookup performance, index size, and index-update performance. Many index designs exhibit logarithmic (O(log(N))) lookup performance and in some applications it is possible to achieve flat (O(1)) performance.

Policing the Database Constraints

Indexes are used to police database constraints, such as UNIQUE, EXCLUSION, PRIMARY KEY and FOREIGN KEY. An index may be declared as UNIQUE, which creates an implicit constraint on the underlying table. Database systems usually implicitly create an index on a set of columns declared PRIMARY KEY, and some are capable of using an already-existing index to police this constraint. Many database systems require that both referencing and referenced sets of columns in a FOREIGN KEY constraint are indexed, thus improving performance of inserts, updates and deletes to the tables participating in the constraint.

Some database systems support an EXCLUSION constraint that ensures that, for a newly inserted or updated record, a certain predicate holds for no other record. This can be used to implement a UNIQUE constraint (with equality predicate) or more complex constraints, like ensuring that no overlapping time ranges or no intersecting geometry objects would be stored in the table. An index supporting fast searching for records satisfying the predicate is required to police such a constraint.

Index Architecture and Indexing Methods

Non-clustered

The data is present in arbitrary order, but the logical ordering is specified by the index. The data rows may be spread throughout the table regardless of the value of the indexed column or expression. The non-clustered index tree contains the index keys in sorted order, with the leaf level of the index containing the pointer to the record (page and the row number in the data page in page-organized engines; row offset in file-organized engines).

In a non-clustered index:

- The physical order of the rows is not the same as the index order.

- The indexed columns are typically non-primary key columns used in JOIN, WHERE, and ORDER BY clauses.

There can be more than one non-clustered index on a database table.

Clustered

Clustering alters the data block into a certain distinct order to match the index, resulting in the row data being stored in order. Therefore, only one clustered index can be created on a given database table. Clustered indices can greatly increase overall speed of retrieval, but usually only where the data is accessed sequentially in the same or reverse order of the clustered index, or when a range of items is selected.

Since the physical records are in this sort order on disk, the next row item in the sequence is immediately before or after the last one, and so fewer data block reads are required. The primary feature of a clustered index is therefore the ordering of the physical data rows in accordance with the index blocks that point to them. Some databases separate the data and index blocks into separate files, others put two completely different data blocks within the same physical files.

Cluster

When multiple databases and multiple tables are joined, it's referred to as a cluster. The records for the tables sharing the value of a cluster key shall be stored together in the same or nearby data blocks. This may improve the joins of these tables on the cluster key, since the matching records are stored together and less I/O is required to locate them. The cluster configuration defines the data layout in the tables that are parts of the cluster. A cluster can be keyed with a B-Tree index or a hash table. The data block where the table record is stored is defined by the value of the cluster key.

Column Order

The order that the index definition defines the columns in is important. It is possible to retrieve a set of row identifiers using only the first indexed column. However, it is not possible or efficient (on most databases) to retrieve the set of row identifiers using only the second or greater indexed column.

For example, imagine a phone book that is organized by city first, then by last name, and then by first name. If you are given the city, you can easily extract the list of all phone numbers for that city. However, in this phone book it would be very tedious to find all the phone numbers for a given last name. You would have to look within each city's section for the entries with that last name. Some databases can do this, others just won't use the index.

In the phone book example with a composite index created on the columns (`city, last_name, first_name`), if we search by giving exact values for all the three fields, search time is minimal—but if we provide the values for `city` and `first_name` only, the search uses only the `city` field to retrieve all matched records. Then a sequential lookup checks the matching with first_name. So, to improve the performance, one must ensure that the index is created on the order of search columns.

Applications and Limitations

Indexes are useful for many applications but come with some limitations. Consider the following SQL statement: `SELECT first_name FROM people WHERE last_name = 'Smith';`. To process this statement without an index the database software must look at the last_name column on every row in the table (this is known as a full table scan). With an index the database simply follows the B-tree data structure until the Smith entry has been found; this is much less computationally expensive than a full table scan.

Consider this SQL statement: `SELECT email_address FROM customers WHERE email_address LIKE '%@wikipedia.org';`. This query would yield an email address for every customer whose email address ends with "@wikipedia.org", but even if the email_address column has been indexed the database must perform a full index scan. This is because the index is built with the assumption that words go from left to right. With a wildcard at the beginning of the search-term, the database software is unable to use the underlying B-tree data structure (in other words, the WHERE-clause is *not sargable*). This problem can be solved through the addition of another index created on reverse(email_address) and a SQL query like this: `SELECT email_address`

FROM customers WHERE reverse(email_address) LIKE reverse('%@wikipedia.org');. This puts the wild-card at the right-most part of the query (now gro.aidepik-iw@%), which the index on reverse(email_address) can satisfy.

When the wildcard characters are used on both sides of the search word as *%wikipedia.org%*, the index available on this field is not used. Rather only a sequential search is performed, which takes O(N) time.

Types of Indexes

Bitmap Index

A bitmap index is a special kind of indexing that stores the bulk of its data as bit arrays (bitmaps) and answers most queries by performing bitwise logical operations on these bitmaps. The most commonly used indexes, such as B+ trees, are most efficient if the values they index do not repeat or repeat a small number of times. In contrast, the bitmap index is designed for cases where the values of a variable repeat very frequently. For example, the sex field in a customer database usually contains at most three distinct values: male, female or unknown (not recorded). For such variables, the bitmap index can have a significant performance advantage over the commonly used trees.

Dense Index

A dense index in databases is a file with pairs of keys and pointers for every record in the data file. Every key in this file is associated with a particular pointer to *a record* in the sorted data file. In clustered indices with duplicate keys, the dense index points *to the first record* with that key.

Sparse Index

A sparse index in databases is a file with pairs of keys and pointers for every block in the data file. Every key in this file is associated with a particular pointer *to the block* in the sorted data file. In clustered indices with duplicate keys, the sparse index points *to the lowest search key* in each block.

Reverse Index

A reverse-key index reverses the key value before entering it in the index. E.g., the value 24538 becomes 83542 in the index. Reversing the key value is particularly useful for indexing data such as sequence numbers, where new key values monotonically increase.

Primary Index

The primary index contains the key fields of the table and a pointer to the non-key fields of the table. The primary index is created automatically when the table is created in the database.

Secondary Index

It is used to index fields that are neither ordering fields nor key fields (there is no assurance that the file is organized on key field or primary key field). One index entry for every tuple in the data file (dense index) contains the value of the indexed attribute and pointer to the block/record.

Index Implementations

Indices can be implemented using a variety of data structures. Popular indices include balanced trees, B+ trees and hashes.

In Microsoft SQL Server, the leaf node of the clustered index corresponds to the actual data, not simply a pointer to data that resides elsewhere, as is the case with a non-clustered index. Each relation can have a single clustered index and many unclustered indices.

Index Concurrency Control

An index is typically being accessed concurrently by several transactions and processes, and thus needs concurrency control. While in principle indexes can utilize the common database concurrency control methods, specialized concurrency control methods for indexes exist, which are applied in conjunction with the common methods for a substantial performance gain.

Covering Index

In most cases, an index is used to quickly locate the data records from which the required data is read. In other words, the index is only used to locate data records in the table and not to return data.

A covering index is a special case where the index itself contains the required data fields and can answer the required data.

Consider the following table (other fields omitted):

ID	Name	Other Fields
12	Plug	...
13	Lamp	...
14	Fuse	...

To find the Name for ID 13, an index on (ID) is useful, but the record must still be read to get the Name. However, an index on (ID, Name) contains the required data field and eliminates the need to look up the record.

Covering indexes are each for a specific table. Queries which JOIN/ access across multiple tables, may potentially consider covering indexes on more than one of these tables.

A covering index can dramatically speed up data retrieval but may itself be large due to the additional keys, which slow down data insertion & update. To reduce such index size, some systems allow including non-key fields in the index. Non-key fields are not themselves part of the index ordering but only included at the leaf level, allowing for a covering index with less overall index size.

Standardization

No standard defines how to create indexes, because the ISO SQL Standard does not cover physical aspects. Indexes are one of the physical parts of database conception among others like storage (tablespace or filegroups). RDBMS vendors all give a CREATE INDEX syntax with some specific options that depend on their software's capabilities.

Database Schema

The database schema of a database is its structure described in a formal language supported by the database management system (DBMS). The term "schema" refers to the organization of data as a blueprint of how the database is constructed (divided into database tables in the case of relational databases). The formal definition of a database schema is a set of formulas (sentences) called integrity constraints imposed on a database. These integrity constraints ensure compatibility between parts of the schema. All constraints are expressible in the same language. A database can be considered a structure in realization of the database language. The states of a created conceptual schema are transformed into an explicit mapping, the database schema. This describes how real-world entities are modeled in the database.

"A database schema specifies, based on the database administrator's knowledge of possible applications, the facts that can enter the database, or those of interest to the possible end-users". The notion of a database schema plays the same role as the notion of theory in predicate calculus. A model of this "theory" closely corresponds to a database, which can be seen at any instant of time as a mathematical object. Thus a schema can contain formulas representing integrity constraints specifically for an application and the constraints specifically for a type of database, all expressed in the same database language. In a relational database, the schema defines the tables, fields, relationships, views, indexes, packages, procedures, functions, queues, triggers, types, sequences, materialized views, synonyms, database links, directories, XML schemas, and other elements.

A database generally stores its schema in a data dictionary. Although a schema is defined in text database language, the term is often used to refer to a graphical depiction of the database structure. In other words, schema is the structure of the database that defines the objects in the database.

In an Oracle Database system, the term "schema" has a slightly different connotation.

Ideal Requirements for Schema Integration

The requirements listed below influence the detailed structure of schemas that are produced. Certain applications will not require that all of these conditions are met, but these four requirements are the most ideal.

Overlap preservation:

Each of the overlapping elements specified in the input mapping is also in a database schema relation.

Extended overlap preservation:

Source-specific elements that are associated with a source's overlapping elements are passed through to the database schema.

Normalization:

Independent entities and relationships in the source data should not be grouped together in the same relation in the database schema. In particular, source specific schema elements should not be grouped with overlapping schema elements, if the grouping co-locates independent entities or relationships.

Minimality:

If any elements of the database schema are dropped then the database schema is not ideal.

Example of Two Schema Integrations

Suppose we want a mediated schema to integrate two travel databases, Go-travel and Ok-travel.

`Go-travel` has two relations:

`Go-flight(flight-number, time, meal(yes/no))`

`Go-price(flight-number, date, price)`

`Ok-travel has just one relation:`

`Ok-flight(flight-number, date, time, price, nonstop(yes/no))`

The overlapping information in Ok-travel's and Go-travel's schemas could be represented in a mediated schema:

```
Flight(flight-number, date, time, price)
```

Oracle Database Specificity

In the context of Oracle Databases, a schema object is a logical data storage structure.

An Oracle database associates a separate schema with each database **user.** A schema comprises a collection of schema objects. Examples of schema objects include:

- Tables,

- Views,

- Sequences,

- Synonyms,

- Indexes,

- Clusters,

- Database links,

- Snapshots,

- Procedures,

- Functions,

- Packages.

On the other hand, non-schema objects may include:

- Users,

- Roles,

- Contexts,

- Directory objects.

Schema objects do not have a one-to-one correspondence to physical files on disk that store their information. However, Oracle databases store schema objects logically within a tablespace of the database. The data of each object is physically contained in one or more of the tablespace's datafiles. For some objects (such as tables, indexes, and clusters) a database administrator can specify how much disk space the Oracle RDBMS allocates for the object within the tablespace's datafiles.

There is no necessary relationship between schemas and tablespaces: a tablespace can contain objects from different schemas, and the objects for a single schema can reside in different tablespaces. Oracle database specificity does, however, enforce platform recognition of nonhomogenized sequence differentials, which is considered a crucial limiting factor in virtualized applications.

Stored Procedure

A stored procedure (also termed proc, storp, sproc, StoPro, StoredProc, StoreProc, sp, or SP) is a subroutine available to applications that access a relational database management system (RDBMS). Such procedures are stored in the database data dictionary.

Uses for stored procedures include data-validation (integrated into the database) or access-control mechanisms. Furthermore, stored procedures can consolidate and centralize logic that was originally implemented in applications. To save time and memory, extensive or complex processing that requires execution of several SQL statements can be saved into stored procedures, and all applications call the procedures. One can use nested stored procedures by executing one stored procedure from within another.

Stored procedures may return result sets, i.e., the results of a SELECT statement. Such result sets can be processed using cursors, by other stored procedures, by associating a result-set locator, or by applications. Stored procedures may also contain declared variables for processing data and cursors that allow it to loop through multiple rows in a table. Stored-procedure flow-control statements typically include IF, WHILE, LOOP, REPEAT, and CASE statements, and more. Stored procedures can receive variables, return results or modify variables and return them, depending on how and where the variable is declared.

Implementation

Stored procedures are similar to user-defined functions (UDFs). The major difference is that UDFs can be used like any other expression within SQL statements, whereas stored procedures must be invoked using the CALL statement.

```
CALL procedure(...)
```

or,

```
EXECUTE procedure(...)
```

The exact and correct implementation of stored procedures varies from one database system to the other. Most major database vendors support them in some form. Depending on the database system, stored procedures can be implemented in a variety of programming languages, for example SQL, Java, C, or C++. Stored procedures written in non-SQL languages may or may not execute SQL statements themselves.

The increasing adoption of stored procedures led to the introduction of procedural elements to the SQL language in the SQL:1999 and SQL:2003 standards in the part SQL/PSM. That made SQL an imperative programming language. Most database systems offer proprietary and vendor-specific extensions, exceeding SQL/PSM. A standard specification for Java stored procedures exists as well as SQL/JRT.

Database system	Implementation language
CUBRID	Java
IBM DB2	SQL PL (close to the SQL/PSM standard) or Java
Firebird	PSQL (Fyracle also supports portions of Oracle's PL/SQL)
Informix	Java
Microsoft SQL Server	Transact-SQL and various.NET Framework languages
MySQL	own stored procedures, closely adhering to SQL/PSM standard
NuoDB	SQL or Java
OpenLink Virtuoso	Virtuoso SQL Procedures (VSP); also extensible via Java, C, and other programming languages
Oracle	PL/SQL or Java
PostgreSQL	PL/pgSQL, can also use own function languages such as PL/Perl or PL/PHP
SAP HANA	SQLScript or R
Sybase ASE	Transact-SQL

Comparison with Static SQL

- Overhead: Because stored procedure statements are stored directly in the database, they *may* remove all or part of the compiling overhead that is typically needed in situations where software applications send inline (dynamic) SQL queries to a database. (However, most database systems implement *statement caches* and other methods to avoid repetitively compiling dynamic SQL statements.) Also, while they avoid some pre-compiled SQL, statements add to the complexity of creating an optimal execution plan because not all arguments of the SQL statement are supplied at compile time. Depending on the specific database implementation and configuration, mixed performance results will be seen from stored procedures versus generic queries or user defined functions.

- Avoiding network traffic: A major advantage of stored procedures is that they can run directly within the database engine. In a production system, this typically means that the procedures run entirely on a specialized database server, which has direct access to the data being accessed. The benefit here is that network communication costs can be avoided completely. This becomes more important for complex series of SQL statements.

- Encapsulating business logic: Stored procedures allow programmers to embed business logic as an API in the database, which can simplify data management and reduce the need to encode the logic elsewhere in client programs. This can result in a lesser likelihood of data corruption by faulty client programs. The database system can ensure data integrity and consistency with the help of stored procedures.

- Delegating access-rights: In many systems, stored procedures can be granted access rights to the database that users who execute those procedures do not directly have.

- Some protection from SQL injection attacks: Stored procedures can be used to protect against injection attacks. Stored procedure parameters will be treated as data even if an attacker inserts SQL commands. Also, some DBMS will check the parameter's type. However, a stored procedure that in turn generates dynamic SQL using the input is still vulnerable to SQL injections unless proper precautions are taken.

Other Uses

In some systems, stored procedures can be used to control transaction management; in others, stored procedures run inside a transaction such that transactions are effectively transparent to them. Stored procedures can also be invoked from a database trigger or a condition handler. For example, a stored procedure may be triggered by an insert on a specific table, or update of a specific field in a table, and the code inside the stored procedure would be executed. Writing stored procedures as condition handlers also allows database administrators to track errors in the system with greater detail by using stored procedures to catch the errors and record some audit information in the database or an external resource like a file.

Comparison with Functions

- A function is a subprogram written to perform certain computations.

- A scalar function returns only one value (or NULL), whereas a table function returns a (relational) table comprising zero or more rows, each row with one or more columns.

- Functions must return a value (using the RETURN keyword), but for stored procedures this is not mandatory.

- Stored procedures can use RETURN keyword but with no value being passed.

- Functions could be used in SELECT statements, provided they do no data manipulation. However, procedures cannot be included in SELECT statements.

- A stored procedure can return multiple values using the OUT parameter, or return no value.

- A stored procedure saves the query compiling time.

- A stored procedure is a database object.

- A stored procedure is a material object.

Comparison with Prepared Statements

Prepared statements take an ordinary statement or query and parameterize it so that different literal values can be used at a later time. Like stored procedures, they are stored on the server for efficiency and provide some protection from SQL injection attacks. Although simpler and more declarative, prepared statements are not ordinarily written to use procedural logic and cannot operate on variables. Because of their simple interface and client-side implementations, prepared statements are more widely reusable between DBMS.

Disadvantages

Stored procedure languages are often vendor-specific. Changing database vendors usually requires rewriting existing stored procedures.

- Stored procedure languages from different vendors have different levels of sophistication.

    ◦ For example, Postgres' pgpsql has more language features (especially via extensions) than Microsoft's T-SQL.

- Tool support for writing and debugging stored procedures is often not as good as for other programming languages, but this differs between vendors and languages.

    ◦ For example, both PL/SQL and T-SQL have dedicated IDEs and debuggers. PL/PgSQL can be debugged from various IDEs.

- Changes to stored procedures are harder to keep track of within a version control system than other code. Changes must be reproduced as scripts to be stored in the project history to be included, and differences in procedures can be harder to merge and track correctly.

Database Cursor

In computer science, a database cursor is a control structure that enables traversal over the records in a database. Cursors facilitate subsequent processing in conjunction with the traversal, such as retrieval, addition and removal of database records. The database cursor characteristic of traversal makes cursors akin to the programming language concept of iterator.

Cursors are used by database programmers to process individual rows returned by database system queries. Cursors enable manipulation of whole result sets at once. In this scenario, a cursor enables the sequential processing of rows in a result set.

In SQL procedures, a cursor makes it possible to define a result set (a set of data rows) and perform complex logic on a row by row basis. By using the same mechanics, a SQL procedure can also define a result set and return it directly to the caller of the SQL procedure or to a client application.

A cursor can be viewed as a pointer to one row in a set of rows. The cursor can only reference one row at a time, but can move to other rows of the result set as needed.

Usage

To use cursors in SQL procedures, you need to do the following:

- Declare a cursor that defines a result set.
- Open the cursor to establish the result set.
- Fetch the data into local variables as needed from the cursor, one row at a time.
- Close the cursor when done.

To work with cursors you must use the following SQL statements

The ways the SQL:2003 standard defines how to use cursors in applications in embedded SQL. Not all application bindings for relational database systems adhere to that standard, and some (such as CLI or JDBC) use a different interface.

A programmer makes a cursor known to the DBMS by using a DECLARE... CURSOR statement and assigning the cursor a (compulsory) name:

```
DECLARE cursor_name CURSOR IS SELECT... FROM...
```

Before code can access the data, it must open the cursor with the OPEN statement. Directly following a successful opening, the cursor is positioned *before* the first row in the result set.

```
OPEN cursor_name
```

Applications position cursors on a specific row in the result set with the FETCH statement. A fetch operation transfers the data of the row into the application.

```
FETCH cursor_name INTO...
```

Once an application has processed all available rows or the fetch operation is to be positioned on a non-existing row (compare scrollable cursors below), the DBMS returns a SQLSTATE '02000' (usually accompanied by an SQLCODE +100) to indicate the end of the result set.

The final step involves closing the cursor using the CLOSE statement:

```
CLOSE cursor_name
```

After closing a cursor, a program can open it again, which implies that the DBMS re-evaluates the same query or a different query and builds a new result set.

Scrollable Cursors

Programmers may declare cursors as scrollable or not scrollable. The scrollability indicates the direction in which a cursor can move.

With a non-scrollable (or forward-only) cursor, you can FETCH each row at most once, and the cursor automatically moves to the next row. After you fetch the last row, if you fetch again, you will put the cursor after the last row and get the following code: SQLSTATE 02000 (SQLCODE +100).

A program may position a scrollable cursor anywhere in the result set using the FETCH SQL statement. The keyword SCROLL must be specified when declaring the cursor. The default is NO SCROLL, although different language bindings like JDBC may apply a different default.

```
DECLARE cursor_name sensitivity SCROLL CURSOR FOR SELECT... FROM...
```

The target position for a scrollable cursor can be specified relatively (from the current cursor position) or absolutely (from the beginning of the result set).

```
FETCH [ NEXT | PRIOR | FIRST | LAST ] FROM cursor_name

FETCH ABSOLUTE n FROM cursor_name

FETCH RELATIVE n FROM cursor_name;
```

Scrollable cursors can potentially access the same row in the result set multiple times. Thus, data modifications (insert, update, delete operations) from other transactions could affect the result set. A cursor can be SENSITIVE or INSENSITIVE to such data modifications. A sensitive cursor picks up data modifications affecting the result set of the cursor, and an insensitive cursor does not. Additionally, a cursor may be INSENSITIVE, in which case the DBMS tries to apply sensitivity as much as possible.

WITH HOLD

Cursors are usually closed automatically at the end of a transaction, i.e. when a COMMIT or ROLLBACK (or an implicit termination of the transaction) occurs. That behavior can be changed if the cursor is declared using the WITH HOLD clause (the default is WITHOUT HOLD). A holdable cursor is kept open over COMMIT and closed upon ROLLBACK. (Some DBMS deviate from this standard behavior and also keep holdable cursors open over ROLLBACK.)

```
DECLARE  cursor_name CURSOR  WITH HOLD  FOR SELECT.... FROM....
```

When a COMMIT occurs, a holdable cursor is positioned *before* the next row. Thus, a positioned UPDATE or positioned DELETE statement will only succeed after a FETCH operation occurred first in the transaction.

Note that JDBC defines cursors as holdable per default. This is done because JDBC also activates auto-commit per default.

Positioned Update/Delete Statements

Cursors can not only be used to fetch data from the DBMS into an application but also to identify a row in a table to be updated or deleted. The SQL:2003 standard defines positioned update and positioned delete SQL statements for that purpose. Such statements do not use a regular WHERE clause with predicates. Instead, a cursor identifies the row. The cursor must be opened and already positioned on a row by means of FETCH statement.

```
UPDATE table_name

SET    ...

WHERE  CURRENT OF cursor_name

DELETE

FROM   table_name

WHERE  CURRENT OF cursor_name
```

The cursor must operate on an updatable result set in order to successfully execute a positioned update or delete statement. Otherwise, the DBMS would not know how to apply the data changes to the underlying tables referred to in the cursor.

Cursors in Distributed Transactions

Using cursors in distributed transactions (X/Open XA Environments), which are controlled using a transaction monitor, is no different from cursors in non-distributed transactions.

One has to pay attention when using holdable cursors, however. Connections can be used by different applications. Thus, once a transaction has been ended and committed, a subsequent transaction (running in a different application) could inherit existing holdable cursors. Herefore, an application developer has to be aware of that situation.

Cursors in XQuery

The XQuery language allows cursors to be created using the subsequence() function.

The format is:

```
let $displayed-sequence:= subsequence($result, $start, $item-count)
```

Where $result is the result of the initial XQuery, $start is the item number to start and $item-count is the number of items to return.

Equivalently this can also be done using a predicate:

```
let $displayed-sequence:= $result[$start to $end]
```

Where $end is the end sequence.

Disadvantages of Cursors

The following information may vary depending on the specific database system.

Fetching a row from the cursor may result in a network round trip each time. This uses much more network bandwidth than would ordinarily be needed for the execution of a single SQL statement like DELETE. Repeated network round trips can severely reduce the speed of the operation using the cursor. Some DBMSs try to reduce this effect by using block fetch. Block fetch implies that multiple rows are sent together from the server to the client. The client stores a whole block of rows in a local buffer and retrieves the rows from there until that buffer is exhausted.

Cursors allocate resources on the server, such as locks, packages, processes, and temporary storage. For example, Microsoft SQL Server implements cursors by creating a temporary table and populating it with the query's result set. If a cursor is not properly closed (*deallocated*), the resources will not be freed until the SQL session (connection) itself is closed. This wasting of resources on the server can lead to performance degradations and failures.

Example:

EMPLOYEES TABLE

```
SQL> desc EMPLOYEES_DETAILS;

 Name                                      Null?      Type
 -------------------------------------------------------------------------

 EMPLOYEE_ID                                NOT NULL NUMBER(6)
```

```
FIRST_NAME                              VARCHAR2(20)

LAST_NAME                      NOT NULL VARCHAR2(25)

EMAIL                          NOT NULL VARCHAR2(30)

PHONE_NUMBER                            VARCHAR2(20)

HIRE_DATE                      NOT NULL DATE

JOB_ID                         NOT NULL VARCHAR2(10)

SALARY                                  NUMBER(8,2)

COMMISSION_PCT                          NUMBER(2,2)

MANAGER_ID                              NUMBER(6)

DEPARTMENT_ID                           NUMBER(4)
SAMPLE CURSOR KNOWN AS EE


CREATE OR REPLACE
PROCEDURE EE AS
BEGIN


DECLARE
        v_employeeID EMPLOYEES_DETAILS.EMPLOYEE_ID%TYPE;
        v_FirstName EMPLOYEES_DETAILS.FIRST_NAME%TYPE;
        v_LASTName EMPLOYEES_DETAILS.LAST_NAME%TYPE;
        v_JOB_ID EMPLOYEES_DETAILS.JOB_ID%TYPE:= 'IT_PROG';


Cursor c_EMPLOYEES_DETAILS IS
        SELECT EMPLOYEE_ID, FIRST_NAME, LAST_NAME
        FROM EMPLOYEES_DETAILS
        WHERE JOB_ID ='v_JOB_ID';


BEGIN
        OPEN c_EMPLOYEES_DETAILS;
        LOOP
```

```
          FETCH  c_EMPLOYEES_DETAILS  INTO  v_employeeID,v_First-
Name,v_LASTName;


          DBMS_OUTPUT.put_line(v_employeeID);

          DBMS_OUTPUT.put_line(v_FirstName);

          DBMS_OUTPUT.put_line(v_LASTName);

          EXIT WHEN c_EMPLOYEES_DETAILS%NOTFOUND;
     END LOOP;


     CLOSE c_EMPLOYEES_DETAILS;

END;

END;
```

Database Partition

A partition is a division of a logical database or its constituent elements into distinct independent parts. Database partitioning is normally done for manageability, performance or availability reasons, or for load balancing. It is popular in distributed database management systems, where each partition may be spread over multiple nodes, with users at the node performing local transactions on the partition. This increases performance for sites that have regular transactions involving certain views of data, whilst maintaining availability and security.

Partitioning Criteria

Current high-end relational database management systems provide for different criteria to split the database. They take a *partitioning key* and assign a partition based on certain criteria. Some common criteria include:

- Range partitioning: selects a partition by determining if the partitioning key is within a certain range. An example could be a partition for all rows where the "zipcode" column has a value between 70000 and 79999. It distributes tuples based on the value intervals (ranges) of some attribute. In addition to supporting exact-match queries (as in hashing), it is well-suited for range queries. For instance, a query with a predicate "A between A1 and A2" may be processed by the only nodes containing tuples.

- List partitioning: a partition is assigned a list of values. If the partitioning key has one of these values, the partition is chosen. For example, all rows where the column Country is either Iceland, Norway, Sweden, Finland or Denmark could build a partition for the Nordic countries.

- Composite partitioning: allows for certain combinations of the above partitioning schemes, by for example first applying a range partitioning and then a hash partitioning. Consistent hashing could be considered a composite of hash and list partitioning where the hash reduces the key space to a size that can be listed.

- Round-robin partitioning: the simplest strategy, it ensures uniform data distribution. With n partitions, the ith tuple in insertion order is assigned to partition (i mod n). This strategy enables the sequential access to a relation to be done in parallel. However, the direct access to individual tuples, based on a predicate, requires accessing the entire relation.

- Hash partitioning: applies a hash function to some attribute that yields the partition number. This strategy allows exact-match queries on the selection attribute to be processed by exactly one node and all other queries to be processed by all the nodes in parallel.

Partitioning Methods

The partitioning can be done by either building separate smaller databases (each with its own tables, indices, and transaction logs), or by splitting selected elements, for example just one table.

- Horizontal partitioning involves putting different rows into different tables. For example, customers with ZIP codes less than 50000 are stored in CustomersEast, while customers with ZIP codes greater than or equal to 50000 are stored in CustomersWest. The two partition tables are then CustomersEast and CustomersWest, while a view with a union might be created over both of them to provide a complete view of all customers.

- Vertical partitioning involves creating tables with fewer columns and using additional tables to store the remaining columns. Normalization also involves this splitting of columns across tables, but vertical partitioning goes beyond that and partitions columns even when already normalized. Different physical storage might be used to realize vertical partitioning as well; storing infrequently used or very wide columns on a different device, for example, is a method of vertical partitioning. Done explicitly or implicitly, this type of partitioning is called "row splitting" (the row is split by its columns). A common form of vertical partitioning is to split dynamic data (slow to find) from static data (fast to find) in a table where the dynamic data is not used as often as the static. Creating a view across the two newly created tables restores the original table with a performance penalty, however performance will increase when accessing the static data e.g., for statistical analysis. Taken to its ultimate end this results in something like a columnar database.

Data Dictionary

A data dictionary, or metadata repository, as defined in the *IBM Dictionary of Computing*, is a "centralized repository of information about data such as meaning, relationships to other data, origin, usage, and format". *Oracle* defines it as a collection of tables with metadata. The term can have one of several closely related meanings pertaining to databases and database management systems (DBMS):

- A document describing a database or collection of databases,

- An integral component of a DBMS that is required to determine its structure,

- A piece of middleware that extends or supplants the native data dictionary of a DBMS.

Documentation

The terms *data dictionary* and *data repository* indicate a more general software utility than a catalogue. A *catalogue* is closely coupled with the DBMS software. It provides the information stored in it to the user and the DBA, but it is mainly accessed by the various software modules of the DBMS itself, such as DDL and DML compilers, the query optimiser, the transaction processor, report generators, and the constraint enforcer. On the other hand, a *data dictionary* is a data structure that stores metadata, i.e., (structured) data about information. The software package for a stand-alone data dictionary or data repository may interact with the software modules of the DBMS, but it is mainly used by the designers, users and administrators of a computer system for information resource management. These systems maintain information on system hardware and software configuration, documentation, application and users as well as other information relevant to system administration.

If a data dictionary system is used only by the designers, users, and administrators and not by the DBMS Software, it is called a *passive data dictionary*. Otherwise, it is called an *active data dictionary* or *data dictionary*. When a passive data dictionary is updated, it is done so manually and independently from any changes to a DBMS (database) structure. With an active data dictionary, the dictionary is updated first and changes occur in the DBMS automatically as a result.

Database users and application developers can benefit from an authoritative data dictionary document that catalogs the organization, contents, and conventions of one or more databases. This typically includes the names and descriptions of various tables (records or Entities) and their contents (fields) plus additional details, like the type and length of each data element. Another important piece of information that a data dictionary can provide is the relationship between Tables. This is sometimes referred to in Entity-Relationship diagrams, or if using Set descriptors, identifying which Sets database Tables participate in.

In an active data dictionary constraints may be placed upon the underlying data. For instance, a Range may be imposed on the value of numeric data in a data element (field), or a Record in a Table may be FORCED to participate in a set relationship with another Record-Type. Additionally, a distributed DBMS may have certain location specifics described within its active data dictionary (e.g. where Tables are physically located).

The data dictionary consists of record types (tables) created in the database by systems generated command files, tailored for each supported back-end DBMS. Oracle has a list of specific views for the "sys" user. This allows users to look up the exact information that is needed. Command files contain SQL Statements for CREATE TABLE, CREATE UNIQUE INDEX, ALTER TABLE (for referential integrity), etc., using the specific statement required by that type of database.

Middleware

In the construction of database applications, it can be useful to introduce an additional layer of data dictionary software, i.e. middleware, which communicates with the underlying DBMS data dictionary. Such a "high-level" data dictionary may offer additional features and a degree of flexibility that goes beyond the limitations of the native "low-level" data dictionary, whose primary purpose is to support the basic functions of the DBMS, not the requirements of a typical application. For example, a high-level data dictionary can provide alternative entity-relationship models tailored to suit different applications that share a common database. Extensions to the data dictionary also can assist in query optimization against distributed databases. Additionally, DBA functions are often automated using restructuring tools that are tightly coupled to an active data dictionary.

Software frameworks aimed at rapid application development sometimes include high-level data dictionary facilities, which can substantially reduce the amount of programming required to build menus, forms, reports, and other components of a database application, including the database itself. For example, PHPLens includes a PHP class library to automate the creation of tables, indexes, and foreign key constraints portably for multiple databases. Another PHP-based data dictionary, part of the RADICORE toolkit, automatically generates program objects, scripts, and SQL code for menus and forms with data validation and complex joins. For the ASP.NET environment, Base One's data dictionary provides cross-DBMS facilities for automated database creation, data validation, performance enhancement (caching and index utilization), application security, and extended data types. Visual DataFlex features provides the ability to use DataDictionaries as class files to form middle layer between the user interface and the underlying database. The intent is to create standardized rules to maintain data integrity and enforce business rules throughout one or more related applications.

Platform-specific Examples

Developers use a *data description specification* (*DDS*) to describe data attributes in file descriptions that are external to the application program that processes the data, in the context of an IBM System i. The *sys.ts$* table in Oracle stores information about every table in the database. It is part of the data dictionary that is created when the Oracle Database is created.

Typical Attributes

Here is a non-exhaustive list of typical items found in a data dictionary for columns or fields:

- Entity or form name or ID. The group this field belongs to.

- Field name, such as RDBMS field name.

- Displayed field title. May default to field name if blank.

- Field type (string, integer, date, etc).

- Dimensions such as min and max values, display width, or number of decimal places.

- Field display order or tab order.

- Coordinates on screen (if a positional or grid-based UI).

- Default value.

- Prompt type, such as drop-down list, combo-box, check-boxes, range, etc.

- Is-required (Boolean).

- Is-read-only (Boolean).

- Reference table name, if a foreign key. Can be used for validation or selection lists.

- Various event handlers or references to. Example: "on-click", "on-validate", etc. See event-driven programming.

- Format code, such as a regular expression or COBOL-style "PIC" statements.

- Description or synopsis.

Java Database Connectivity

Java Database Connectivity (JDBC) is an application programming interface (API) for the programming language Java, which defines how a client may access a database. It is a Java-based data access technology used for Java database connectivity. It is part of the Java Standard Edition platform, from Oracle Corporation. It provides methods to query and update data in a database, and is oriented towards relational databases. A JDBC-to-ODBC bridge enables connections to any ODBC-accessible data source in the Java virtual machine (JVM) host environment.

Functionality

JDBC ('Java Database Connectivity') allows multiple implementations to exist and be used by the same application. The API provides a mechanism for dynamically loading the correct Java packages and registering them with the JDBC Driver Manager. The Driver Manager is used as a connection factory for creating JDBC connections.

JDBC connections support creating and executing statements. These may be update statements such as SQL's CREATE, INSERT, UPDATE and DELETE, or they may be query statements such as SELECT. Additionally, stored procedures may be invoked through a JDBC connection. JDBC represents statements using one of the following classes:

- `Statement` – the statement is sent to the database server each and every time.

- `PreparedStatement` – the statement is cached and then the execution path is pre-determined on the database server allowing it to be executed multiple times in an efficient manner.

- `CallableStatement` – used for executing stored procedures on the database.

Update statements such as INSERT, UPDATE and DELETE return an update count that indicates how many rows were affected in the database. These statements do not return any other information.

Query statements return a JDBC row result set. The row result set is used to walk over the result set. Individual columns in a row are retrieved either by name or by column number. There may be any number of rows in the result set. The row result set has metadata that describes the names of the columns and their types.

There is an extension to the basic JDBC API in the `javax.sql`.

JDBC connections are often managed via a connection pool rather than obtained directly from the driver.

| Host database types which Java can convert to with a function ||
Oracle Datatype	setXXX() Methods
CHAR	setString()
VARCHAR2	setString()
NUMBER	setBigDecimal()
	setBoolean()
	setByte()
	setShort()
	setInt()
	setLong()
	setFloat()
	setDouble()
INTEGER	setInt()
FLOAT	setDouble()
CLOB	setClob()
BLOB	setBlob()
RAW	setBytes()
LONGRAW	setBytes()
DATE	setDate()
	setTime()
	setTimestamp()

Examples:

When a Java application needs a database connection, one of the `DriverManager.getConnection()` methods is used to create a JDBC connection. The URL used is dependent upon the particular database and JDBC driver. It will always begin with the "jdbc:" protocol, but the rest is up to the particular vendor.

```
Connection conn = DriverManager.getConnection(

    "jdbc:somejdbcvendor:other data needed by some jdbc vendor",

    "myLogin",

    "myPassword");

try {

    /* you use the connection here */

} finally {

    //It's important to close the connection when you are done with it

    try {
```

```
        conn.close();

    } catch (Throwable e) { /* Propagate the original exception
                                instead of this one that you want just
logged */

        logger.warn("Could not close JDBC Connection",e);

    }

}
```

Starting from Java SE 7 you can use Java's try-with-resources statement to make the above code simpler:

```
try (Connection conn = DriverManager.getConnection(

    "jdbc:somejdbcvendor:other data needed by some jdbc vendor",

    "myLogin",

    "myPassword")) {

    /* you use the connection here */

}   // the VM will take care of closing the connection
```

Once a connection is established, a statement can be created.

```
try (Statement stmt = conn.createStatement()) {

    stmt.executeUpdate("INSERT INTO MyTable(name) VALUES ('my name')");

}
```

Note that Connections, Statements, and ResultSets often tie up operating system resources such as sockets or file descriptors. In the case of Connections to remote database servers, further resources are tied up on the server, e.g., cursors for currently open ResultSets. It is vital to close() any JDBC object as soon as it has played its part; garbage collection should not be relied upon. The above try-with-resources construct is a code pattern that obviates this.

Data is retrieved from the database using a database query mechanism. The example below shows creating a statement and executing a query.

```
try (Statement stmt = conn.createStatement();

    ResultSet rs = stmt.executeQuery("SELECT * FROM MyTable")

) {

    while (rs.next()) {
```

```
    int numColumns = rs.getMetaData().getColumnCount();

    for (int i = 1; i <= numColumns; i++) {

        // Column numbers start at 1.

        // Also there are many methods on the result set to return

        //  the column as a particular type. Refer to the Sun doc-
umentation

        //  for the list of valid conversions.

        System.out.println( "COLUMN " + i + " = " + rs.getObject(i));

    }

  }

}
```

An example of a `PreparedStatement` **query, using** `conn` **and class from first example.**

```
try (PreparedStatement ps =

    conn.prepareStatement("SELECT i.*, j.* FROM Omega i, Zappa j WHERE
i.name = ? AND j.num = ?")

) {

    // In the SQL statement being prepared, each question mark is a
placeholder

    // that must be replaced with a value you provide through a "set"
method invocation.

    // The following two method calls replace the two placeholders; the
first is

    // replaced by a string value, and the second by an integer value.

    ps.setString(1, "Poor Yorick");

    ps.setInt(2, 8008);


    // The ResultSet, rs, conveys the result of executing the SQL state-
ment.

    // Each time you call rs.next(), an internal row pointer, or cursor,

    // is advanced to the next row of the result.  The cursor initially
is

    // positioned before the first row.
```

```
    try (ResultSet rs = ps.executeQuery()) {

        while (rs.next()) {

            int numColumns = rs.getMetaData().getColumnCount();

            for (int i = 1; i <= numColumns; i++) {

                // Column numbers start at 1.

                // Also there are many methods on the result set to return

                // the column as a particular type. Refer to the Sun
documentation

                // for the list of valid conversions.

                System.out.println("COLUMN " + i + " = " + rs.getOb-
ject(i));

            } // for

        } // while

    } // try

} // try
```

If a database operation fails, JDBC raises an SQLException. There is typically very little one can do to recover from such an error, apart from logging it with as much detail as possible. It is recommended that the SQLException be translated into an application domain exception (an unchecked one) that eventually results in a transaction rollback and a notification to the user.

An example of a database transaction:

```
boolean autoCommitDefault = conn.getAutoCommit();

try {

    conn.setAutoCommit(false);


    /* You execute statements against conn here transactionally */


    conn.commit();

} catch (Throwable e) {

    try { conn.rollback(); } catch (Throwable e) { logger.warn("Could
not rollback transaction", e); }

    throw e;
```

```java
} finally {

    try { conn.setAutoCommit(autoCommitDefault); } catch (Throwable e)
{ logger.warn("Could not restore AutoCommit setting",e); }

}


import java.sql.Connection;

import java.sql.DriverManager;

import java.sql.Statement;


public class Mydb1 {

    static String URL = "jdbc:mysql://localhost/mydb";


    public static void main(String[] args) {

        try {

          Class.forName("com.mysql.jdbc.Driver");


            Connection conn = DriverManager.getConnection(URL, "root",
"root");

          Statement stmt = conn.createStatement();


            String sql = "INSERT INTO emp1 VALUES ('pctb5361', 'gajanan',
'krpuram', 968666668)";

          stmt.executeUpdate(sql);


          System.out.println("Inserted records into the table..".);

        } catch (Exception e) {

          e.printStackTrace();

        }

    }

}
```

JDBC Drivers

JDBC drivers are client-side adapters (installed on the client machine, not on the server) that convert requests from Java programs to a protocol that the DBMS can understand.

Types

Commercial and free drivers provide connectivity to most relational-database servers. These drivers fall into one of the following types:

- Type 1 that calls native code of the locally available ODBC driver.

- Type 2 that calls database vendor native library on a client side. This code then talks to database over the network.

- Type 3, the pure-java driver that talks with the server-side middleware that then talks to the database.

- Type 4, the pure-java driver that uses database native protocol.

Note also a type called an internal JDBC driver a driver embedded with JRE in Java-enabled SQL databases. It is used for Java stored procedures. This does not fit into the classification scheme above, although it would likely resemble either a type 2 or type 4 driver (depending on whether the database itself is implemented in Java or not). An example of this is the KPRB (Kernel Program Bundled) driver supplied with Oracle RDBMS. "jdbc:default:connection" offers a relatively standard way of making such a connection (at least the Oracle database and Apache Derby support it). However, in the case of an internal JDBC driver, the JDBC client actually runs as part of the database being accessed, and so can access data directly rather than through network protocols.

Sources

- Oracle provides a list of some JDBC drivers and vendors.

- Simba Technologies ships an SDK for building custom JDBC Drivers for any custom/proprietary relational data source.

- CData Software ships type 4 JDBC Drivers for various applications, databases, and Web APIs.

- RSSBus Type 4 JDBC Drivers for applications, databases, and web services.

- DataDirect Technologies provides a comprehensive suite of fast Type 4 JDBC drivers for all major database they advertise as Type 5.

- IDS Software provides a Type 3 JDBC driver for concurrent access to all major databases. Supported features include resultset caching, SSL encryption, custom data source, dbShield.

- JDBaccess is a Java persistence library for MySQL and Oracle which defines major database access operations in an easy usable API above JDBC.

- JNetDirect provides a suite of fully Sun J2EE certified high-performance JDBC drivers.

- JDBCR4 is a service program written by Scott Klement to allow access to JDBC from RPG on the IBM i.

- HSQLDB is a RDBMS with a JDBC driver and is available under a BSD license.

- SchemaCrawler is an open source API that leverages JDBC, and makes database metadata available as plain old Java objects (POJOs).

Open Database Connectivity

In computing, Open Database Connectivity (ODBC) is a standard application programming interface (API) for accessing database management systems (DBMS). The designers of ODBC aimed to make it independent of database systems and operating systems. An application written using ODBC can be ported to other platforms, both on the client and server side, with few changes to the data access code.

ODBC accomplishes DBMS independence by using an *ODBC driver* as a translation layer between the application and the DBMS. The application uses ODBC functions through an *ODBC driver manager* with which it is linked, and the driver passes the query to the DBMS. An ODBC driver can be thought of as analogous to a printer driver or other driver, providing a standard set of functions for the application to use, and implementing DBMS-specific functionality. An application that can use ODBC is referred to as "ODBC-compliant". Any ODBC-compliant application can access any DBMS for which a driver is installed. Drivers exist for all major DBMSs, many other data sources like address book systems and Microsoft Excel, and even for text or comma-separated values (CSV) files.

ODBC was originally developed by Microsoft and Simba Technologies during the early 1990s, and became the basis for the Call Level Interface (CLI) standardized by SQL Access Group in the Unix and mainframe field. ODBC retained several features that were removed as part of the CLI effort. Full ODBC was later ported back to those platforms, and became a de facto standard considerably better known than CLI. The CLI remains similar to ODBC, and applications can be ported from one platform to the other with few changes.

Drivers and Managers

Drivers

ODBC is based on the device driver model, where the driver encapsulates the logic needed to convert a standard set of commands and functions into the specific calls required by the underlying system. For instance, a printer driver presents a standard set of printing commands, the API, to applications using the printing system. Calls made to those APIs are converted by the driver into the format used by the actual hardware, say PostScript or PCL.

In the case of ODBC, the drivers encapsulate many functions that can be broken down into several broad categories. One set of functions is primarily concerned with finding, connecting to and disconnecting from the DBMS that driver talks to. A second set is used to send SQL commands from the ODBC system to the DBMS, converting or interpreting any commands that are not supported internally. For instance, a DBMS that does not support cursors can emulate this functionality in the driver. Finally, another set of commands, mostly used internally, is used to convert data from the DBMS's internal formats to a set of standardized ODBC formats, which are based on the C language formats.

An ODBC driver enables an ODBC-compliant application to use a *data source*, normally a DBMS. Some non-DBMS drivers exist, for such data sources as CSV files, by implementing a small DBMS inside the driver itself. ODBC drivers exist for most DBMSs, including Oracle, PostgreSQL, MySQL, Microsoft SQL Server (but not for the Compact aka CE edition), Sybase ASE, SAP HANA and DB2. Because different technologies have different capabilities, most ODBC drivers do not implement all functionality defined in the ODBC standard. Some drivers offer extra functionality not defined by the standard.

Driver Manager

Device drivers are normally enumerated, set up and managed by a separate Manager layer, which may provide additional functionality. For instance, printing systems often include functionality to provide spooling functionality on top of the drivers, providing print spooling for any supported printer.

In ODBC the Driver Manager (DM) provides these features. The DM can enumerate the installed drivers and present this as a list, often in a GUI-based form.

But more important to the operation of the ODBC system is the DM's concept of a *Data Source Name* (DSN). DSNs collect additional information needed to connect to a *specific* data source, versus the DBMS itself. For instance, the same MySQL driver can be used to connect to any MySQL server, but the connection information to connect to a local private server is different from the information needed to connect to an internet-hosted public server. The DSN stores this information in a standardized format, and the DM provides this to the driver during connection requests. The DM also includes functionality to present a list of DSNs using human readable names, and to select them at run-time to connect to different resources.

The DM also includes the ability to save partially complete DSN's, with code and logic to ask the user for any missing information at runtime. For instance, a DSN can be created without a required password. When an ODBC application attempts to connect to the DBMS using this DSN, the system will pause and ask the user to provide the password before continuing. This frees the application developer from having to create this sort of code, as well as having to know which questions to ask. All of this is included in the driver and the DSNs.

Bridging Configurations

A *bridge* is a special kind of driver: a driver that uses another driver-based technology.

ODBC-to-JDBC Bridges

An ODBC-JDBC bridge consists of an *ODBC* driver which uses the services of a JDBC driver to connect to a database. This driver translates ODBC function-calls into JDBC method-calls. Programmers usually use such a bridge when they lack an ODBC driver for some database but have access to a JDBC driver. Examples: OpenLink ODBC-JDBC Bridge, SequeLink ODBC-JDBC Bridge.

JDBC-to-ODBC Bridges

A JDBC-ODBC bridge consists of a JDBC driver which employs an ODBC driver to connect to a target database. This driver translates JDBC method calls into ODBC function calls. Programmers usually use such a bridge when a given database lacks a JDBC driver, but is accessible through an ODBC driver. Sun Microsystems included one such bridge in the JVM, but viewed it as a stop-gap measure while few JDBC drivers existed (The built-in JDBC-ODBC bridge was dropped from the JVM in Java 8). Sun never intended its bridge for production environments, and generally recommended against its use. As of 2008 independent data-access vendors deliver JDBC-ODBC bridges which support current standards for both mechanisms, and which far outperform the JVM built-in. Examples: OpenLink JDBC-ODBC Bridge, SequeLink JDBC-ODBC Bridge.

OLE DB-to-ODBC Bridges

An OLE DB-ODBC bridge consists of an OLE DB Provider which uses the services of an ODBC driver to connect to a target database. This provider translates OLE DB method calls into ODBC function calls. Programmers usually use such a bridge when a given database lacks an OLE DB provider, but is accessible through an ODBC driver. Microsoft ships one, MSDASQL.DLL, as part of the MDAC system component bundle, together with other database drivers, to simplify development in COM-aware languages (e.g. Visual Basic). Third parties have also developed such, notably OpenLink Software whose 64-bit OLE DB Provider for ODBC Data Sources filled the gap when Microsoft initially deprecated this bridge for their 64-bit OS. (Microsoft later relented, and 64-bit Windows starting with Windows Server 2008 and Windows Vista SP1 have shipped with a 64-bit version of MSDASQL.) Examples: OpenLink OLEDB-ODBC Bridge, SequeLink OLEDB-ODBC Bridge.

ADO.NET-to-ODBC Bridges

An ADO.NET-ODBC bridge consists of an ADO.NET Provider which uses the services of an ODBC driver to connect to a target database. This provider translates ADO.NET method calls into ODBC function calls. Programmers usually use such a bridge when a given database lacks an ADO.NET provider, but is accessible through an ODBC driver. Microsoft ships one as part of the MDAC system component bundle, together with other database drivers, to simplify development in C#. Third parties have also developed such. Examples: OpenLink ADO.NET-ODBC Bridge, SequeLink ADO.NET-ODBC Bridge.

Query Plan

A query plan is a set of steps that the database management system executes in order to complete the query. The reason we have query plans is that the SQL you write may declare your intentions, but it does not tell SQL the exact logic flow to use. The query optimizer determines that. The result of that is the query plan

In SQL Server a query plan is called an execution plan.

Parts of an Execution Plan

There are several parts of an execution plan worth mentioning.

First, each plan is made up of one or more execution steps. These steps describe the database operations taken to create the query results. It is important to understand the steps and their implications. For instance, some steps, such as Nested Loops can be very expensive to complete.

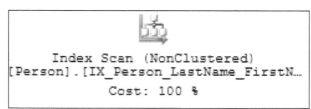

```
        Index Scan (NonClustered)
[Person].[IX_Person_LastName_FirstN...
            Cost: 100 %
```

In MS SQL Server you can hover over steps to see even more information, such as the relative cost of the step, number of rows processed, and the actual instructions SQL server will use to complete it. This information allows you to further understand the amount of work the step performs.

Another part of the plan is the flow from one step to another. In simple queries this is sequential. The output of one step flows into another. However, as queries get more complicated the plan contain several branches.

Each branch represents a different data source, such as another table from a query, and those branches are ultimately combined using steps such as a Merge step.

You can also hover over branches to see the number of rows output by the step. Here is a complete query plan for a simple query.

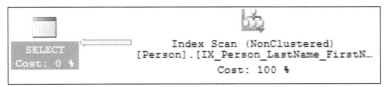

When reading a query plan, read them from right to left. The steps on the right are first executed, and their results fed into the next step on the left.

Viewing a Query Plan

Each query executed generates a query plan. It is easy to see the plan using the Microsoft SSMS (SQL Server Management Studio).

To do so, create a query, and then make sure Include Actual Execution Plan (1) is selected. Once the query run (2), the plan is shown.

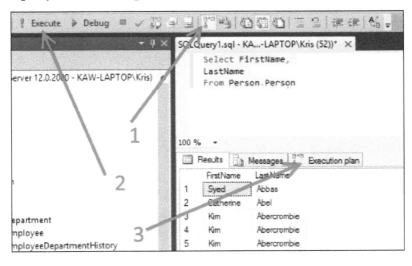

One you have created the plan, run the query and then select the Execution plan tab (3) to view it.

Explain Query Plan

The EXPLAIN QUERY PLAN SQL command is used to obtain a high-level description of the strategy or plan that SQLite uses to implement a specific SQL query. Most significantly, EXPLAIN QUERY PLAN reports on the way in which the query uses database indices.

A query plan is represented as a tree. In raw form, as returned by sqlite3_step(), each node of the tree consists of four fields: An integer node id, an integer parent id, an auxiliary integer field that is not currently used, and a description of the node. The entire tree is therefore a table with four columns and zero or more rows. The command-line shell will usually intercept this table and renders it as an ASCII-art graph for more convenient viewing. To disable the shells automatic graph rendering and to display EXPLAIN QUERY PLAN output in its tabular format, run the command ".explain off" to set the "EXPLAIN formatting mode" to off. To restore automatic graph rendering, run ".explain auto". You can see the current "EXPLAIN formatting mode" setting using the ".show" command.

One can also set the CLI into automatic EXPLAIN QUERY PLAN mode using the ".eqp on" command:

```
sqlite>.eqp on
```

In automatic EXPLAIN QUERY PLAN mode, the shell automatically runs a separate EXPLAIN QUERY PLAN query for each statement you enter and displays the result before actually running the query. Use the ".eqp off" command to turn automatic EXPLAIN QUERY PLAN mode back off.

EXPLAIN QUERY PLAN is most useful on a SELECT statement, but may also appear with other statements that read data from database tables (e.g. UPDATE, DELETE, INSERT INTO SELECT).

Table and Index Scans

When processing a SELECT (or other) statement, SQLite may retrieve data from database tables in a variety of ways. It may scan through all the records in a table (a full-table scan), scan a contiguous subset of the records in a table based on the rowid index, scan a contiguous subset of the entries in a database index, or use a combination of the above strategies in a single scan.

For each table read by the query, the output of EXPLAIN QUERY PLAN includes a record for which the value in the "detail" column begins with either "SCAN" or "SEARCH". "SCAN" is used for a full-table scan, including cases where SQLite iterates through all records in a table in an order defined by an index. "SEARCH" indicates that only a subset of the table rows are visited. Each SCAN or SEARCH record includes the following information:

- The name of the table data is read from.
- Whether or not an index or automatic index is used.
- Whether or not the covering index optimization applies.
- Which terms of the WHERE clause are used for indexing.

For example, the following EXPLAIN QUERY PLAN command operates on a SELECT statement that is implemented by performing a full-table scan on table t1:

```
sqlite> EXPLAIN QUERY PLAN SELECT a, b FROM t1 WHERE a=1;

QUERY PLAN

`--SCAN TABLE t1
```

The example above shows SQLite picking full-table scan will visit all rows in the table. If the query were able to use an index, then the SCAN/SEARCH record would include the name of the index and, for a SEARCH record, an indication of how the subset of rows visited is identified. For example:

```
sqlite> CREATE INDEX i1 ON t1(a);

sqlite> EXPLAIN QUERY PLAN SELECT a, b FROM t1 WHERE a=1;

QUERY PLAN

`--SEARCH TABLE t1 USING INDEX i1 (a=?)
```

The previous example, SQLite uses index "i1" to optimize a WHERE clause term of the form (a=?) in this case "a=1". The previous example could not use a covering index, but the following example can, and that fact is reflected in the output:

```
sqlite> CREATE INDEX i2 ON t1(a, b);

sqlite> EXPLAIN QUERY PLAN SELECT a, b FROM t1 WHERE a=1;
```

QUERY PLAN

```
`--SEARCH TABLE t1 USING COVERING INDEX i2 (a=?)
```

All joins in SQLite are implemented using nested scans. When a SELECT query that features a join is analyzed using EXPLAIN QUERY PLAN, one SCAN or SEARCH record is output for each nested loop. For example:

```
sqlite> EXPLAIN QUERY PLAN SELECT t1.*, t2.* FROM t1, t2 WHERE t1.a=1
AND t1.b>2;

QUERY PLAN

|--SEARCH TABLE t1 USING INDEX i2 (a=? AND b>?)

`--SCAN TABLE t2
```

The order of the entries indicates the nesting order. In this case, the scan of table t1 using index i2 is the outer loop (since it appears first) and the full-table scan of table t2 is the inner loop (since it appears last). In the following example, the positions of t1 and t2 in the FROM clause of the SELECT are reversed. The query strategy remains the same. The output from EXPLAIN QUERY PLAN shows how the query is actually evaluated, not how it is specified in the SQL statement.

```
sqlite> EXPLAIN QUERY PLAN SELECT t1.*, t2.* FROM t2, t1 WHERE t1.a=1
AND t1.b>2;

QUERY PLAN

|--SEARCH TABLE t1 USING INDEX i2 (a=? AND b>?)

`--SCAN TABLE t2
```

If the WHERE clause of a query contains an OR expression, then SQLite might use the "OR by union" strategy (also known as the OR optimization). In this case there will be single top-level record for the search, with two sub-records, one for each index:

```
sqlite> CREATE INDEX i3 ON t1(b);

sqlite> EXPLAIN QUERY PLAN SELECT * FROM t1 WHERE a=1 OR b=2;

QUERY PLAN

`--MULTI-INDEX OR

   |--SEARCH TABLE t1 USING COVERING INDEX i2 (a=?)

   `--SEARCH TABLE t1 USING INDEX i3 (b=?)
```

Temporary Sorting B-Trees

If a SELECT query contains an ORDER BY, GROUP BY or DISTINCT clause, SQLite may need to use a temporary b-tree structure to sort the output rows. Or, it might use an index. Using an index is almost always much more efficient than performing a sort. If a temporary b-tree is required, a record is added to the EXPLAIN QUERY PLAN output with the "detail" field set to a string value of the form "USE TEMP B-TREE FOR xxx", where xxx is one of "ORDER BY", "GROUP BY" or "DISTINCT". For example:

```
sqlite> EXPLAIN QUERY PLAN SELECT c, d FROM t2 ORDER BY c;

QUERY PLAN

|--SCAN TABLE t2

`--USE TEMP B-TREE FOR ORDER BY
```

In this case using the temporary b-tree can be avoided by creating an index on t2(c), as follows:

```
sqlite> CREATE INDEX i4 ON t2(c);

sqlite> EXPLAIN QUERY PLAN SELECT c, d FROM t2 ORDER BY c;
```

```
QUERY PLAN

`--SCAN TABLE t2 USING INDEX i4
```

Subqueries

In all the examples above, there has only been a single SELECT statement. If a query contains sub-selects, those are shown as being children of the outer SELECT. For example:

sqlite> EXPLAIN QUERY PLAN SELECT (SELECT b FROM t1 WHERE a=0), (SELECT a FROM t1 WHERE b=t2.c) FROM t2;

```
|--SCAN TABLE t2 USING COVERING INDEX i4

|--SCALAR SUBQUERY

|   `--SEARCH TABLE t1 USING COVERING INDEX i2 (a=?)

`--CORRELATED SCALAR SUBQUERY

    `--SEARCH TABLE t1 USING INDEX i3 (b=?)
```

The example above contains two "SCALAR" subqueries. The subqueries are SCALAR in the sense that they return a single value a one-row, one-column table. If the actual query returns more than that, then only the first column of the first row is used.

The first subquery above is constant with respect to the outer query. The value for the first subquery can be computed once and then reused for each row of the outer SELECT. The second subquery, however, is "CORRELATED". The value of the second subquery changes depending on values in the current row of the outer query. Hence, the second subquery must be run once for each output row in the outer SELECT.

Unless the flattening optimization is applied, if a subquery appears in the FROM clause of a SELECT statement, SQLite can either run the subquery and stores the results in a temporary table, or it can run the subquery as a co-routine. The following query is an example of the latter. The subquery is run by a co-routine. The outer query blocks whenever it needs another row of input from the subquery. Control switches to the co-routine which produces the desired output row, then control switches back to the main routine which continues processing.

```
sqlite> EXPLAIN QUERY PLAN SELECT count(*) FROM (SELECT max(b) AS x
FROM t1 GROUP BY a) GROUP BY x;

QUERY PLAN

|--CO-ROUTINE 0x20FC3E0
```

```
|   `--SCAN TABLE t1 USING COVERING INDEX i2

|--SCAN SUBQUERY 0x20FC3E0

`--USE TEMP B-TREE FOR GROUP BY
```

If the flattening optimization is used on a subquery in the FROM clause of a SELECT statement, that effectively merges the subquery into the outer query. The output of EX-PLAIN QUERY PLAN reflects this, as in the following example:

```
sqlite> EXPLAIN QUERY PLAN SELECT * FROM (SELECT * FROM t2 WHERE c=1),
t1;

QUERY PLAN

|--SEARCH TABLE t2 USING INDEX i4 (c=?)

`--SCAN TABLE t1
```

If the content of a subquery might need to be visited more than once, then the use of a co-routine is undesirable, as the co-routine would then have to compute the data more than once. And if the subquery cannot be flattened, that means the subquery must be manifested into a transient table.

```
sqlite> SELECT * FROM

       >    (SELECT * FROM t1 WHERE a=1 ORDER BY b LIMIT 2) AS x,

       >    (SELECT * FROM t2 WHERE c=1 ORDER BY d LIMIT 2) AS y;
```

QUERY PLAN

```
|--MATERIALIZE 0x18F06F0

|   `--SEARCH TABLE t1 USING COVERING INDEX i2 (a=?)

|--MATERIALIZE 0x18F80D0

|   |--SEARCH TABLE t2 USING INDEX i4 (c=?)

|   `--USE TEMP B-TREE FOR ORDER BY

|--SCAN SUBQUERY 0x18F06F0 AS x

`--SCAN SUBQUERY 0x18F80D0 AS y
```

Compound Queries

Each component query of a compound query (UNION, UNION ALL, EXCEPT or INTERSECT) is assigned computed separately and is given its own line in the EXPLAIN QUERY PLAN output.

```
sqlite> EXPLAIN QUERY PLAN SELECT a FROM t1 UNION SELECT c FROM t2;
```

```
QUERY PLAN

`--COMPOUND QUERY

   |--LEFT-MOST SUBQUERY

   |   `--SCAN TABLE t1 USING COVERING INDEX i1

   `--UNION USING TEMP B-TREE

       `--SCAN TABLE t2 USING COVERING INDEX i4
```

The "USING TEMP B-TREE" clause in the above output indicates that a temporary b-tree structure is used to implement the UNION of the results of the two sub-selects. An alternative method of computing a compound is to run each subquery as a co-routine, arrange for their outputs to appear in sorted order, and merge the results together. When the query planner chooses this latter approach, the EXPLAIN QUERY PLAN output looks like this:

```
sqlite> EXPLAIN QUERY PLAN SELECT a FROM t1 EXCEPT SELECT d FROM t2
ORDER BY 1;

QUERY PLAN

`--MERGE (EXCEPT)

   |--LEFT

   |   `--SCAN TABLE t1 USING COVERING INDEX i1

   `--RIGHT

       |--SCAN TABLE t2

       `--USE TEMP B-TREE FOR ORDER BY
```

References

- The-components-of-a-table, sql-basic: w3resource.com, Retrieved 15 July, 2020

- Özsu, M. Tamer; Valduriez, Patrick (2011). Principles of Distributed Database Systems, Third Edition. Springer. doi:10.1007/978-1-4419-8834-8. ISBN 978-1-4419-8833-1

- What-is-a-query-plan: essentialsql.com, Retrieved 23 April, 2020

- Pottinger, P.; Berstein, P. (2008). Schema merging and mapping creation for relational sources. Proceedings of the 11th International Conference on Extending Database Technology: Advances in Database Technology (EDBT '08). New York, NY: ACM. pp. 73–84. CiteSeerX 10.1.1.405.2990. doi:10.1145/1353343.1353357. ISBN 9781595939265

- Procedures-and-functions.dbms-collapse2: tutorialink.com, Retrieved 19 June, 2020

- Bryla, Bob; Thomas, Biju (2006). OCP: Oracle 10g New Features for Administrators Study Guide: Exam 1Z0-040. John Wiley & Sons. p. 90. ISBN 9780782150858. Retrieved 2015-08-14

Database Models 3

- Data Modeling
- Entity–relationship Model
- Enhanced Entity-relationship Model
- Network Model
- Hierarchical Model
- Object Oriented Data Model
- Object Relation Model
- Semi Structured Model
- Associative Model
- Conceptual Schema
- Logical Data Model
- Physical Data Model
- Data Structure Diagram
- Generic Data Model
- Semantic Data Model
- Object-role Modeling
- Cloud Database Deployment Models

A type of data model that determines the logical structure of a database is called a database model. It includes network model, object oriented data model, object relation model, associative model, generic data model, semantic data model, etc. All the aspects related to these database models have been carefully analyzed in this chapter.

A database model shows the logical structure of a database, including the relationships and constraints that determine how data can be stored and accessed. Individual database models are designed based on the rules and concepts of whichever broader data model the designers adopt. Most data models can be represented by an accompanying database diagram.

Types of Database Models

There are many kinds of data models. Some of the most common ones include:

- Hierarchical database model.

- Relational model.

- Network model.

- Object-oriented database model.

- Entity-relationship model.

- Document model.

- Entity-attribute-value model.

- Star schema.

- The object-relational model, which combines the two that make up its name.

You may choose to describe a database with any one of these depending on several factors. The biggest factor is whether the database management system you are using supports a particular model. Most database management systems are built with a particular data model in mind and require their users to adopt that model, although some do support multiple models.

In addition, different models apply to different stages of the database design process. High-level conceptual data models are best for mapping out relationships between data in ways that people perceive that data. Record-based logical models, on the other hand, more closely reflect ways that the data is stored on the server.

Selecting a data model is also a matter of aligning your priorities for the database with the strengths of a particular model, whether those priorities include speed, cost reduction, usability, or something else.

A variety of other database models has been or is still used today.

Inverted File Model

A database built with the inverted file structure is designed to facilitate fast full text searches. In this model, data content is indexed as a series of keys in a lookup table, with the values pointing to the location of the associated files. This structure can provide nearly instantaneous reporting in big data and analytics, for instance.

This model has been used by the ADABAS database management system of Software AG since 1970, and it is still supported today.

Flat Model

The flat model is the earliest, simplest data model. It simply lists all the data in a single table, consisting of columns and rows. In order to access or manipulate the data, the computer has to read the entire flat file into memory, which makes this model inefficient for all but the smallest data sets.

Multidimensional Model

This is a variation of the relational model designed to facilitate improved analytical processing. While the relational model is optimized for online transaction processing (OLTP), this model is designed for online analytical processing (OLAP).

Each cell in a dimensional database contains data about the dimensions tracked by the database. Visually, it's like a collection of cubes, rather than two-dimensional tables.

Semistructured Model

In this model, the structural data usually contained in the database schema is embedded with the data itself. Here the distinction between data and schema is vague at best. This model is useful for describing systems, such as certain Web-based data sources, which we treat as databases but cannot constrain with a schema. It's also useful for describing interactions between databases that don't adhere to the same schema.

Context Model

This model can incorporate elements from other database models as needed. It cobbles together elements from object-oriented, semistructured, and network models.

Associative Model

This model divides all the data points based on whether they describe an entity or an association. In this model, an entity is anything that exists independently, whereas an association is something that only exists in relation to something else.

The associative model structures the data into two sets:

- A set of items, each with a unique identifier, a name, and a type.

- A set of links, each with a unique identifier and the unique identifiers of a source, verb, and target. The stored fact has to do with the source, and each of the three identifiers may refer either to a link or an item.

Other, less common database models include:

- Semantic model, which includes information about how the stored data relates to the real world.

- XML database, which allows data to be specified and even stored in XML format.

- Named graph.

- Triplestore.

NoSQL Database Models

In addition to the object database model, other non-SQL models have emerged in contrast to the relational model.

The graph database model, which is even more flexible than a network model, allowing any node to connect with any other.

The multivalue model, which breaks from the relational model by allowing attributes to contain a list of data rather than a single data point.

The document model, which is designed for storing and managing documents or semi-structured data, rather than atomic data.

Databases on the Web

Most websites rely on some kind of database to organize and present data to users. Whenever someone uses the search functions on these sites, their search terms are converted into queries for a database server to process. Typically, middleware connects the web server with the database.

The broad presence of databases allows them to be used in almost any field, from online shopping to micro-targeting a voter segment as part of a political campaign. Various industries have developed their own norms for database design, from air transport to vehicle manufacturing.

Data Modeling

Data modeling is the process of creating a data model for the data to be stored in a Database. This data model is a conceptual representation of Data objects, the associations between different data objects and the rules. Data modeling helps in the visual representation of data and enforces business rules, regulatory compliances, and government policies on the data. Data Models ensure consistency in naming conventions, default values, semantics, security while ensuring quality of the data.

Data model emphasizes on what data is needed and how it should be organized instead of what operations need to be performed on the data. Data Model is like architect's building plan which helps to build a conceptual model and set the relationship between data items.

The two types of Data Models techniques are:

- Entity Relationship (E-R) Model.

- UML (Unified Modelling Language).

The primary goals of using data model are:

- Ensures that all data objects required by the database are accurately represented. Omission of data will lead to creation of faulty reports and produce incorrect results.

- A data model helps design the database at the conceptual, physical and logical levels.

- Data Model structure helps to define the relational tables, primary and foreign keys and stored procedures.

- It provides a clear picture of the base data and can be used by database developers to create a physical database.

- It is also helpful to identify missing and redundant data.

- Though the initial creation of data model is labor and time consuming, in the long run, it makes your IT infrastructure upgrade and maintenance cheaper and faster.

Types of Data Models

There are mainly three different types of data models:

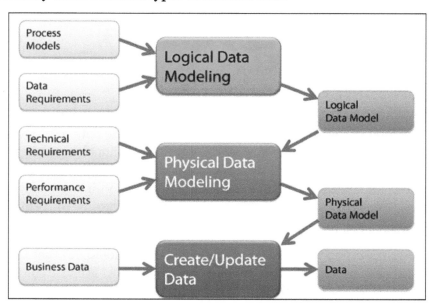

- Conceptual: This Data Model defines WHAT the system contains. This model is typically created by Business stakeholders and Data Architects. The purpose is to organize, scope and define business concepts and rules.

- Logical: Defines HOW the system should be implemented regardless of the DBMS. This model is typically created by Data Architects and Business Analysts. The purpose is to developed technical map of rules and data structures.

- Physical: This Data Model describes HOW the system will be implemented using a specific DBMS system. This model is typically created by DBA and developers. The purpose is actual implementation of the database.

Conceptual Model

The main aim of this model is to establish the entities, their attributes, and their relationships. In this Data modeling level, there is hardly any detail available of the actual Database structure.

The 3 basic tenants of Data Model are:

- Entity: A real-world thing.

- Attribute: Characteristics or properties of an entity.

- Relationship: Dependency or association between two entities.

For example:

- Customer and Product are two entities. Customer number and name are attributes of the Customer entity.

- Product name and price are attributes of product entity.

- Sale is the relationship between the customer and product.

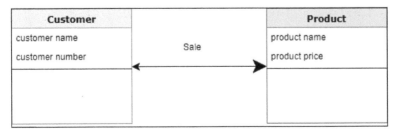

Characteristics of a Conceptual Data Model

- Offers Organisation-wide coverage of the business concepts.

- This type of Data Models are designed and developed for a business audience.

- The conceptual model is developed independently of hardware specifications like data storage capacity, location or software specifications like DBMS vendor and technology. The focus is to represent data as a user will see it in the "real world".

Conceptual data models known as Domain models create a common vocabulary for all stakeholders by establishing basic concepts and scope.

Logical Data Model

Logical data models add further information to the conceptual model elements. It defines the structure of the data elements and set the relationships between them.

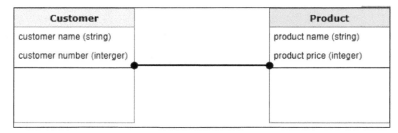

The advantage of the Logical data model is to provide a foundation to form the base for the Physical model. However, the modeling structure remains generic.

At this Data Modeling level, no primary or secondary key is defined. At this Data modeling level, you need to verify and adjust the connector details that were set earlier for relationships.

Characteristics of a Logical Data Model

- Describes data needs for a single project but could integrate with other logical data models based on the scope of the project.

- Designed and developed independently from the DBMS.

- Data attributes will have datatypes with exact precisions and length.

- Normalization processes to the model is applied typically till 3NF.

Physical Data Model

A Physical Data Model describes the database specific implementation of the data model. It offers an abstraction of the database and helps generate schema. This is because of the richness of meta-data offered by a Physical Data Model.

This type of Data model also helps to visualize database structure. It helps to model database columns keys, constraints, indexes, triggers, and other RDBMS features.

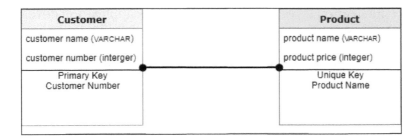

Characteristics of a Physical Data Model

- The physical data model describes data need for a single project or application though it maybe integrated with other physical data models based on project scope.

- Data Model contains relationships between tables that which addresses cardinality and nullability of the relationships.

- Developed for a specific version of a DBMS, location, data storage or technology to be used in the project.

- Columns should have exact datatypes, lengths assigned and default values.

- Primary and Foreign keys, views, indexes, access profiles, and authorizations, etc. are defined.

Advantages and Disadvantages of Data Model

Advantages of Data Model

- The main goal of a designing data model is to make certain that data objects offered by the functional team are represented accurately.

- The data model should be detailed enough to be used for building the physical database.

- The information in the data model can be used for defining the relationship between tables, primary and foreign keys, and stored procedures.

- Data Model helps business to communicate the within and across organizations.

- Data model helps to documents data mappings in ETL process.

- Help to recognize correct sources of data to populate the model.

Disadvantages of Data Model

- To develop Data model one should know physical data stored characteristics.

- This is a navigational system produces complex application development, management. Thus, it requires knowledge of the biographical truth.

- Even smaller change made in structure requires modification in the entire application.

- There is no set data manipulation language in DBMS.

Entity–relationship Model

An entity–relationship model (or ER model) describes interrelated things of interest in a specific domain of knowledge. A basic ER model is composed of entity types (which classify the things of interest) and specifies relationships that can exist between entities (instances of those entity types).

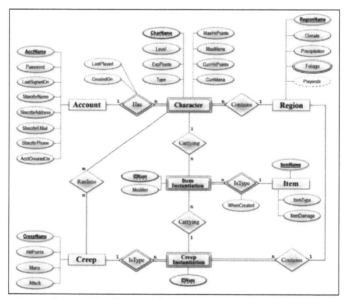

An entity–relationship diagram for a MMORPG using Chen's notation.

In software engineering, an ER model is commonly formed to represent things a business needs to remember in order to perform business processes. Consequently, the ER model becomes an abstract data model, that defines a data or information structure which can be implemented in a database, typically a relational database.

Entity–relationship modeling was developed for database and design by Peter Chen and published in a 1976 paper. However, variants of the idea existed previously. Some ER models show super and subtype entities connected by generalization-specialization relationships, and an ER model can be used also in the specification of domain-specific ontologies.

An E-R model is usually the result of systematic analysis to define and describe what is important to processes in an area of a business. It does not define the business processes; it only presents a business data schema in graphical form. It is usually drawn in a graphical form as boxes (*entities*) that are connected by lines (*relationships*) which express the associations and dependencies between entities. An ER model can also be expressed in a verbal form, for example: one building may be divided into zero or more apartments, but one apartment can only be located in one building.

Entities may be characterized not only by relationships, but also by additional properties (*attributes*), which include identifiers called "primary keys". Diagrams created to represent attributes as well as entities and relationships may be called entity-attribute-relationship diagrams, rather than entity–relationship models.

An ER model is typically implemented as a database. In a simple relational database implementation, each row of a table represents one instance of an entity type, and each field in a table represents an attribute type. In a relational database a relationship between entities is implemented by storing the primary key of one entity as a pointer or "foreign key" in the table of another entity.

There is a tradition for ER/data models to be built at two or three levels of abstraction. Note that the conceptual-logical-physical hierarchy below is used in other kinds of specification, and is different from the three schema approach to software engineering.

Conceptual Data Model

This is the highest level ER model in that it contains the least granular detail but establishes the overall scope of what is to be included within the model set. The conceptual ER model normally defines master reference data entities that are commonly used by the organization. Developing an enterprise-wide conceptual ER model is useful to support documenting the data architecture for an organization.

A conceptual ER model may be used as the foundation for one or more *logical data models*. The purpose of the conceptual ER model is then to establish structural metadata commonality for the master data entities between the set of logical ER models. The conceptual data model may be used to form commonality relationships between ER models as a basis for data model integration.

Logical Data Model

A logical ER model does not require a conceptual ER model, especially if the scope of the logical ER model includes only the development of a distinct information system. The logical ER model contains more detail than the conceptual ER model. In addition to master data entities, operational and transactional data entities are now defined. The details of each data entity are developed and the relationships between these data entities are established. The logical ER model is however developed independently of the specific database management system into which it can be implemented.

Physical Data Model

One or more physical ER models may be developed from each logical ER model. The physical ER model is normally developed to be instantiated as a database. Therefore, each physical ER model must contain enough detail to produce a database and each physical ER model is technology dependent since each database management system is somewhat different.

The physical model is normally instantiated in the structural metadata of a database management system as relational database objects such as database tables, database indexes such as unique key indexes, and database constraints such as a foreign key constraint or a commonality constraint. The ER model is also normally used to design modifications to the relational database objects and to maintain the structural metadata of the database.

The first stage of information system design uses these models during the requirements analysis to describe information needs or the type of information that is to be stored in a database. The data modeling technique can be used to describe any ontology (i.e. an overview and classifications of used terms and their relationships) for a certain area of interest. In the case of the design of an information system that is based on a database, the conceptual data model is, at a later stage (usually called logical design), mapped to a logical data model, such as the relational model; this in turn is mapped to a physical model during physical design. Note that sometimes, both of these phases are referred to as "physical design".

Entity–relationship Model

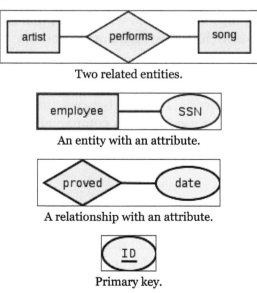

Two related entities.

An entity with an attribute.

A relationship with an attribute.

Primary key.

An entity may be defined as a thing capable of an independent existence that can be uniquely identified. An entity is an abstraction from the complexities of a domain. When we speak of an entity, we normally speak of some aspect of the real world that can be distinguished from other aspects of the real world.

An entity is a thing that exists either physically or logically. An entity may be a physical object such as a house or a car (they exist physically), an event such as a house sale or a car service, or a concept such as a customer transaction or order (they exist logically—as a concept). Although the term entity is the one most commonly used, following Chen we should really distinguish between an entity and an entity-type. An entity-type is a category. An entity, strictly speaking, is an instance of a given entity-type. There are usually many instances of an entity-type. Because the term entity-type is somewhat cumbersome, most people tend to use the term entity as a synonym for this term.

Entities can be thought of as nouns. Examples: a computer, an employee, a song, a mathematical theorem, etc.

A relationship captures how entities are related to one another. Relationships can be thought of as verbs, linking two or more nouns. Examples: an *owns* relationship between a company and a computer, a *supervises* relationship between an employee and a department, a *performs* relationship between an artist and a song, a *proves* relationship between a mathematician and a conjecture, etc.

The model's linguistic aspect described above is utilized in the declarative database query language ERROL, which mimics natural language constructs. ERROL's semantics and implementation are based on reshaped relational algebra (RRA), a relational algebra that is adapted to the entity–relationship model and captures its linguistic aspect.

Entities and relationships can both have attributes. Examples: an *employee* entity might have a *Social Security Number* (SSN) attribute, while a *proved* relationship may have a *date* attribute.

Every entity (unless it is a weak entity) must have a minimal set of uniquely identifying attributes, which is called the entity's primary key.

Entity–relationship diagrams don't show single entities or single instances of relations. Rather, they show entity sets (all entities of the same entity type) and relationship sets (all relationships of the same relationship type). Examples: a particular *song* is an entity; the collection of all songs in a database is an entity set; the *eaten* relationship between a child and his lunch is a single relationship; the set of all such child-lunch relationships in a database is a relationship set. In other words, a relationship set corresponds to a relation in mathematics, while a relationship corresponds to a member of the relation. Certain cardinality constraints on relationship sets may be indicated as well.

Mapping Natural Language

Chen proposed the following "rules of thumb" for mapping natural language descriptions into ER diagrams:

English grammar structure	ER structure
Common noun	Entity type
Proper noun	Entity
Transitive verb	Relationship type
Intransitive verb	Attribute type
Adjective	Attribute for entity
Adverb	Attribute for relationship

Physical view show how data is actually stored.

Relationships, Roles and Cardinalities

In Chen's original paper he gives an example of a relationship and its roles. He describes a relationship "marriage" and its two roles "husband" and "wife".

A person plays the role of husband in a marriage (relationship) and another person plays the role of wife in the (same) marriage. These words are nouns. That is no surprise; naming things requires a noun.

Chen's terminology has also been applied to earlier ideas. The lines, arrows and crow's-feet of some diagrams owes more to the earlier Bachman diagrams than to Chen's relationship diagrams.

Another common extension to Chen's model is to "name" relationships and roles as verbs or phrases.

Role Naming

It has also become prevalent to name roles with phrases such as *is the owner of* and *is owned by*. Correct nouns in this case are *owner* and *possession*. Thus person plays the role of owner and car plays the role of possession rather than person plays the role of, is the owner of, etc.

The use of nouns has direct benefit when generating physical implementations from semantic models. When a *person* has two relationships with *car* then it is possible to generate names such as *owner_person* and *driver_person*, which are immediately meaningful.

Cardinalities

Modifications to the original specification can be beneficial. Chen described look-across cardinalities. As an aside, the Barker–Ellis notation, used in Oracle Designer, uses same-side for minimum cardinality (analogous to optionality) and role, but look-across for maximum cardinality (the crows foot).

In Merise, Elmasri & Navathe and others there is a preference for same-side for roles and both minimum and maximum cardinalities. Recent researchers (Feinerer, Dullea) have shown that this is more coherent when applied to n-ary relationships of order greater than 2.

In Dullea one reads "A 'look across' notation such as used in the UML does not effectively represent the semantics of participation constraints imposed on relationships where the degree is higher than binary".

In Feinerer it says "Problems arise if we operate under the look-across semantics as used for UML associations. Hartmann investigates this situation and shows how and why different transformations fail". (Although the "reduction" mentioned is spurious as the two diagrams 3.4 and 3.5 are in fact the same) and also "As we will see on the next few pages, the look-across interpretation introduces several difficulties that prevent the extension of simple mechanisms from binary to n-ary associations".

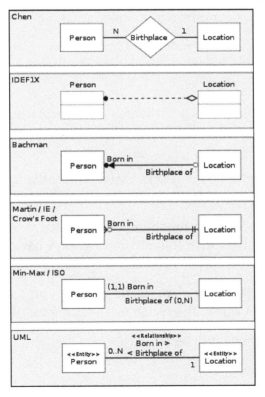

Various methods of representing the same one to many relationship. In each case, the diagram shows the relationship between a person and a place of birth: each person must have been born at one, and only one, location, but each location may have had zero or more people born at it.

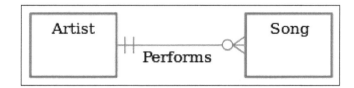

Two related entities shown using Crow's Foot notation. In this example, an optional relationship is shown between Artist and Song; the symbols closest to the song entity represents "zero, one, or many", whereas a song has "one and only one" Artist. The former is therefore read as, an Artist (can) performs "zero, one, or many" songs.

Chen's notation for entity–relationship modeling uses rectangles to represent entity sets, and diamonds to represent relationships appropriate for first-class objects: they can have attributes and relationships of their own. If an entity set participates in a relationship set, they are connected with a line.

Attributes are drawn as ovals and are connected with a line to exactly one entity or relationship set.

Cardinality constraints are expressed as follows:

- A double line indicates a *participation constraint*, totality or surjectivity: All entities in the entity set must participate in *at least one* relationship in the relationship set.

- An arrow from entity set to relationship set indicates a key constraint, i.e. injectivity: Each entity of the entity set can participate in *at most one* relationship in the relationship set.

- A thick line indicates both, i.e. bijectivity: each entity in the entity set is involved in *exactly one* relationship.

- An underlined name of an attribute indicates that it is a key: Two different entities or relationships with this attribute always have different values for this attribute.

Attributes are often omitted as they can clutter up a diagram; other diagram techniques often list entity attributes within the rectangles drawn for entity sets.

Related diagramming convention techniques:

- Bachman notation.

- Barker's notation.

- EXPRESS.

- IDEF1X.

- Crow's foot notation (also Martin notation).

- (min, max)-notation of Jean-Raymond Abrial in 1974.

- UML class diagrams.

- Merise.

- Object-role modeling.

Crow's Foot Notation

Crow's foot notation, the beginning of which dates back to an article by Gordon Everest, is used in Barker's notation, Structured Systems Analysis and Design Method (SSADM) and information technology engineering. Crow's foot diagrams represent entities as boxes, and relationships as lines between the boxes. Different shapes at the ends of these lines represent the relative cardinality of the relationship.

Crow's foot notation was used in the consultancy practice CACI. Many of the consultants at CACI (including Richard Barker) subsequently moved to Oracle UK, where they developed the early versions of Oracle's CASE tools, introducing the notation to a wider audience.

With this notation, relationships cannot have attributes. Where necessary, relationships are promoted to entities in their own right: for example, if it is necessary to capture where and when an artist performed a song, a new entity "performance" is introduced (with attributes reflecting the time and place), and the relationship of an artist to a song becomes an indirect relationship via the performance (artist-performs-performance, performance-features-song).

Three symbols are used to represent cardinality:

- The ring represents "zero".

- The dash represents "one".

- The crow's foot represents "many" or "infinite".

These symbols are used in pairs to represent the four types of cardinality that an entity may have in a relationship. The inner component of the notation represents the minimum, and the outer component represents the maximum.

- Ring and dash: Minimum zero, maximum one (optional).

- Dash and dash: Minimum one, maximum one (mandatory).

- Ring and crow's foot: Minimum zero, maximum many (optional).

- Dash and crow's foot: Minimum one, maximum many (mandatory).

Model Usability Issues

In using a modeled database, users can encounter two well known issues where the returned results mean something other than the results assumed by the query author.

The first is the 'fan trap'. It occurs with a (master) table that links to multiple tables in a one-to-many relationship. The issue derives its name from the way the model looks when it's drawn in an entity–relationship diagram: the linked tables 'fan out' from the master table. This type of model looks similar to a star schema, a type of model used in data warehouses. When trying to calculate sums over aggregates using standard SQL over the master table, unexpected (and incorrect) results. The solution is to either adjust the model or the SQL. This issue occurs mostly in databases for decision support systems, and software that queries such systems sometimes includes specific methods for handling this issue.

The second issue is a 'chasm trap'. A chasm trap occurs when a model suggests the existence of a relationship between entity types, but the pathway does not exist between certain entity occurrences. For example, a Building has one-or-more Rooms, that hold zero-or-more Computers. One would expect to be able to query the model to see all the Computers in the Building. However, Computers not currently assigned to a Room (because they are under repair or somewhere else) are not shown on the list. Another relation between Building and Computers is needed to capture all the computers in the building. This last modelling issue is the result of a failure to capture all the relationships that exist in the real world in the model.

Entity–relationships and Semantic Modeling

Semantic Model

A semantic model is a model of concepts, it is sometimes called a "platform independent model". It is an intensional model. At the latest since Carnap, it is well known that:

> "The full meaning of a concept is constituted by two aspects, its intension and its extension. The first part comprises the embedding of a concept in the world of concepts as a whole, i.e. the totality of all relations to other concepts. The second part establishes the referential meaning of the concept, i.e. its counterpart in the real or in a possible world".

Extension Model

An extensional model is one that maps to the elements of a particular methodology or technology, and is thus a "platform specific model". The UML specification explicitly states that associations in class models are extensional and this is in fact self-evident by considering the extensive array of additional "adornments" provided by the specification over and above those provided by any of the prior candidate "semantic modelling languages".

Entity–relationship Origins

Peter Chen, the father of ER modeling said in his seminal paper:

> "The entity-relationship model adopts the more natural view that the real world consists of entities and relationships. It incorporates some of the important semantic information about the real world".

In his original 1976 article Chen explicitly contrasts entity–relationship diagrams with record modelling techniques:

> "The data structure diagram is a representation of the organization of records and is not an exact representation of entities and relationships".

Philosophical Alignment

Chen is in accord with philosophic and theoretical traditions from the time of the Ancient Greek philosophers: Socrates, Plato and Aristotle through to modern epistemology, semiotics and logic of Peirce, Frege and Russell.

Plato himself associates knowledge with the apprehension of unchanging Forms (The forms, according to Socrates, are roughly speaking archetypes or abstract representations of the many types of things, and properties) and their relationships to one another.

Limitations

- ER assume information content that can readily be represented in a relational database. They describe only a relational structure for this information.

- They are inadequate for systems in which the information cannot readily be represented in relational form, such as with semi-structured data.

- For many systems, possible changes to information contained are nontrivial and important enough to warrant explicit specification.

- Some authors have extended ER modeling with constructs to represent change, an approach supported by the original author; an example is Anchor Modeling. An alternative is to model change separately, using a process modeling technique. Additional techniques can be used for other aspects of systems. For instance, ER models roughly correspond to just 1 of the 14 different modeling techniques offered by UML.

- Even where it is suitable in principle, ER modeling is rarely used as a separate activity. One reason for this is today's abundance of tools to support diagramming and other design support directly on relational database management systems. These tools can readily extract database diagrams that are very close to ER diagrams from existing databases, and they provide alternative views on the information contained in such diagrams.

- In a survey, Brodie and Liu could not find a single instance of entity–relationship modeling inside a sample of ten Fortune 100 companies. Badia and Lemire blame this lack of use on the lack of guidance but also on the lack of benefits, such as lack of support for data integration.

- The enhanced entity–relationship model (EER modeling) introduces several concepts not in ER modeling, but are closely related to object-oriented design, like is-a relationships.

- For modelling temporal databases, numerous ER extensions have been considered. Similarly, the ER model was found unsuitable for multidimensional databases (used in OLAP applications); no dominant conceptual model has emerged in this field yet, although they generally revolve around the concept of OLAP cube (also known as *data cube* within the field).

Enhanced Entity–relationship Model

The enhanced entity–relationship (EER) model (or extended entity–relationship model) in computer science is a high-level or conceptual data model incorporating extensions to the original entity–relationship (ER) model, used in the design of databases.

It was developed to reflect more precisely the properties and constraints that are found in more complex databases, such as in engineering design and manufacturing (CAD/ CAM), telecommunications, complex software systems and geographic information systems (GIS).

Mechanics

The EER model includes all of the concepts introduced by the ER model. Additionally it includes the concepts of a subclass and superclass (Is-a), along with the concepts of specialization and generalization. Furthermore, it introduces the concept of a union type or category, which is used to represent a collection of objects that is the union of objects of different entity types. EER model also includes EER diagrams that are conceptual models that accurately represent the requirements of complex databases.

Subclass and Superclass

Entity type Y is a subtype (subclass) of an entity type X if and only if every Y is necessarily an X. A subclass entity inherits all attributes and relationships of its superclass entity. This property is called the attribute and relationship inheritance. A subclass entity may have its own specific attributes and relationships (together with all the attributes and relationships it inherits from the superclass). A common superclass example is a Vehicle superclass along with the subclasses of Car and Truck. There are a number of common attributes between a car and a truck, which would be part of the superclass, while the attributes specific to a car or a truck (such as max payload, truck type) would make up two subclass.

Tools

- The MySQL Workbench offers creating, editing and exporting EER Models. Exporting to PNG and PDF allows easy sharing for presentations.

- Skipper allows users to create, import and export from ORM schema definitions to editable EER models.

- SAP PowerDesigner is a complex tool for modelling and transforming different models.

Network Model

The network model is a database model conceived as a flexible way of representing objects and their relationships. Its distinguishing feature is that the schema, viewed as a graph in which object types are nodes and relationship types are arcs, is not restricted to being a hierarchy or lattice.

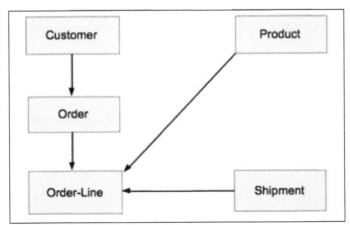

Bachman diagram of a simple network database.

While the hierarchical database model structures data as a tree of records, with each record having one parent record and many children, the network model allows each record to have multiple parent and child records, forming a generalized graph structure. This property applies at two levels: the schema is a generalized graph of record types connected by relationship types (called "set types" in CODASYL), and the database itself is a generalized graph of record occurrences connected by relationships (CODASYL "sets"). Cycles are permitted at both levels. The chief argument in favour of the network model, in comparison to the hierarchical model, was that it allowed a more natural modeling of relationships between entities. Although the model was widely implemented and used, it failed to become dominant for two main reasons. Firstly, IBM chose to stick to the hierarchical model with semi-network extensions in their established products such as IMS and DL/I. Secondly, it was eventually displaced by the relational model, which offered a higher-level, more declarative interface. Until the early 1980s the performance benefits of the low-level navigational interfaces offered by hierarchical and network databases were persuasive for many large-scale applications, but as hardware became faster, the extra productivity and flexibility of the relational model led to the gradual obsolescence of the network model in corporate enterprise usage.

Database Systems

Some well-known database systems that use the network model include:

- Integrated Data Store (IDS).

- IDMS (Integrated Database Management System).

- Raima Database Manager.

- TurboIMAGE.

- Univac DMS-1100.

Hierarchical Model

A hierarchical database model is a data model in which the data are organized into a tree-like structure. The data are stored as records which are connected to one another through links. A record is a collection of fields, with each field containing only one value. The type of a record defines which fields the record contains.

The hierarchical database model mandates that each child record has only one parent, whereas each parent record can have one or more child records. In order to retrieve data from a hierarchical database the whole tree needs to be traversed starting from the root node. This model is recognized as the first database model created by IBM in the 1960s.

The hierarchical structure was developed by IBM in the 1960s, and used in early mainframe DBMS. Records' relationships form a treelike model. This structure is simple but inflexible because the relationship is confined to a one-to-many relationship. The IBM Information Management System (IMS) and the RDM Mobile are examples of a hierarchical database system with multiple hierarchies over the same data. RDM Mobile is a newly designed embedded database for a mobile computer system.

The hierarchical data model lost traction as Codd's relational model became the de facto standard used by virtually all mainstream database management systems. A relational-database implementation of a hierarchical model was first discussed in published form in 1992. Hierarchical data organization schemes resurfaced with the advent of XML in the late 1990s. The hierarchical structure is used primarily today for storing geographic information and file systems.

Currently hierarchical databases are still widely used especially in applications that require very high performance and availability such as banking and telecommunications. One of the most widely used commercial hierarchical databases is IMS. Another example of the use of hierarchical databases is Windows Registry in the Microsoft Windows operating systems.

Examples of Hierarchical Data Represented as Relational Tables

An organization could store employee information in a table that contains attributes/columns such as employee number, first name, last name, and department number. The organization provides each employee with computer hardware as needed, but computer equipment may only be used by the employee to which it is assigned. The organization could store the computer hardware information in a separate table that includes each part's serial number, type, and the employee that uses it. The tables might look like this:

employee table			
EmpNo	First Name	Last Name	Dept. Num
100	Mahwish	Faki	10-L
101	Hamadh	Hashim	10-L
102	Nirun	Ar	20-B
103	Chaaya	Sandakelum	20-B

computer table		
Serial Num	Type	User EmpNo
3009734-4	Computer	100
3-23-283742	Monitor	100
2-22-723423	Monitor	100
232342	Printer	100

In this model, the employee data table represents the "parent" part of the hierarchy, while the computer table represents the "child" part of the hierarchy. In contrast to tree structures usually found in computer software algorithms, in this model the children point to the parents. As shown, each employee may possess several pieces of computer equipment, but each individual piece of computer equipment may have only one employee owner.

Consider the following structure:

EmpNo	Designation	ReportsTo
10	Director	
20	Senior Manager	10
30	Typist	20
40	Programmer	20

In this, the "child" is the same type as the "parent". The hierarchy stating EmpNo 10 is boss of 20, and 30 and 40 each report to 20 is represented by the "ReportsTo" column. In Relational database terms, the ReportsTo column is a foreign key referencing the EmpNo column. If the "child" data type were different, it would be in a different table, but there would still be a foreign key referencing the EmpNo column of the employees table.

This simple model is commonly known as the adjacency list model, and was introduced by Dr. Edgar F. Codd after initial criticisms surfaced that the relational model could not model hierarchical data. However, the model is only a special case of a general adjacency list for a graph.

Object Oriented Data Model

Object oriented data model is based upon real world situations. These situations are represented as objects, with different attributes. All these object have multiple relationships between them.

Elements of Object Oriented Data Model

Objects

The real world entities and situations are represented as objects in the Object oriented database model.

Attributes and Method

Every object has certain characteristics. These are represented using Attributes. The behaviour of the objects is represented using Methods.

Class

Similar attributes and methods are grouped together using a class. An object can be called as an instance of the class.

Inheritance

A new class can be derived from the original class. The derived class contains attributes and methods of the original class as well as its own.

An Example of the Object Oriented data model is:

- Shape, Circle, Rectangle and Triangle are all objects in this model.

- Circle has the attributes Center and Radius.

- Rectangle has the attributes Length and Breath.

- Triangle has the attributes Base and Height.

- The objects Circle, Rectangle and Triangle inherit from the object Shape.

Object Relation Model

An Object relational model is a combination of a Object oriented database model and a Relational database model. So, it supports objects, classes, inheritance etc. just like Object Oriented models and has support for data types, tabular structures etc. like Relational data model.

One of the major goals of Object relational data model is to close the gap between relational databases and the object oriented practises frequently used in many programming languages such as C++, C#, Java etc.

Both Relational data models and Object oriented data models are very useful. But it was felt that they both were lacking in some characteristics and so work was started to build a model that was a combination of them both. Hence, Object relational data model was created as a result of research that was carried out in the 1990's.

Advantages of Object Relaotional Model

The advantages of the Object Relational model are:

Inheritance

The Object Relational data model allows its users to inherit objects, tables etc. so that they can extend their functionality. Inherited objects contains new attributes as well as the attributes that were inherited.

Complex Data Types

Complex data types can be formed using existing data types. This is useful in Object relational data model as complex data types allow better manipulation of the data.

Extensibility

The functionality of the system can be extended in Object relational data model. This can be achieved using complex data types as well as advanced concepts of object oriented model such as inheritance.

Disadvantages of Object Relational Model

The object relational data model can get quite complicated and difficult to handle at times as it is a combination of the Object oriented data model and Relational data model and utilizes the functionalities of both of them.

Semi Structured Model

The semi-structured model is a database model where there is no separation between the data and the schema, and the amount of structure used depends on the purpose.

The advantages of this model are the following:

- It can represent the information of some data sources that cannot be constrained by schema.

- It provides a flexible format for data exchange between different types of databases.

- It can be helpful to view structured data as semi-structured (for browsing purposes).

- The schema can easily be changed.

- The data transfer format may be portable.

The primary trade-off being made in using a semi-structured database model is that queries cannot be made as efficiently as in a more constrained structure, such as in the relational model. Typically the records in a semi-structured database are stored with unique IDs that are referenced with pointers to their location on disk. This makes navigational or path-based queries quite efficient, but for doing searches over many records (as is typical in SQL), it is not as efficient because it has to seek around the disk following pointers.

The Object Exchange Model (OEM) is one standard to express semi-structured data, another way is XML.

Associative Model

The associative model of data is a data model for database systems. Other data models, such as the relational model and the object data model, are record-based. These models involve encompassing attributes about a thing, such as a car, in a record structure. Such attributes might be registration, colour, make, model, etc. In the associative model, everything which has "discrete independent existence" is modeled as an entity, and relationships between them are modeled as associations. The granularity at which data is represented is similar to schemes presented by Chen (Entity-relationship model); Bracchi, Paolini and Pelagatti (Binary Relations); and Senko (The Entity Set Model).

A number of claims made about the model by Simon Williams, in his book *The Associative Model of Data*, distinguish the associative model from more traditional models.

In an associative database management system, data and metadata (data about data) are stored as two types of things:

- Items, each of which has a unique identifier and a name.

- Links, each of which has a unique identifier, together with the unique identifiers of three other things, that represent the source, verb and target of a fact that is recorded about the source in the database. Each of the three things identified by the source, verb and target may each be either a link or an item.

Here's how the associative model would use these two structures to store the piece of information *Flight BA1234 arrived at London Heathrow on 12-Dec-05 at 10:25 am*. There are seven items: the four nouns *Flight BA1234*, *London Heathrow*, *12-Dec-05* and *10:25 am*, and the three verbs *arrived at*, *on* and *at*. Three links are needed to store the data. They are:

> Flight BA1234 arrived at London Heathrow,

> ... on 12-Dec-05,

> ... at 10:25 am.

The first link has Flight BA1234 as its source, arrived at as its verb and London Heathrow as its target. The second link has the first link as its source, on as its verb and the item 12-Dec-05 as its target. (A link that begins with an ellipsis has the previous link as its source.) The third link has the second link as its source, at as its verb and 10:25 am as its target.

Here is an alternative way to write the same thing using parentheses:

((Flight BA1234 arrived at London Heathrow) on 12-Dec-05) at 10:25 am.

An associative database may be regarded as comprising two tables: one for items and one for links. Each item and each link has an arbitrary number (called a surrogate) as an identifier:

Items	
Identifier	Name
77	Flight BA1234
08	London Heathrow
32	12-Dec-05
48	10:25am
12	arrived at
67	on
09	at

Links			
Identifier	Source	Verb	Target
74	77	12	08
03	74	67	32
64	03	09	48

Conceptual Schema

A 'conceptual schema' is a high-level description of a business's informational needs. It typically includes only the main concepts and the main relationships among them. Typically this is a first-cut model, with insufficient detail to build an actual database. This level describes the structure of the whole database for a group of users. The conceptual model is also known as the data model that can be used to describe the conceptual schema when a database system is implemented. It hides the internal details of physical storage and targets on describing entities, datatype, relationships and constraints.

A conceptual schema or conceptual data model is a map of concepts and their relationships used for databases. This describes the semantics of an organization and represents a series of assertions about its nature. Specifically, it describes the things of significance to an organization (*entity classes*), about which it is inclined to collect information, and characteristics of (*attributes*) and associations between pairs of those things of significance (*relationships*).

Because a conceptual schema represents the semantics of an organization, and not a database design, it may exist on various levels of abstraction. The original ANSI four-schema architecture began with the set of *external schema* that each represent one person's view of the world around him or her. These are consolidated into a single *conceptual schema* that is the superset of all of those external views. A data model can be as concrete as each person's perspective, but this tends to make it inflexible. If that person's world changes, the model must change. Conceptual data models take a more abstract perspective, identifying the fundamental things, of which the things an individual deals with are just examples.

The model does allow for what is called inheritance in object oriented terms. The set of instances of an entity class may be subdivided into entity classes in their own right. Thus, each instance of a *sub-type* entity class is also an instance of the entity class's *super-type*. Each instance of the super-type entity class, then is also an instance of one of the sub-type entity classes.

Super-type/sub-type relationships may be *exclusive* or not. A methodology may require that each instance of a super-type may *only* be an instance of *one* sub-type. Similarly, a super-type/sub-type relationship may be *exhaustive* or not. It is exhaustive if the methodology requires that each instance of a super-type *must be* an instance of a sub-type. A sub-type named other is often necessary.

Example Relationships

- Each PERSON may be *the vendor in* one or more ORDERS.

- Each ORDER must be *from* one and only one PERSON.

- PERSON is *a sub-type of* PARTY. (Meaning that every instance of PERSON is also an instance of PARTY.)

- Each EMPLOYEE may have a *supervisor* who is also an EMPLOYEE.

Logical Data Model

A logical data model or logical schema is a data model of a specific problem domain expressed independently of a particular database management product or storage technology (physical data model) but in terms of data structures such as relational tables and columns, object-oriented classes, or XML tags. This is as opposed to a conceptual data model, which describes the semantics of an organization without reference to technology.

Logical data models represent the abstract structure of a domain of information. They are often diagrammatic in nature and are most typically used in business processes that seek to capture things of importance to an organization and how they relate to one another. Once validated and approved, the logical data model can become the basis of a physical data model and form the design of a database.

Logical data models should be based on the structures identified in a preceding conceptual data model, since this describes the semantics of the information context, which the logical model should also reflect. Even so, since the logical data model anticipates implementation on a specific computing system, the content of the logical data model is adjusted to achieve certain efficiencies.

The term 'Logical Data Model' is sometimes used as a synonym of 'domain model' or as an alternative to the domain model. While the two concepts are closely related, and have overlapping goals, a domain model is more focused on capturing the concepts in the problem domain rather than the structure of the data associated with that domain.

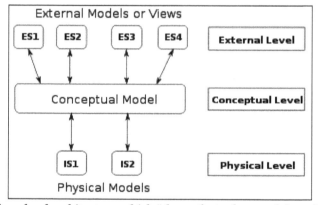

The ANSI/SPARC three level architecture, which "shows that a data model can be an external model (or view), a conceptual model, or a physical model. This is not the only way to look at data models, but it is a useful way, particularly when comparing models".

When ANSI first laid out the idea of a *logical schema* in 1975, the choices were *hierarchical* and *network*. The relational model – where data is described in terms of tables and columns – had just been recognized as a data organization theory but no software existed to support that approach. Since that time, an object-oriented approach to data modelling – where data is described in terms of classes, attributes, and associations – has also been introduced.

Logical Data Model Topics

Reasons for Building a Logical Data Structure

- Helps common understanding of business data elements and requirements.

- Provides foundation for designing a database.

- Facilitates avoidance of data redundancy and thus prevent data & business transaction inconsistency.

- Facilitates data re-use and sharing.

- Decreases development and maintenance time and cost.

- Confirms a logical process model and helps impact analysis.

Conceptual, Logical and Physical Data Model

A logical data model is sometimes incorrectly called a physical data model, which is not what the ANSI people had in mind. The physical design of a database involves deep use of particular database management technology. For example, a table/column design could be implemented on a collection of computers, located in different parts of the world. That is the domain of the physical model.

Conceptual, logical and physical data models are very different in their objectives, goals and content. Key differences noted below.

Conceptual Data Model (CDM)	Logical Data Model (LDM)	Physical Data Model (PDM)
Includes high-level data constructs	Includes entities (tables), attributes (columns/fields) and relationships (keys)	Includes tables, columns, keys, data types, validation rules, database triggers, stored procedures, domains, and access constraints
Non-technical names, so that executives and managers at all levels can understand the data basis of Architectural Description	Uses business names for entities & attributes	Uses more defined and less generic specific names for tables and columns, such as abbreviated column names, limited by the database management system (DBMS) and any company defined standards
Uses general high-level data constructs from which Architectural Descriptions are created in non-technical terms	Is independent of technology (platform, DBMS)	Includes primary keys and indices for fast data access.
Represented in the DIV-1 Viewpoint (DoDAF V2.0)	Represented in the DIV-2 Viewpoint (DoDAF V2.0), and OV-7 View (DoDAF V1.5)	Represented in the DIV-3 Viewpoint (DoDAF V2.0), and SV-11 View (DoDAF V1.5)

Physical Data Model

A physical data model (or database design) is a representation of a data design as implemented, or intended to be implemented, in a database management system. In the lifecycle of a project it typically derives from a logical data model, though it may be reverse-engineered from a given database implementation. A complete physical data model will include all the database artifacts required to create relationships between tables or to achieve performance goals, such as indexes, constraint definitions, linking tables, partitioned tables or clusters. Analysts can usually use a physical data model to calculate storage estimates; it may include specific storage allocation details for a given database system.

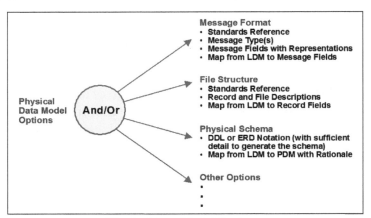

Physical Data Model Options.

As of 2012 seven main databases dominate the commercial marketplace: Informix, Oracle, Postgres, SQL Server, Sybase, DB2 and MySQL. Other RDBMS systems tend either to be legacy databases or used within academia such as universities or further education colleges. Physical data models for each implementation would differ significantly, not least due to underlying operating-system requirements that may sit underneath them. For example: SQL Server runs only on Microsoft Windows operating-systems (Starting with SQL Server 2017, SQL Server runs on Linux. It's the same SQL Server database engine, with many similar features and services regardless of your operating system), while Oracle and MySQL can run on Solaris, Linux and other UNIX-based operating-systems as well as on Windows. This means that the disk requirements, security requirements and many other aspects of a physical data model will be influenced by the RDBMS that a database administrator (or an organization) chooses to use.

Physical Schema

Physical schema is a term used in data management to describe how data is to be represented and stored (files, indices,) in secondary storage using a particular database management system (DBMS) (e.g., Oracle RDBMS, Sybase SQL Server, etc.).

In the ANSI/SPARC Architecture three schema approach, the *internal schema* is the view of data that involved data management technology. This is as opposed to an *external schema* that reflects an individual's view of the data, or the *conceptual schema* that is the integration of a set of external schemas.

Subsequently the internal schema was recognized to have two parts:

The logical schema was the way data were represented to conform to the constraints of a particular approach to database management. At that time the choices were hierarchical and network. Describing the logical schema, however, still did not describe how physically data would be stored on disk drives. That is the domain of the *physical schema*. Now logical schemas describe data in terms of relational *tables and columns*, object-oriented *classes*, and XML *tags*.

A single set of tables, for example, can be implemented in numerous ways, up to and including an architecture where table rows are maintained on computers in different countries.

Data Structure Diagram

Data structure diagram (DSD) is a diagram of the conceptual data model which documents the entities and their relationships, as well as the constraints that connect to them.

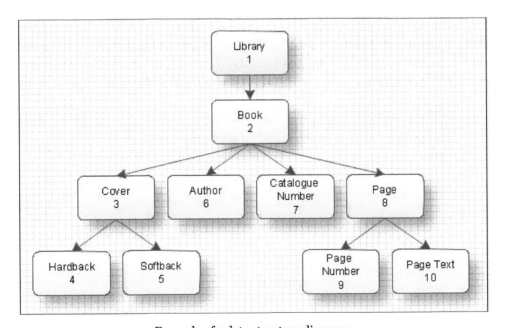

Example of a data structure diagram.

The basic graphic notation elements of DSDs are boxes which represent entities. The arrow symbol represents relationships. Data structure diagrams are most useful for documenting complex data entities.

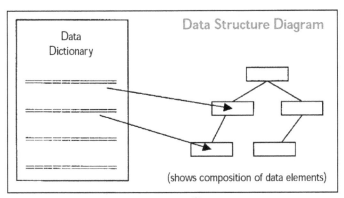

Data structure diagram.

Data Structure Diagram is a diagram type that is used to depict the structure of data elements in the data dictionary. The data structure diagram is a graphical alternative to the composition specifications within such data dictionary entries.

The data structure diagrams is a predecessor of the entity–relationship model (E–R model). In DSDs, attributes are specified inside the entity boxes rather than outside of them, while relationships are drawn as boxes composed of attributes which specify the constraints that bind entities together. DSDs differ from the E–R model in that the E–R model focuses on the relationships between different entities, whereas DSDs focus on the relationships of the elements within an entity.

There are several styles for representing data structure diagrams, with the notable difference in the manner of defining cardinality. The choices are between arrow heads, inverted arrow heads (crow's feet), or numerical representation of the cardinality.

Bachman Diagram

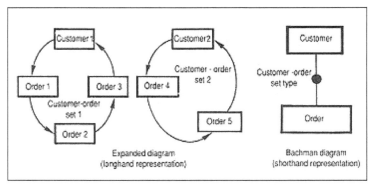

Illustration of set type using a Bachman diagram.

A Bachman diagram is a certain type of data structure diagram, and is used to design the data with a network or relational "logical" model, separating the data model from the way the data is stored in the system. The model is named after database pioneer Charles Bachman, and mostly used in computer software design.

In a relational model, a relation is the cohesion of attributes that are fully and not transitive functional dependent of every key in that relation. The coupling between the relations is based on accordant attributes. For every relation, a rectangle has to be drawn and every coupling is illustrated by a line that connects the relations. On the edge of each line, arrows indicate the cardinality. We have 1-to-n, 1-to-1 and n-to-n. The latter has to be avoided and must be replaced by two (or more) 1-to-n couplings.

Generic Data Model

Generic data models are generalizations of conventional data models. They define standardised general relation types, together with the kinds of things that may be related by such a relation type.

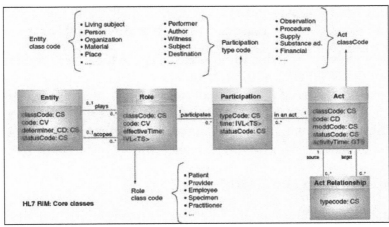

Example of a Generic data model.

The definition of generic data model is similar to the definition of a natural language. For example, a generic data model may define relation types such as a 'classification relation', being a binary relation between an individual thing and a kind of thing (a class) and a 'part-whole relation', being a binary relation between two things, one with the role of part, the other with the role of whole, regardless the kind of things that are related. Given an extensible list of classes, this allows the classification of any individual thing and to specify part-whole relations for any individual object. By standardisation of an extensible list of relation types, a generic data model enables the expression of an unlimited number of kinds of facts and will approach the capabilities of natural languages. Conventional data models, on the other hand, have a fixed and limited domain scope, because the instantiation (usage) of such a model only allows expressions of kinds of facts that are predefined in the model.

Generic data models are developed as an approach to solve some shortcomings of conventional data models. For example, different modelers usually produce different conventional data models of the same domain. This can lead to difficulty in bringing the models of different people together and is an obstacle for data exchange and data integration. Invariably, however, this difference is attributable to different levels of abstraction in the models and differences in the kinds of facts that can be instantiated (the semantic expression capabilities of the models). The modelers need to communicate and agree on certain elements which are to be rendered more concretely, in order to make the differences less significant.

Generic Data Model Topics

Generic Patterns

There are generic patterns that can be used to advantage for modeling business. These include entity types for PARTY (with included PERSON and ORGANIZATION), PRODUCT TYPE, PRODUCT INSTANCE, ACTIVITY TYPE, ACTIVITY INSTANCE, CONTRACT, GEOGRAPHIC AREA, and SITE. A model which explicitly includes versions of these entity classes will be both reasonably robust and reasonably easy to understand.

More abstract models are suitable for general purpose tools, and consist of variations on THING and THING TYPE, with all actual data being instances of these. Such abstract models are on one hand more difficult to manage, since they are not very expressive of real world things, but on the other hand they have a much wider applicability, especially if they are accompanied by a standardised dictionary. More concrete and specific data models will risk having to change as the scope or environment changes.

Approach to Generic Data Modeling

One approach to generic data modeling has the following characteristics:

- A generic data model shall consist of generic entity types, such as 'individual thing', 'class', 'relationship', and possibly a number of their subtypes.

- Every individual thing is an instance of a generic entity called 'individual thing' or one of its subtypes.

- Every individual thing is explicitly classified by a kind of thing ('class') using an explicit classification relationship.

- The classes used for that classification are separately defined as standard instances of the entity 'class' or one of its subtypes, such as 'class of relationship'. These standard classes are usually called 'reference data'. This means that domain specific knowledge is captured in those standard instances and not as entity types. For example, concepts such as car, wheel, building, ship, and also temperature, length, etc. are standard instances. But also standard types of relationship, such as 'is composed of' and 'is involved in' can be defined as standard instances.

This way of modeling allows the addition of standard classes and standard relation types as data (instances), which makes the data model flexible and prevents data model changes when the scope of the application changes.

Generic Data Model Rules

A generic data model obeys the following rules:

- Candidate attributes are treated as representing relationships to other entity types.

- Entity types are represented, and are named after, the underlying nature of a thing, not the role it plays in a particular context. Entity types are chosen. Thus as a result of this principle, any occurrence of an entity type will belong to it from the time it is created to the time it is destroyed, not just whilst it is of interest. This is important when managing the underlying data, rather than the views on it used by applications. We call entity types that conform to this principle generic entity types.

- Entities have a local identifier within a database or exchange file. These should be artificial and managed to be unique. Relationships are not used as part of the local identifier.

- Activities, relationships and event-effects are represented by entity types (not attributes).

- Entity types are part of a sub-type/super-type hierarchy of entity types, in order to define a universal context for the model. As types of relationships are also entity types, they are also arranged in a sub-type/super-type hierarchy of types of relationship.

- Types of relationships are defined on a high (generic) level, being the highest level where the type of relationship is still valid. For example, a composition relationship (indicated by the phrase: 'is composed of') is defined as a relationship between an 'individual thing' and another 'individual thing' (and not just between e.g. an order and an order line). This generic level means that the type of relation may in principle be applied between any individual thing and any other individual thing. Additional constraints are defined in the 'reference data', being standard instances of relationships between kinds of things.

Examples of generic data models are:

- ISO 10303-221.

- ISO 15926.

- Gellish or Gellish English.

- Found in *Data Model Patterns: Conventions of Thought* by David C. Hay. 1995.

- Found in *Enterprise Model Patterns: Describing the World* by David C. Hay. 2011.

Semantic Data Model

Semantic data model (SDM) is a high-level semantics-based database description and structuring formalism (database model) for databases. This database model is designed to capture more of the meaning of an application environment than is possible with contemporary database models. An SDM specification describes a database in terms of the kinds of entities that exist in the application environment, the classifications and groupings of those entities, and the structural interconnections among them. SDM provides a collection of high-level modeling primitives to capture the semantics of an application environment. By accommodating derived information in a database structural specification, SDM allows the same information to be viewed in several ways; this makes it possible to directly accommodate the variety of needs and processing requirements typically present in database applications. The design of the present SDM is based on our experience in using a preliminary version of it. SDM is designed to enhance the effectiveness and usability of database systems. An SDM database description can serve as a formal specification and documentation tool for a database; it can provide a basis for supporting a variety of powerful user interface facilities, it can serve as a conceptual database model in the database design process; and, it can be used as the database model for a new kind of database management system.

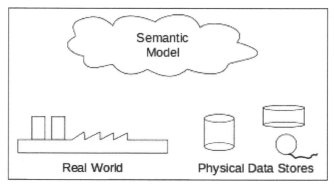

Semantic data models.

A semantic data model in software engineering has various meanings:

- It is a conceptual data model in which semantic information is included. This means that the model describes the meaning of its instances. Such a semantic data model is an abstraction that defines how the stored symbols (the instance data) relate to the real world.

- It is a conceptual data model that includes the capability to express information that enables parties to the information exchange to interpret meaning (semantics) from the instances, without the need to know the meta-model. Such semantic models are fact-oriented (as opposed to object-oriented). Facts are typically expressed by binary relations between data elements, whereas higher order relations are expressed as collections of binary relations. Typically binary relations have the form of triples: Object-RelationType-Object. For example: the Eiffel Tower <is located in> Paris.

Typically the instance data of semantic data models explicitly include the kinds of relationships between the various data elements, such as <is located in>. To interpret the meaning of the facts from the instances it is required that the meaning of the kinds of relations (relation types) be known. Therefore, semantic data models typically standardize such relation types. This means that the second kind of semantic data models enable that the instances express facts that include their own meaning. The second kind of semantic data models are usually meant to create semantic databases. The ability to include meaning in semantic databases facilitates building distributed databases that enable applications to interpret the meaning from the content. This implies that semantic databases can be integrated when they use the same (standard) relation types. This also implies that in general they have a wider applicability than relational or object-oriented databases.

The logical data structure of a database management system (DBMS), whether hierarchical, network, or relational, cannot totally satisfy the requirements for a conceptual definition of data, because it is limited in scope and biased toward the implementation strategy employed by the DBMS. Therefore, the need to define data from a conceptual view has led to the development of semantic data modeling techniques. That is, techniques to define the meaning of data within the context of its interrelationships with other data, as illustrated in the figure. The real world, in terms of resources, ideas, events, etc., are symbolically defined within physical data stores. A semantic data model is an abstraction which defines how the stored symbols relate to the real world. Thus, the model must be a true representation of the real world.

According to Klas and Schrefl, the "overall goal of semantic data models is to capture more meaning of data by integrating relational concepts with more powerful abstraction concepts known from the Artificial Intelligence field. The idea is to provide high level modeling primitives as an integral part of a data model in order to facilitate the representation of real world situations".

The need for semantic data models was first recognized by the U.S. Air Force in the mid-1970s as a result of the Integrated Computer-Aided Manufacturing (ICAM) Program. The objective of this program was to increase manufacturing productivity through the systematic application of computer technology. The ICAM Program identified a need for better analysis and communication techniques for people involved in improving manufacturing productivity. As a result, the ICAM Program developed a series of techniques known as the IDEF (ICAM Definition) Methods which included the following:

- IDEF0 used to produce a "function model" which is a structured representation of the activities or processes within the environment or system.

- IDEF1 used to produce an "information model" which represents the structure and semantics of information within the environment or system.

    ○ IDEF1X is a semantic data modeling technique. It is used to produce a graphical information model which represents the structure and semantics of information within an environment or system. Use of this standard permits the construction of semantic data models which may serve to support the management of data as a resource, the integration of information systems, and the building of computer databases.

- IDEF2 used to produce a "dynamics model" which represents the time varying behavioral characteristics of the environment or system.

During the 1990s the application of semantic modelling techniques resulted in the semantic data models of the second kind. An example of such is the semantic data model that is standardised as ISO 15926-2, which is further developed into the semantic modelling language Gellish. The definition of the Gellish language is documented in the form of a semantic data model. Gellish itself is a semantic modelling language, that can be used to create other semantic models. Those semantic models can be stored in Gellish Databases, being semantic databases.

Applications

A semantic data model can be used to serve many purposes. Some key objectives include:

- Planning of Data Resources: A preliminary data model can be used to provide an overall view of the data required to run an enterprise. The model can then be analyzed to identify and scope projects to build shared data resources.

- Building of Shareable Databases: A fully developed model can be used to define an application independent view of data which can be validated by users and then transformed into a physical database design for any of the various DBMS technologies. In addition to generating databases which are consistent and shareable, development costs can be drastically reduced through data modeling.

- Evaluation of Vendor Software: Since a data model actually represents the infrastructure of an organization, vendor software can be evaluated against a company's data model in order to identify possible inconsistencies between the infrastructure implied by the software and the way the company actually does business.

- Integration of Existing Databases: By defining the contents of existing databases with semantic data models, an integrated data definition can be derived. With the proper technology, the resulting conceptual schema can be used to control transaction processing in a distributed database environment. The U.S. Air Force Integrated Information Support System (I2S2) is an experimental development and demonstration of this type of technology applied to a heterogeneous DBMS environment

Object-role Modeling

Object-role modeling (ORM) is used to model the semantics of a universe of discourse. ORM is often used for data modeling and software engineering.

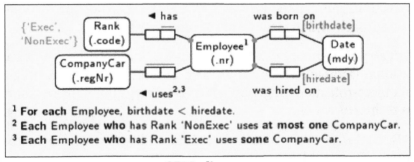

ORM2 diagram.

An object-role model uses graphical symbols that are based on first order predicate logic and set theory to enable the modeler to create an unambiguous definition of an arbitrary universe of discourse. Attribute free, the predicates of an ORM Model lend themselves to the analysis and design of graph database models in as much as ORM was originally conceived to benefit relational database design.

The term "object-role model" was coined in the 1970s and ORM based tools have been used for more than 30 years – principally for data modeling. More recently ORM has been used to model business rules, XML-Schemas, data warehouses, requirements engineering and web forms.

The roots of ORM can be traced to research into semantic modeling for information systems in Europe during the 1970s. There were many pioneers and this short summary does not by any means mention them all. An early contribution came in 1973 when Michael Senko wrote about "data structuring" in the IBM Systems Journal. In 1974 Jean-Raymond Abrial contributed an article about "Data Semantics". In June 1975,

Eckhard Falkenberg's doctoral thesis was published and in 1976 one of Falkenberg's papers mentions the term "object-role model".

G.M. Nijssen made fundamental contributions by introducing the "circle-box" notation for object types and roles, and by formulating the first version of the conceptual schema design procedure. Robert Meersman extended the approach by adding subtyping, and introducing the first truly conceptual query language.

Object role modeling also evolved from the *Natural language Information Analysis Method*, a methodology that was initially developed by the academic researcher, G.M. Nijssen in the Netherlands (Europe) in the mid-1970s and his research team at the Control Data Corporation Research Laboratory in Belgium, and later at the University of Queensland, Australia in the 1980s. The acronym NIAM originally stood for "Nijssen's Information Analysis Methodology", and later generalised to "Natural language Information Analysis Methodology" and *Binary Relationship Modeling* since G. M. Nijssen was only one of many people involved in the development of the method.

In 1989 Terry Halpin completed his PhD thesis on ORM, providing the first full formalization of the approach and incorporating several extensions.

Also in 1989, Terry Halpin and G.M. Nijssen co-authored the book "Conceptual Schema and Relational Database Design" and several joint papers, providing the first formalization of object-role modeling. Since then Dr. Terry Halpin has authored six books and over 160 technical papers.

A graphical NIAM design tool which included the ability to generate database-creation scripts for Oracle, DB2 and DBQ was developed in the early 1990s in Paris. It was originally named Genesys and was marketed successfully in France and later Canada. It could also handle ER diagram design. It was ported to SCO Unix, SunOs, DEC 3151's and Windows 3.0 platforms, and was later migrated to succeeding Microsoft operating systems, utilising XVT for cross operating system graphical portability. The tool was renamed OORIANE and is currently being used for large data warehouse and SOA projects.

Also evolving from NIAM is *"Fully Communication Oriented Information Modeling"* FCO-IM. It distinguishes itself from traditional ORM in that it takes a strict communication-oriented perspective. Rather than attempting to model the domain and its essential concepts, it models the communication in this domain (universe of discourse). Another important difference is that it does this on instance level, deriving type level and object/fact level during analysis.

Another recent development is the use of ORM in combination with standardised relation types with associated roles and a standard machine-readable dictionary and taxonomy of concepts as are provided in the Gellish English dictionary. Standardisation of relation types (fact types), roles and concepts enables increased possibilities for model integration and model reuse.

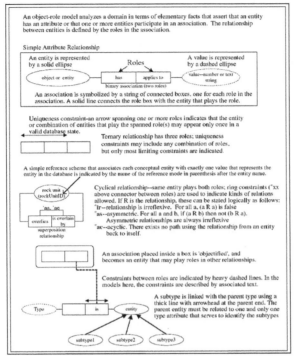

Overview of object-role model notation.

Facts

Object-role models are based on elementary facts, and expressed in diagrams that can be verbalised into natural language. A fact is a proposition such as "John Smith was hired on 5 January 1995" or "Mary Jones was hired on 3 March 2010".

With ORM, propositions such as these, are abstracted into "fact types" for example "Person was hired on Date" and the individual propositions are regarded as sample data. The difference between a "fact" and an "elementary fact" is that an elementary fact cannot be simplified without loss of meaning. This "fact-based" approach facilitates modeling, transforming, and querying information from any domain.

Attribute-free

ORM is attribute-free: unlike models in the entity–relationship (ER) and Unified Modeling Language (UML) methods, ORM treats all elementary facts as relationships and so treats decisions for grouping facts into structures (e.g. attribute-based entity types, classes, relation schemes, XML schemas) as implementation concerns irrelevant to semantics. By avoiding attributes, ORM improves semantic stability and enables verbalization into natural language.

Fact-based Modeling

Fact-based modelling includes procedures for mapping facts to attribute-based structures, such as those of ER or UML.

Fact-based textual representations are based on formal subsets of native languages. ORM proponents argue that ORM models are easier to understand by people without a technical education. For example, proponents argue that object-role models are easier to understand than declarative languages such as Object Constraint Language (OCL) and other graphical languages such as UML class models. Fact-based graphical notations are more expressive than those of ER and UML. An object-role model can be automatically mapped to relational and deductive databases.

ORM 2 Graphical Notation

ORM2 is the latest generation of object-role modeling. The main objectives for the ORM 2 graphical notation are:

- More compact display of ORM models without compromising clarity.

- Improved internationalization (e.g. avoid English language symbols).

- Simplified drawing rules to facilitate creation of a graphical editor.

- Extended use of views for selectively displaying/suppressing detail.

- Support for new features (e.g. role path delineation, closure aspects, modalities).

Design Procedure

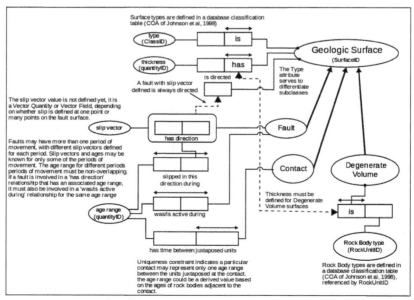

Example of the application of Object Role Modeling.

System development typically involves several stages such as: feasibility study; requirements analysis; conceptual design of data and operations; logical design; external design; prototyping; internal design and implementation; testing and validation; and maintenance. The seven steps of the conceptual schema design procedure are:

- Transform familiar information examples into elementary facts, and apply quality checks.

- Draw the fact types, and apply a population check.

- Check for entity types that should be combined, and note any arithmetic derivations.

- Add uniqueness constraints, and check arity of fact types.

- Add mandatory role constraints, and check for logical derivations.

- Add value, set comparison and subtyping constraints.

- Add other constraints and perform final checks.

ORM's conceptual schema design procedure (CSDP) focuses on the analysis and design of data.

Cloud Database Deployment Models

There are two primary cloud database models:

- Traditional, which is very similar to an onsite, in-house managed database—except for infrastructure provisioning. In this case, an organization purchases virtual machine space from a cloud services provider, and the database is deployed to the cloud. The organization's developers use a DevOps model or traditional IT staff to control the database. The organization is responsible for oversight and database management.

- Database as a service (DBaaS), in which an organization contracts with a cloud services provider through a fee-based subscription service. The service provider offers a variety of real-time operational, maintenance, administrative, and database management tasks to the end user. The database runs on the service provider's infrastructure. This usage model typically includes automation in the areas of provisioning, backup, scaling, high availability, security, patching, and health monitoring. The DBaaS model provides organizations with the greatest value, allowing them to use outsourced database management optimized by software automation rather than hire and manage in-house database experts.

The Benefits of having a Cloud-based Database

Cloud databases offer many of the same benefits as other cloud services, including:

- Improved agility and innovation: Cloud databases can be set up very quickly and decommissioned just as quickly—making testing, validating, and operationalizing new business ideas easy and fast. If the organization decides not to operationalize a project, it can simply abandon the project (and its database) and move on to the next innovation.

- Faster time to market: When using a cloud database, there's no need to order hardware or spend time waiting for shipments, installation, and network setup when a new product is in the development queue. Database access can be available within minutes.

- Reduced risks: Cloud databases offer numerous opportunities to reduce risk across the business, particularly for DBaaS models. Cloud services providers can use automation to enforce security best practices and features and to lower the probability of human error—the primary cause of software downtime. Automated high-availability features and service level agreements (SLAs) can reduce or eliminate loss of revenue due to downtime. And capacity forecasting is no longer a critical issue when implementing projects, because the cloud can be an infinite pool of just-in-time infrastructure and services.

- Lower costs: Pay-per-use subscription models and dynamic scaling allow end users to provision for steady state, then scale up for peak demand during busy periods, and then scale back down when demand returns to steady state. This is much less costly than maintaining these capabilities in-house, where organizations must purchase physical servers that can handle peak demand even though they may only need peak capabilities a couple of days per quarter. Enterprises can save money by literally turning services off when they're not needed. They can also reduce costs by executing global initiatives with marginal infrastructure investment. In many instances, cloud software automation takes the place of high-cost database administrators (DBAs)—thereby reducing operational expenses by eliminating the need for expensive in-house resources.

Cloud Database Management Choices

Enterprises have choices in how to manage their cloud databases. Database management styles can be generalized into the following four categories:

- Self-managed cloud databases: In this model, an organization runs its database on a cloud infrastructure but manages the database itself, using in-house resources, without any automation being integrated by the cloud vendor. This model offers some of the standard benefits of locating a database in the cloud—including improved flexibility and agility—but the organization maintains responsibility and control over database management.

- Automated cloud databases: In this model, organizations use database cloud service application programming interfaces (APIs) to assist with lifecycle operations, but they maintain access to the database servers and control database configuration and operating systems. Automated database services feature limited SLAs and typically exclude planned activities, such as patching and maintenance.

- Managed cloud databases: This model is similar to automated cloud databases, but the cloud vendor does not allow consumer access to servers hosting the database. Configuration is limited to cloud vendor–supported configurations, because end users are not allowed to install their own software.

- Autonomous cloud databases: This is a new, hands-free operating model in which automation and machine learning eliminate the human labor associated with database management and performance tuning. Services include SLAs for business-critical applications, such as zero-downtime operations for unplanned and planned database and service lifecycle activities.

Types of Cloud Databases and the Move to Multimodel

There are numerous types of cloud databases, all of which are intended to meet specific needs and handle specific types of workloads. For example, there are databases specially designed to manage transactions, others designed to run internet-scale applications, and others that serve as data warehouses for analytics. Applying specific database models to address the needs of specific applications or workloads is referred to as polyglot persistence.

OLTP workloads are supported by data models that differ from those used in OLAP workloads. Document and multimedia data relies on formats like XML and JavaScript Object Notation (JSON). Other types of databases include graph databases used for connectivity analysis, spatial databases for geographic analysis, and key-value stores for high-performance storage and lookup of simple data types.

As commercial, enterprise databases have developed over time, they've begun to encompass multiple data models and access methods within a single database management system. What's emerging in the industry today is a move toward the multimodel database that allows an end user to work across different types of workloads from one underlying database.

Oracle refers to this concept as multimodel polyglot persistence. This new capability allows many applications to use the same database management system while the enterprise continues to benefit from the unique data models necessary for a specific application.

These new database architectures are allowing enterprises to significantly streamline the number of databases they use and prevent the creation of data silos that lock an organization's most valuable asset (data) away from broader use by the company.

Cloud Database Solutions: What should Run in the Cloud?

Most every industry, from financial services to healthcare, can benefit from using cloud database solutions. The choice is not whether or not to use a cloud database. The choice is which model and type will work best to meet an enterprise's specific needs.

Many organizations choose to take a staged approach to cloud database utilization, blending traditional cloud database models with DBaaS models. For others, such as those in the financial services industry, keeping mission-critical applications in-house could remain a priority.

However, things are changing quickly. As DBaaS models become more robust and the move to autonomous cloud databases takes hold, it's likely that enterprises will find greater opportunities, and greater benefits, in fully migrating their databases to the cloud.

The Database of the Future: Self-driving Cloud Databases

The newest and most innovative type of cloud database is the self-driving cloud database (also known as the autonomous database, referenced earlier). Whereas on-premises databases require a dedicated DBA to manage them, that same deep DBA expertise is not necessary for managing a self-driving cloud database. This database type uses cloud technology and machine learning to automate database tuning, security, backups, updates, and other routine management tasks that have traditionally been performed by DBAs.

Self-driving databases are designed to automatically withstand hardware failures, including those at cloud platform sites, and offer online full-stack patching of software, firmware, virtualization, and clustering. They easily scale performance and capacity as needed. Additionally, they protect data from both external attacks and malicious internal users, and they avoid many of the downtime-related issues of the other models—including planned maintenance.

IDC research indicates that as much as 75% of an enterprise's total data management costs can be in labor alone. A self-driving database could potentially save the average enterprise hundreds, or perhaps thousands, of full-time employee hours annually for every one of its major enterprise databases. In addition, it's been estimated that 72% of enterprise IT budgets goes to maintaining existing systems, leaving a mere 25% for innovation.

Self-driving databases could go a long way toward eliminating these high costs and allowing enterprises to utilize their DBAs on higher value work—such as data modeling, assisting programmers with data architecture, and planning for future capacity.

References

- Database-models, database-diagram: lucidchart.com, Retrieved 11 April, 2020

- Beynon-Davies, Paul (2004). Database Systems. Basingstoke, UK: Palgrave: Houndmills. ISBN 978-1403916013

- Data-modelling-conceptual-logical: guru99.com, Retrieved 08 June, 2020

- Elmasri, Ramez; Navathe, Shamkant B. (2015). Fundamentals of database systems (Seventhition ed.). Pearson. p. 1280. ISBN 978-0133970777

- Object-relational-Data-Model: tutorialspoint.com, Retrieved 29 August, 2020

- RICCARDO TORLONE (2003). "Conceptual Multidimensional Models" (PDF). In Maurizio Rafanelli (ed.). Multidimensional Databases: Problems and Solutions. Idea Group Inc (IGI). ISBN 978-1-59140-053-0

- What-is-a-cloud-database, database: oracle.com, Retrieved 24 March, 2020

Database Management Systems 4

Database management system is a software that stores and retrieves users' data for managing it by taking appropriate security measures. A few of its types are hierarchical database, network database, relational database, object-oriented database, document database, etc. This chapter discusses database management system in detail.

Database Management System (DBMS) is a software for storing and retrieving users' data while considering appropriate security measures. It consists of a group of programs which manipulate the database. The DBMS accepts the request for data from an application and instructs the operating system to provide the specific data. In large systems, a DBMS helps users and other third-party software to store and retrieve data.

DBMS allows users to create their own databases as per their requirement. The term "DBMS" includes the user of the database and other application programs. It provides an interface between the data and the software application.

A simple example of a university database. This database is maintaining information concerning students, courses, and grades in a university environment. The database is organized as five files:

- The STUDENT file stores data of each student.

- The COURSE file stores contain data on each course.

- The SECTION stores the information about sections in a particular course.

- The GRADE file stores the grades which students receive in the various sections.

- The TUTOR file contains information about each professor.

To define a database system:

- We need to specify the structure of the records of each file by defining the different types of data elements to be stored in each record.

- We can also use a coding scheme to represent the values of a data item.

- Basically, your Database will have 5 tables with a foreign key defined amongst the various tables.

Characteristics of Database Management System

- Provides security and removes redundancy.

- Self-describing nature of a database system.

- Insulation between programs and data abstraction.

- Support of multiple views of the data.

- Sharing of data and multiuser transaction processing.

- DBMS allows entities and relations among them to form tables.

- It follows the ACID concept (Atomicity, Consistency, Isolation, and Durability).

- DBMS supports multi-user environment that allows users to access and manipulate data in parallel.

DBMS vs. Flat File

DBMS	Flat File Management System
Multi-user access	It does not support multi-user access.
Design to fulfill the need for small and large businesses	It is only limited to smaller DBMS system.
Remove redundancy and Integrity	Redundancy and Integrity issues.

Expensive. But in the long term Total Cost of Ownership is cheap	It's cheaper.
Easy to implement complicated transactions	No support for complicated transactions.

Users in a DBMS Environment

Following are the various category of users of a DBMS system:

Component Name	Task
Application Programmers	The Application programmers write programs in various programming languages to interact with databases.
Database Administrators	Database Admin is responsible for managing the entire DBMS system. He/She is called Database admin or DBA.
End-Users	The end users are the people who interact with the database management system. They conduct various operations on database like retrieving, updating, deleting, etc.

Popular DBMS Software

Here, is the list of some popular DBMS system:

- MySQL,
- Microsoft Access,
- Oracle,
- PostgreSQL,
- dBASE,
- FoxPro,
- SQLite,
- IBM DB2,
- LibreOffice Base,
- MariaDB,
- Microsoft SQL Server etc.

Application of DBMS

Sector	Use of DBMS
Banking	For customer information, account activities, payments, deposits, loans, etc.

Airlines	For reservations and schedule information.
Universities	For student information, course registrations, colleges and grades.
Telecom-munication	It helps to keep call records, monthly bills, maintaining balances, etc.
Finance	For storing information about stock, sales, and purchases of financial instruments like stocks and bonds.
Sales	Use for storing customer, product & sales information.
Manufac-turing	It is used for the management of supply chain and for tracking production of items. Inventories status in warehouses.
HR Man-agement	For information about employees, salaries, payroll, deduction, generation of paychecks, etc.

Types of DBMS

Types of DBMS.

Four Types of DBMS systems are: Hierarchical, Network, Relational & Object-Oriented DBMS.

Hierarchical DBMS

In a Hierarchical database, model data is organized in a tree-like structure. Data is Stored Hierarchically (top down or bottom up) format. Data is represented using a parent-child relationship. In Hierarchical DBMS parent may have many children, but children have only one parent.

Network Model

The network database model allows each child to have multiple parents. It helps you to address the need to model more complex relationships like as the orders/parts many-to-many relationship. In this model, entities are organized in a graph which can be accessed through several paths.

Relational Model

Relational DBMS is the most widely used DBMS model because it is one of the easiest. This model is based on normalizing data in the rows and columns of the tables. Relational model stored in fixed structures and manipulated using SQL.

Object-oriented Model

In Object-oriented Model data stored in the form of objects. The structure which is called classes which display data within it. It defines a database as a collection of objects which stores both data member's values and operations.

Advantages of DBMS

- DBMS offers a variety of techniques to store & retrieve data.

- DBMS serves as an efficient handler to balance the needs of multiple applications using the same data.

- Uniform administration procedures for data.

- Application programmers never exposed to details of data representation and storage.

- A DBMS uses various powerful functions to store and retrieve data efficiently.

- Offers Data Integrity and Security.

- The DBMS implies integrity constraints to get a high level of protection against prohibited access to data.

- A DBMS schedules concurrent access to the data in such a manner that only one user can access the same data at a time.

- Reduced Application Development Time.

Disadvantage of DBMS

DBMS may offer plenty of advantages but, it has certain flaws:

- Cost of Hardware and Software of a DBMS is quite high which increases the budget of your organization.

- Most database management systems are often complex systems, so the training for users to use the DBMS is required.

- In some organizations, all data is integrated into a single database which can be damaged because of electric failure or database is corrupted on the storage media.

- Use of the same program at a time by many users sometimes lead to the loss of some data.

- DBMS can't perform sophisticated calculations.

DBMS architecture helps in design, development, implementation, and maintenance of a database. A database stores critical information for a business. Selecting the correct Database Architecture helps in quick and secure access to this data.

1-tier Architecture

1-tier Architecture Diagram.

The simplest of Database Architecture are 1 tier where the Client, Server, and Database all reside on the same machine. Anytime you install a DB in your system and access it to practise SQL queries it is 1 tier architecture. But such architecture is rarely used in production.

2-tier Architecture

A two-tier architecture is a database architecture where:

- Presentation layer runs on a client (PC, Mobile, Tablet, etc).

- Data is stored on a Server.

An application interface which is called ODBC (Open Database Connectivity) an API which allows the client-side program to call the DBMS. Today most of the DBMS offers ODBC drivers for their DBMS. 2 tier architecture provides added security to the DBMS as it is not exposed to the end user directly.

Example of Two-tier Architecture is a Contact Management System created using MS-Access.

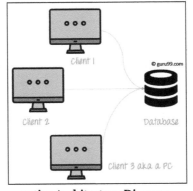

2-tier Architecture Diagram.

In the above 2-teir architecture we can see that one server is connected with clients 1, 2m and 3. This architecture provides Direct and faster communication.

3-tier Architecture

3-tier schema is an extension of the 2-tier architecture. 3-tier architecture has following layers:

- Presentation layer (your PC, Tablet, Mobile, etc.).

- Application layer (server).

- Database Server.

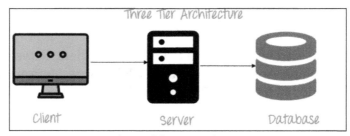

3-tier Architecture Diagram.

This DBMS architecture contains an Application layer between the user and the DBMS, which is responsible for communicating the user's request to the DBMS system and send the response from the DBMS to the user.

The application layer(business logic layer) also processes functional logic, constraint, and rules before passing data to the user or down to the DBMS.

Three tier architecture is the most popular DBMS architecture.

The goals of three-tier architecture are:

- To separate the user applications and physical database.

- Proposed to support DBMS characteristics.

- Program-data independence.

- Support of multiple views of the data.

Database systems comprise of complex data structures. Thus, to make the system efficient for retrieval of data and reduce the complexity of the users, developers use the method of Data Abstraction.

There are mainly three levels of data abstraction:

- Internal Level: Actual PHYSICAL storage structure and access paths.

- Conceptual or Logical Level: Structure and constraints for the entire database.

- External or View level: Describes various user views.

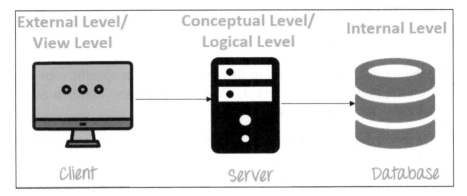

Internal Level/Schema

The internal schema defines the physical storage structure of the database. The internal schema is a very low-level representation of the entire database. It contains multiple occurrences of multiple types of internal record. In the ANSI term, it is also called "stored record'.

Facts about Internal Schema

- The internal schema is the lowest level of data abstraction.

- It helps you to keeps information about the actual representation of the entire database. Like the actual storage of the data on the disk in the form of records.

- The internal view tells us what data is stored in the database and how.

- It never deals with the physical devices. Instead, internal schema views a physical device as a collection of physical pages.

Conceptual Schema/Level

The conceptual schema describes the Database structure of the whole database for the community of users. This schema hides information about the physical storage structures and focuses on describing data types, entities, relationships, etc.

This logical level comes between the user level and physical storage view. However, there is only single conceptual view of a single database.

Facts about Conceptual Schema

- Defines all database entities, their attributes, and their relationships.

- Security and integrity information.

- In the conceptual level, the data available to a user must be contained in or derivable from the physical level.

External Schema/Level

An external schema describes the part of the database which specific user is interested in. It hides the unrelated details of the database from the user. There may be "n" number of external views for each database.

Each external view is defined using an external schema, which consists of definitions of various types of external record of that specific view.

An external view is just the content of the database as it is seen by some specific particular user. For example, a user from the sales department will see only sales related data.

Facts about External Schema

- An external level is only related to the data which is viewed by specific end users.

- This level includes some external schemas.

- External schema level is nearest to the user.

- The external schema describes the segment of the database which is needed for a certain user group and hides the remaining details from the database from the specific user group.

Goal of 3 Level/Schema of Database

Here, are some Objectives of using three schema architecture:

- Every user should be able to access the same data but able to see a customized view of the data.

- The user needs not to deal directly with physical database storage detail.

- The DBA should be able to change the database storage structure without disturbing the user's views.

- The internal structure of the database should remain unaffected when changes made to the physical aspects of storage.

Advantages Database Schema

- You can manage data independent of the physical storage.

- Faster Migration to new graphical environments.

- DBMS Architecture allows you to make changes on the presentation level without affecting the other two layers.

- As each tier is separate, it is possible to use different sets of developers.

- It is more secure as the client doesn't have direct access to the database business logic.

- In case of the failure of the one-tier no data loss as you are always secure by accessing the other tier.

Disadvantages Database Schema

- Complete DB Schema is a complex structure which is difficult to understand for everyone.

- Difficult to set up and maintain.

- The physical separation of the tiers can affect the performance of the Database.

Components of DBMS

A database management system (DBMS) consists of several components. Each component plays very important role in the database management system environment. The major components of database management system are:

- Software,
- Hardware,
- Data,
- Procedures,
- Database Access Language.

Software

The main component of a DBMS is the software. It is the set of programs used to handle the database and to control and manage the overall computerized database:

- DBMS software itself is the most important software component in the overall system.

- Operating system including network software being used in network, to share the data of database among multiple users.

- Application programs developed in programming languages such as C++,

Visual Basic that are used to access database in database management system. Each program contains statements that request the DBMS to perform operation on database. The operations may include retrieving, updating, deleting data etc. The application program may be conventional or online workstations or terminals.

Hardware

Hardware consists of a set of physical electronic devices such as computers (together with associated I/O devices like disk drives), storage devices, I/O channels, electromechanical devices that make interface between computers and the real world systems etc, and so on. It is impossible to implement the DBMS without the hardware devices, in a network, a powerful computer with high data processing speed and a storage device with large storage capacity is required as database server.

Data

Data is the most important component of the DBMS. The main purpose of DBMS is to process the data. In DBMS, databases are defined, constructed and then data is stored, updated and retrieved to and from the databases. The database contains both the actual (or operational) data and the metadata (data about data or description about data).

Procedures

Procedures refer to the instructions and rules that help to design the database and to use the DBMS. The users that operate and manage the DBMS require documented procedures on hot use or run the database management system. These may include:

- Procedure to install the new DBMS.

- To log on to the DBMS.

- To use the DBMS or application program.

- To make backup copies of database.

- To change the structure of database.

- To generate the reports of data retrieved from database.

Database Access Language

The database access language is used to access the data to and from the database. The users use the database access language to enter new data, change the existing data in database and to retrieve required data from databases. The user writes a set of appropriate commands in a database access language and submits these to the DBMS. The

DBMS translates the user commands and sends it to a specific part of the DBMS called the Database Jet Engine. The database engine generates a set of results according to the commands submitted by user, converts these into a user readable form called an Inquiry Report and then displays them on the screen. The administrators may also use the database access language to create and maintain the databases.

The most popular database access language is SQL (Structured Query Language). Relational databases are required to have a database query language.

Users

The users are the people who manage the databases and perform different operations on the databases in the database system. There are three kinds of people who play different roles in database system:

- Application Programmers.

- Database Administrators.

- End-users.

Application Programmers

The people who write application programs in programming languages (such as Visual Basic, Java, or C++) to interact with databases are called Application Programmer.

Database Administrators

A person who is responsible for managing the overall database management system is called database administrator or simply DBA.

End-users

The end-users are the people who interact with database management system to perform different operations on database such as retrieving, updating, inserting, deleting data etc.

Array Database Management Systems

Array database management systems (array DBMSs) provide database services specifically for arrays (also called raster data), that is: homogeneous collections of data items (often called pixels, voxels, etc.), sitting on a regular grid of one, two, or more dimensions. Often arrays are used to represent sensor, simulation, image, or statistics data. Such arrays tend to be Big Data, with single objects frequently ranging into Terabyte and soon Petabyte sizes, for example, today's earth and space observation archives typically grow by Terabytes a day. Array databases aim at offering flexible, scalable storage and retrieval on this information category.

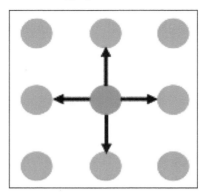

Euclidean neighborhood of elements in arrays.

In the same style as standard database systems do on sets, Array DBMSs offer scalable, flexible storage and flexible retrieval/manipulation on arrays of (conceptually) unlimited size. As in practice arrays never appear standalone, such an array model normally is embedded into some overall data model, such as the relational model. Some systems implement arrays as an analogy to tables, some introduce arrays as an additional attribute type.

Management of arrays requires novel techniques, particularly due to the fact that traditional database tuples and objects tend to fit well into a single database page – a unit of disk access on server, typically 4 KB – while array objects easily can span several media. The prime task of the array storage manager is to give fast access to large arrays and sub-arrays. To this end, arrays get partitioned, during insertion, into so-called *tiles* or *chunks* of convenient size which then act as units of access during query evaluation.

Array DBMSs offer query languages giving declarative access to such arrays, allowing to create, manipulate, search, and delete them. Like with, e.g., SQL, expressions of arbitrary complexity can be built on top of a set of core array operations. Due to the extensions made in the data and query model, Array DBMSs sometimes are subsumed under the NoSQL category, in the sense of "not only SQL". Query optimization and parallelization are important for achieving scalability, actually, many array operators lend themselves well towards parallel evaluation, by processing each tile on separate nodes or cores.

Important application domains of Array DBMSs include Earth, Space, Life, and Social sciences, as well as the related commercial applications (such as hydrocarbon exploration in industry and OLAP in business). The variety occurring can be observed, e.g., in geo data where 1-D environmental sensor time series, 2-D satellite images, 3-D x/y/t image time series and x/y/z geophysics data, as well as 4-D x/y/z/t climate and ocean data can be found.

The relational data model, which is prevailing today, does not directly support the array paradigm to the same extent as sets and tuples. ISO SQL lists an array-valued attribute type, but this is only one-dimensional, with almost no operational support, and not usable for the application domains of Array DBMSs. Another option is to resort to BLOBs ("binary large objects") which are the equivalent to files: byte strings of (conceptually) unlimited length, but again without any query language functionality, such as multi-dimensional subsetting.

First significant work in going beyond BLOBs has been established with PICDMS. This system offers the precursor of a 2-D array query language, albeit still procedural and without suitable storage support.

A first declarative query language suitable for multiple dimensions and with an algebra-based semantics has been published by Baumann, together with a scalable architecture. Another array database language, constrained to 2-D, has been presented by Marathe and Salem. Seminal theoretical work has been accomplished by Libkin, in their model, called NCRA, they extend a nested relational calculus with multidimensional arrays; among the results are important contributions on array query complexity analysis. A map algebra, suitable for 2-D and 3-D spatial raster data.

In terms of Array DBMS implementations, the rasdaman system has the longest implementation track record of n-D arrays with full query support. Oracle GeoRaster offers chunked storage of 2-D raster maps, albeit without SQL integration. TerraLib is an open-source GIS software that extends object-relational DBMS technology to handle spatio-temporal data types, while main focus is on vector data, there is also some support for rasters. Starting with version 2.0, PostGIS embeds raster support for 2-D rasters, a special function offers declarative raster query functionality. SciQL is an array query language being added to the MonetDB DBMS. SciDB is a more recent initiative to establish array database support. Like SciQL, arrays are seen as an equivalent to tables, rather than a new attribute type as in rasdaman and PostGIS.

For the special case of sparse data, OLAP data cubes are well established, they store cell values together with their location – an adequate compression technique in face of the few locations carrying valid information at all – and operate with SQL on them. As this technique does not scale in density, standard databases are not used today for dense data, like satellite images, where most cells carry meaningful information, rather, proprietary ad-hoc implementations prevail in scientific data management and similar situations. Hence, this is where Array DBMSs can make a particular contribution.

Generally, Array DBMSs are an emerging technology. While operationally deployed systems exist, like Oracle GeoRaster, PostGIS 2.0 and rasdaman, there are still many open research questions, including query language design and formalization, query optimization, parallelization and distributed processing, and scalability issues in general.

Besides, scientific communities still appear reluctant in taking up array database technology and tend to favor specialized, proprietary technology.

When adding arrays to databases, all facets of database design need to be reconsidered – ranging from conceptual modeling (such as suitable operators) over storage management (such as management of arrays spanning multiple media) to query processing (such as efficient processing strategies).

Conceptual Modeling

Formally, an array A is given by a (total or partial) function A: $X \rightarrow V$ where X, the domain is a d-dimensional integer interval for some d > 0 and V, called range, is some (non-empty) value set, in set notation, this can be rewritten as {(p,v) | p in X, v in V }. Each (p,v) in A denotes an array element or cell, and following common notation we write A[p] = v. Examples for X include {0..767} × {0..1023} (for XGA sized images), examples for V include {0..255} for 8-bit greyscale images and {0..255} × {0..255} × {0..255} for standard RGB imagery.

Following established database practice, an array query language should be declarative and safe in evaluation. As iteration over an array is at the heart of array processing, declarativeness very much centers on this aspect. The requirement, then, is that conceptually all cells should be inspected simultaneously – in other words, the query does not enforce any explicit iteration sequence over the array cells during evaluation. Evaluation safety is achieved when every query terminates after a finite number of (finite-time) steps, again, avoiding general loops and recursion is a way of achieving this. At the same time, avoiding explicit loop sequences opens up manifold optimization opportunities.

Array Querying

As an example for array query operators the rasdaman algebra and query language can serve, which establish an expression language over a minimal set of array primitives. We begin with the generic core operators and then present common special cases and shorthands.

The marray operator creates an array over some given domain extent and initializes its cells:

```
marray index-range-specification

values cell-value-expression
```

where *index-range-specification* defines the result domain and binds an iteration variable to it, without specifying iteration sequence. The *cell-value-expression* is evaluated at each location of the domain.

Example: "A cutout of array A given by the corner points (10,20) and (40,50)".

```
marray p in [10:20,40:50]

values A[p]
```

This special case, pure subsetting, can be abbreviated as:

```
A[10:20,40:50]
```

This subsetting keeps the dimension of the array, to reduce dimension by extracting slices, a single slicepoint value is indicated in the slicing dimension.

Example: "A slice through an x/y/t timeseries at position t=100, retrieving all available data in x and y".

```
A[*:*,*:*,100]
```

The wildcard operator * indicates that the current boundary of the array is to be used, note that arrays where dimension boundaries are left open at definition time may change size in that dimensions over the array's lifetime.

The above examples have simply copied the original values, instead, these values may be manipulated.

Example: "Array A, with a log() applied to each cell value".

```
marray p in domain(A)

values log( A[p] )
```

This can be abbreviated as:

```
log( A )
```

Through a principle called induced operations, the query language offers all operations the cell type offers on array level, too. Hence, on numeric values all the usual unary and binary arithmetic, exponential, and trigonometric operations are available in a straightforward manner, plus the standard set of Boolean operators.

The condense operator aggregates cell values into one scalar result, similar to SQL aggregates. Its application has the general form:

```
condense condense-op

over index-range-specification

using cell-value-expression
```

As with marray before, the index-range-specification specifies the domain to be iterated over and binds an iteration variable to it – again, without specifying iteration sequence.

Likewise, cell-value-expression is evaluated at each domain location. The condense-op clause specifies the aggregating operation used to combine the cell value expressions into one single value.

Example: "The sum over all values in A".

```
condense +

over p in sdom(A)

using A[p]
```

A shorthand for this operation is:

```
add_cells( A )
```

In the same manner and in analogy to SQL aggregates, a number of further shorthands are provided, including counting, average, minimum, maximum, and Boolean quantifiers.

The next example demonstrates combination of marray and condense operators by deriving a histogram.

Example: "A histogram over 8-bit greyscale image A".

```
marray bucket in [0:255]

values count_cells( A = bucket )
```

The induced comparison, A=bucket, establishes a Boolean array of the same extent as A. The aggregation operator counts the occurrences of true for each value of bucket, which subsequently is put into the proper array cell of the 1-D histogram array.

Such languages allow formulating statistical and imaging operations which can be expressed analytically without using loops. It has been proven that the expressive power of such array languages in principle is equivalent to relational query languages with ranking.

Array Storage

Array storage has to accommodate arrays of different dimensions and typically large sizes. A core task is to maintain spatial proximity on disk so as to reduce the number of disk accesses during subsetting. Note that an emulation of multi-dimensional arrays as nested lists (or 1-D arrays) will not per se accomplish this and, therefore, in general will not lead to scalable architectures.

Commonly arrays are partitioned into sub-arrays which form the unit of access. Regular partitioning where all partitions have the same size (except possibly for boundaries) is referred to as chunking. A generalization which removes the restriction to equally sized partitions by supporting any kind of partitioning is tiling. Array partitioning can improve access to array subsets significantly: by adjusting tiling to the access pattern, the server ideally can fetch all required data with only one disk access.

Compression of tiles can sometimes reduce substantially the amount of storage needed. Also for transmission of results compression is useful, as for the large amounts of data under consideration networks bandwidth often constitutes a limiting factor.

Query Processing

A tile-based storage structure suggests a tile-by-tile processing strategy (in rasdaman called tile streaming). A large class of practically relevant queries can be evaluated by loading tile after tile, thereby allowing servers to process arrays orders of magnitude beyond their main memory.

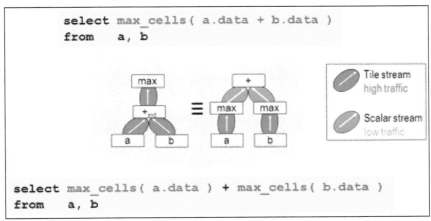

Transformation of a query to a more efficient, but equivalent version during array query optimization.

Due to the massive sizes of arrays in scientific/technical applications in combination with often complex queries, optimization plays a central role in making array queries efficient. Both hardware and software parallelization can be applied. An example for heuristic optimization is the rule "maximum value of an array resulting from the cell-wise addition of two input images is equivalent to adding the maximum values of each input array". By replacing the left-hand variant by the right-hand expression, costs shrink from three (costly) array traversals to two array traversals plus one (cheap) scalar operation.

Application Domains

In many – if not most – cases where some phenomenon is sampled or simulated the result is a rasterized data set which can conveniently be stored, retrieved, and forwarded as an array. Typically, the array data are ornamented with metadata describing them further, for example, geographically referenced imagery will carry its geographic position and the coordinate reference system in which it is expressed.

The following are representative domains in which large-scale multi-dimensional array data are handled:

- Earth sciences: geodesy/mapping, remote sensing, geology, oceanography, hydrology, atmospheric sciences, cryospheric sciences.

- Space sciences: Planetary sciences, astrophysics (optical and radio telescope observations, cosmological simulations).

- Life sciences: gene data, confocal microscopy, CAT scans.

- Social sciences: statistical data cubes.

- Business: OLAP, data warehousing.

These are but examples, generally, arrays frequently represent sensor, simulation, image, and statistics data. More and more spatial and time dimensions are combined with abstract axes, such as sales and products, one example where such abstract axes are explicitly foreseen is the [Open_Geospatial_Consortium |Open Geospatial Consortium] (OGC) coverage model.

Standardization

Many communities have established data exchange formats, such as HDF, NetCDF, and TIFF. A de facto standard in the Earth Science communities is OPeNDAP, a data transport architecture and protocol. While this is not a database specification, it offers important components that characterize a database system, such as a conceptual model and client/server implementations.

A declarative geo raster query language, Web Coverage Processing Service (WCPS), has been standardized by the Open Geospatial Consortium (OGC).

In June 2014, ISO/IEC JTC1 SC32 WG3, which maintains the SQL database standard, has decided to add multi-dimensional array support to SQL as a new column type, based on the initial array support available since the 2003 version of SQL. The new standard, adopted in Fall 2018, is named ISO 9075 SQL Part 15: MDA (Multi-Dimensional Arrays).

List of Array DBMSs
- Oracle GeoRaster,
- MonetDB/SciQL,
- PostGIS,
- Rasdaman,
- SciDB.

Column-oriented DBMS

A column-oriented DBMS (or columnar database management system) is a database management system (DBMS) that stores data tables by column rather than by row. Practical use of a column store versus a row store differs little in the relational DBMS world. Both columnar and row databases can use traditional database query languages like SQL to load data and perform queries. Both row and columnar databases can become the backbone in a system to serve data for common extract, transform, load (ETL) and data visualization tools. However, by storing data in columns rather than rows, the database can more precisely access the data it needs to answer a query rather than scanning and discarding unwanted data in rows. Query performance is increased for certain workloads.

A relational database management system provides data that represents a two-dimensional table, of columns and rows. For example, a database might have this table:

RowId	EmpId	Lastname	Firstname	Salary
001	10	Smith	Joe	60000
002	12	Jones	Mary	80000
003	11	Johnson	Cathy	94000
004	22	Jones	Bob	55000

This simple table includes an employee identifier (EmpId), name fields (Lastname and Firstname) and a salary (Salary). This two-dimensional format is an abstraction. In an actual implementation, storage hardware requires the data to be serialized into one form or another.

The most expensive operations involving hard disks are seeks. In order to improve overall performance, related data should be stored in a fashion to minimize the number of seeks. This is known as locality of reference, and the basic concept appears in a number of different contexts. Hard disks are organized into a series of blocks of a fixed size, typically enough to store several rows of the table. By organizing the table's data so rows fit within these blocks, and grouping related rows onto sequential blocks, the number of blocks that need to be read or sought is minimized in many cases, along with the number of seeks.

A survey by Pinnecke covers techniques for column-/row hybridization as of 2017.

Row-oriented Systems

A common method of storing a table is to serialize each row of data, like this:

```
001:10,Smith,Joe,60000;

002:12,Jones,Mary,80000;
```

```
003:11,Johnson,Cathy,94000;
```

```
004:22,Jones,Bob,55000;
```

As data is inserted into the table, it is assigned an internal ID, the rowid that is used internally in the system to refer to data. In this case the records have sequential rowids independent of the user-assigned empid. In this example, the DBMS uses short integers to store rowids. In practice, larger numbers, 64-bit or 128-bit, are normally used.

Row-based systems are designed to efficiently return data for an entire row, or record, in as few operations as possible. This matches the common use-case where the system is attempting to retrieve information about a particular object, say the contact information for a user in a rolodex system, or product information for an online shopping system. By storing the record's data in a single block on the disk, along with related records, the system can quickly retrieve records with a minimum of disk operations.

Row-based systems are not efficient at performing set-wide operations on the whole table, as opposed to a small number of specific records. For instance, in order to find all records in the example table with salaries between 40,000 and 50,000, the DBMS would have to fully scan through the entire table looking for matching records. While the example table shown above will likely fit in a single disk block, a table with even a few hundred rows would not, and multiple disk operations would be needed to retrieve the data and examine it.

To improve the performance of these sorts of operations (which are very common, and generally the point of using a DBMS), most DBMSs support the use of database indexes, which store all the values from a set of columns along with rowid pointers back into the original table. An index on the salary column would look something like this:

```
001:60000;
```

```
003:94000;
```

```
002:80000;
```

```
004:55000;
```

As they store only single pieces of data, rather than entire rows, indexes are generally much smaller than the main table stores. Scanning this smaller set of data reduces the number of disk operations. If the index is heavily used, it can dramatically reduce the time for common operations. However, maintaining indexes adds overhead to the system, especially when new data is written to the database. Records not only need to be stored in the main table, but any attached indexes have to be updated as well.

The main reason why indexes dramatically improve performance on large datasets is that database indexes on one or more columns are typically sorted by value, which makes range queries operations (like the above "find all records with salaries between 40,000 and 50,000" example) very fast (lower time-complexity).

A number of row-oriented databases are designed to fit entirely in RAM, an in-memory database. These systems do not depend on disk operations, and have equal-time access to the entire dataset. This reduces the need for indexes, as it requires the same amount of operations to fully scan the original data as a complete index for typical aggregation purposes. Such systems may be therefore simpler and smaller, but can only manage databases that will fit in memory.

Column-oriented Systems

A column-oriented database serializes all of the values of a column together, then the values of the next column, and so on. For our example table, the data would be stored in this fashion:

```
10:001,12:002,11:003,22:004;

Smith:001,Jones:002,Johnson:003,Jones:004;

Joe:001,Mary:002,Cathy:003,Bob:004;

60000:001,80000:002,94000:003,55000:004;
```

In this layout, any one of the columns more closely matches the structure of an index in a row-based system. This may cause confusion that can lead to the mistaken belief a column-oriented store "is really just" a row-store with an index on every column. However, it is the mapping of the data that differs dramatically. In a row-oriented indexed system, the primary key is the rowid that is mapped from indexed data. In the column-oriented system, the primary key is the data, which is mapped from rowids. This may seem subtle, but the difference can be seen in this common modification to the same store wherein the two "Jones" items, above, are compressed into a single item with two rowids:

```
...;Smith:001;Jones:002,004;Johnson:003;...
```

Whether or not a column-oriented system will be more efficient in operation depends heavily on the workload being automated. Operations that retrieve all the data for a given object (the entire row) are slower. A row-based system can retrieve the row in a single disk read, whereas numerous disk operations to collect data from multiple columns are required from a columnar database. However, these whole-row operations are generally rare. In the majority of cases, only a limited subset of data is retrieved. In a rolodex application, for instance, collecting the first and last names from many rows to build a list of contacts is far more common than reading all data for any single address. This is even more true for writing data into the database, especially if the data tends to be "sparse" with many optional columns. For this reason, column stores have demonstrated excellent real-world performance in spite of many theoretical disadvantages.

Partitioning, indexing, caching, views, OLAP cubes, and transactional systems such as write-ahead logging or multiversion concurrency control all dramatically affect the physical organization of either system. That said, online transaction processing (OLTP)-focused RDBMS systems are more row-oriented, while online analytical processing (OLAP)-focused systems are a balance of row-oriented and column-oriented.

Benefits

Comparisons between row-oriented and column-oriented databases are typically concerned with the efficiency of hard-disk access for a given workload, as seek time is incredibly long compared to the other bottlenecks in computers. For example, a typical Serial ATA (SATA) hard drive has an average seek time of between 16 and 22 milliseconds while DRAM access on an Intel Core i7 processor takes on average 60 nanoseconds, nearly 400,000 times as fast. Clearly, disk access is a major bottleneck in handling big data. Columnar databases boost performance by reducing the amount of data that needs to be read from disk, both by efficiently compressing the similar columnar data and by reading only the data necessary to answer the query.

In practice, columnar databases are well-suited for OLAP-like workloads (e.g., data warehouses) which typically involve highly complex queries over all data (possibly petabytes). However, some work must be done to write data into a columnar database. Transactions (INSERTs) must be separated into columns and compressed as they are stored, making it less suited for OLTP workloads. Row-oriented databases are well-suited for OLTP-like workloads which are more heavily loaded with interactive transactions. For example, retrieving all data from a single row is more efficient when that data is located in a single location (minimizing disk seeks), as in row-oriented architectures. However, column-oriented systems have been developed as hybrids capable of both OLTP and OLAP operations, with some of the OLTP constraints column-oriented systems face mediated using (amongst other qualities) in-memory data storage. Column-oriented systems suitable for both OLAP and OLTP roles effectively reduce the total data footprint by removing the need for separate systems.

Compression

Column data is of uniform type, therefore, there are some opportunities for storage size optimizations available in column-oriented data that are not available in row-oriented data. For example, many popular modern compression schemes, such as LZW or run-length encoding, make use of the similarity of adjacent data to compress. Missing values and repeated values, common in clinical data, can be represented by a two-bit marker. While the same techniques may be used on row-oriented data, a typical implementation will achieve less effective results.

To improve compression, sorting rows can also help. For example, using bitmap indexes, sorting can improve compression by an order of magnitude. To maximize the compression benefits of the lexicographical order with respect to run-length encoding, it is best to use low-cardinality columns as the first sort keys. For example, given a table with columns sex, age, name, it would be best to sort first on the value sex (cardinality of two), then age (cardinality of <150), then name.

Columnar compression achieves a reduction in disk space at the expense of efficiency of retrieval. The greater adjacent compression achieved, the more difficult random-access may become, as data might need to be uncompressed to be read. Therefore, column-oriented architectures are sometimes enriched by additional mechanisms aimed at minimizing the need for access to compressed data.

Object-relational Database Management System

An object-relational database (ORD), or object-relational database management system (ORDBMS), is a database management system (DBMS) similar to a relational database, but with an object-oriented database model: objects, classes and inheritance are directly supported in database schemas and in the query language. In addition, just as with pure relational systems, it supports extension of the data model with custom data types and methods.

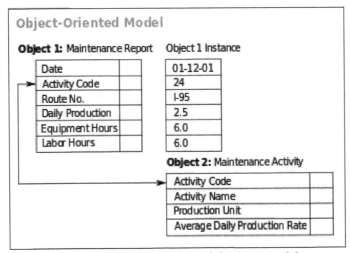

Example of an object-oriented database model.

An object-relational database can be said to provide a middle ground between relational databases and object-oriented databases. In object-relational databases, the approach is essentially that of relational databases: the data resides in the database and is manipulated collectively with queries in a query language, at the other extreme are OODBMSes in which the database is essentially a persistent object store for software written in an object-oriented programming language, with a programming API for storing and retrieving objects, and little or no specific support for querying.

The basic need of Object-relational database arises from the fact that both Relational and Object database have their individual advantages and drawbacks. The isomorphism of the relational database system with a mathematical relation allows it to exploit many useful techniques and theorems from set theory. But these types of databases are not useful when the matter comes to data complexity and mismatch between application and the DBMS. An object oriented database model allows containers like sets and lists, arbitrary user-defined datatypes as well as nested objects. This brings commonality between the application type systems and database type systems which removes any issue of impedance mismatch. But Object databases, unlike relational do not provide any mathematical base for their deep analysis.

The basic goal for the Object-relational database is to bridge the gap between relational databases and the object-oriented modeling techniques used in programming languages such as Java, C++, Visual Basic.NET or C#. However, a more popular alternative for achieving such a bridge is to use a standard relational database systems with some form of object-relational mapping (ORM) software. Whereas traditional RDBMS or SQL-DBMS products focused on the efficient management of data drawn from a limited set of data-types (defined by the relevant language standards), an object-relational DBMS allows software developers to integrate their own types and the methods that apply to them into the DBMS.

The ORDBMS (like ODBMS or OODBMS) is integrated with an object-oriented programming language. The characteristic properties of ORDBMS are 1) complex data, 2) type inheritance, and 3) object behavior. Complex data creation in most SQL ORDBMSs is based on preliminary schema definition via the user-defined type (UDT). Hierarchy within structured complex data offers an additional property, type inheritance. That is, a structured type can have subtypes that reuse all of its attributes and contain additional attributes specific to the subtype. Another advantage, the object behavior, is related with access to the program objects. Such program objects must be storable and transportable for database processing, therefore they usually are named as persistent objects. Inside a database, all the relations with a persistent program object are relations with its object identifier (OID). All of these points can be addressed in a proper relational system, although the SQL standard and its implementations impose arbitrary restrictions and additional complexity.

In object-oriented programming (OOP), object behavior is described through the methods (object functions). The methods denoted by one name are distinguished by the type of their parameters and type of objects for which they attached (method signature). The OOP languages call this the polymorphism principle, which briefly is defined as "one interface, many implementations". Other OOP principles, inheritance and encapsulation, are related both to methods and attributes. Method inheritance is included in type inheritance. Encapsulation in OOP is a visibility degree declared, for example, through the `public`, `private` and `protected` access modifiers.

Object-relational database management systems grew out of research that occurred in the early 1990s. That research extended existing relational database concepts by adding object concepts. The researchers aimed to retain a declarative query-language based on predicate calculus as a central component of the architecture. Probably the most notable research project, Postgres (UC Berkeley), spawned two products tracing their lineage to that research: Illustra and PostgreSQL.

In the mid-1990s, early commercial products appeared. These included Illustra (Illustra Information Systems, acquired by Informix Software, which was in turn acquired by IBM), Omniscience (Omniscience Corporation, acquired by Oracle Corporation and became the original Oracle Lite), and UniSQL (UniSQL, Inc., acquired by KCOMS). Ukrainian developer Ruslan Zasukhin, founder of Paradigma Software, Inc., developed and shipped the first version of Valentina database in the mid-1990s as a C++ SDK. By the next decade, PostgreSQL had become a commercially viable database, and is the basis for several current products that maintain its ORDBMS features.

Computer scientists came to refer to these products as "object-relational database management systems" or ORDBMSs.

Many of the ideas of early object-relational database efforts have largely become incorporated into SQL:1999 via structured types. In fact, any product that adheres to the object-oriented aspects of SQL:1999 could be described as an object-relational database management product. For example, IBM's DB2, Oracle database, and Microsoft SQL Server, make claims to support this technology and do so with varying degrees of success.

Comparison to RDBMS

An RDBMS might commonly involve SQL statements such as these:

```
CREATE TABLE Customers   (

    Id          CHAR(12)     NOT NULL PRIMARY KEY,

    Surname     VARCHAR(32)  NOT NULL,

    FirstName   VARCHAR(32)  NOT NULL,

    DOB         DATE         NOT NULL

);

SELECT InitCap(Surname) || ', ' || InitCap(FirstName)

   FROM Customers

 WHERE Month(DOB)  =  Month(getdate())

   AND Day(DOB)  =  Day(getdate())
```

Most current SQL databases allow the crafting of custom functions, which would allow the query to appear as:

```
SELECT Formal(Id)
   FROM Customers
  WHERE Birthday(DOB) = Today()
```

In an object-relational database, one might see something like this, with user-defined data-types and expressions such as BirthDay():

```
CREATE TABLE Customers (
   Id          Cust_Id      NOT NULL  PRIMARY KEY,
   Name        PersonName   NOT NULL,
   DOB         DATE         NOT NULL
);
SELECT Formal( C.Id )
   FROM Customers C
  WHERE BirthDay ( C.DOB ) = TODAY;
```

The object-relational model can offer another advantage in that the database can make use of the relationships between data to easily collect related records. In an address book application, an additional table would be added to the ones above to hold zero or more addresses for each customer. Using a traditional RDBMS, collecting information for both the user and their address requires a "join":

```
SELECT InitCap(C.Surname) || ', ' || InitCap(C.FirstName), A.city
   FROM Customers C join Addresses A ON A.Cust_Id=C.Id -- the join
   WHERE A.city="New York"
```

The same query in an object-relational database appears more simply:

```
SELECT Formal( C.Name )
   FROM Customers C
   WHERE C.address.city="New York" -- the linkage is 'understood' by
the ORDB
```

Surrogate Key

A surrogate key (or synthetic key, entity identifier, system-generated key, database sequence number, factless key, technical key, or arbitrary unique identifier) in a database is a unique identifier for either an entity in the modeled world or an object in the database. The surrogate key is not derived from application data, unlike a natural (or business) key which is derived from application data.

There are at least two definitions of a surrogate:

Surrogate (1): A surrogate represents an entity in the outside world. The surrogate is internally generated by the system but is nevertheless visible to the user or application.

Surrogate (2): A surrogate represents an object in the database itself. The surrogate is internally generated by the system and is invisible to the user or application.

An important distinction between a surrogate and a primary key depends on whether the database is a current database or a temporal database. Since a current database stores only currently valid data, there is a one-to-one correspondence between a surrogate in the modeled world and the primary key of the database. In this case the surrogate may be used as a primary key, resulting in the term surrogate key. In a temporal database, however, there is a many-to-one relationship between primary keys and the surrogate. Since there may be several objects in the database corresponding to a single surrogate, we cannot use the surrogate as a primary key; another attribute is required, in addition to the surrogate, to uniquely identify each object.

Although Hall say nothing about this, others have argued that a surrogate should have the following characteristics:

- The value is unique system-wide, hence never reused.

- The value is system generated.

- The value is not manipulable by the user or application.

- The value contains no semantic meaning.

- The value is not visible to the user or application.

- The value is not composed of several values from different domains.

Surrogates in Practice

In a current database, the surrogate key can be the primary key, generated by the database management system and *not* derived from any application data in the database. The only significance of the surrogate key is to act as the primary key. It is also possible that the surrogate key exists in addition to the database-generated UUID (for example, an HR number for each employee other than the UUID of each employee).

A surrogate key is frequently a sequential number (e.g. a Sybase or SQL Server "identity column", a PostgreSQL or Informix `serial`, an Oracle or SQL Server SEQUENCE or a column defined with `AUTO_INCREMENT` in MySQL). Some databases provide UUID/GUID as a possible data type for surrogate keys (e.g. PostgreSQL `UUID` or SQL Server `UNIQUEIDENTIFIER`).

Having the key independent of all other columns insulates the database relationships from changes in data values or database design (making the database more agile) and guarantees uniqueness.

In a temporal database, it is necessary to distinguish between the surrogate key and the business key. Every row would have both a business key and a surrogate key. The surrogate key identifies one unique row in the database, the business key identifies one unique entity of the modeled world. One table row represents a slice of time holding all the entity's attributes for a defined timespan. Those slices depict the whole lifespan of one business entity. For example, a table EmployeeContracts may hold temporal information to keep track of contracted working hours. The business key for one contract will be identical (non-unique) in both rows however the surrogate key for each row is unique.

Surro-gateKey	Business-Key	Employ-eeName	WorkingHour-sPerWeek	RowValid-From	RowValidTo
1	BOS0120	John Smith	40	2000-01-01	2000-12-31
56	P0000123	Bob Brown	25	1999-01-01	2011-12-31
234	BOS0120	John Smith	35	2001-01-01	2009-12-31

Some database designers use surrogate keys systematically regardless of the suitability of other candidate keys, while others will use a key already present in the data, if there is one.

Some of the alternate names ("system-generated key") describe the way of generating new surrogate values rather than the nature of the surrogate concept.

Approaches to generating surrogates include:

- Universally Unique Identifiers (UUIDs).

- Globally Unique Identifiers (GUIDs).

- Object Identifiers (OIDs).

- Sybase or SQL Server identity column `IDENTITY` OR `IDENTITY(n,n)`.

- Oracle `SEQUENCE`, or `GENERATED AS IDENTITY` (starting from version 12.1).

- SQL Server `SEQUENCE` (starting from SQL Server 2012).

- PostgreSQL or IBM Informix serial.

- MySQL `AUTO_INCREMENT`.

- SQLite `AUTOINCREMENT`.

- AutoNumber data type in Microsoft Access.

- AS `IDENTITY GENERATED BY DEFAULT` in IBM DB2.

- Identity column (implemented in DDL) in Teradata.

- Table Sequence when the sequence is calculated by a procedure and a sequence table with fields: id, sequenceName, sequenceValue and incrementValue.

Advantages

Immutability

Surrogate keys do not change while the row exists. This has the following advantages:

- Applications cannot lose their reference to a row in the database (since the identifier never changes).

- The primary or natural key data can always be modified, even with databases that do not support cascading updates across related foreign keys.

Requirement Changes

Attributes that uniquely identify an entity might change, which might invalidate the suitability of natural keys. Consider the following example:

An employee's network user name is chosen as a natural key. Upon merging with another company, new employees must be inserted. Some of the new network user names create conflicts because their user names were generated independently (when the companies were separate).

In these cases, generally a new attribute must be added to the natural key (for example, an original_company column). With a surrogate key, only the table that defines the surrogate key must be changed. With natural keys, all tables (and possibly other, related software) that use the natural key will have to change.

Some problem domains do not clearly identify a suitable natural key. Surrogate keys avoid choosing a natural key that might be incorrect.

Performance

Surrogate keys tend to be a compact data type, such as a four-byte integer. This allows the database to query the single key column faster than it could multiple columns. Furthermore, a non-redundant distribution of keys causes the resulting b-tree index to be completely balanced. Surrogate keys are also less expensive to join (fewer columns to compare) than compound keys.

Compatibility

While using several database application development systems, drivers, and object-relational mapping systems, such as Ruby on Rails or Hibernate, it is much easier to use an integer or GUID surrogate keys for every table instead of natural keys in order to support database-system-agnostic operations and object-to-row mapping.

Uniformity

When every table has a uniform surrogate key, some tasks can be easily automated by writing the code in a table-independent way.

Validation

It is possible to design key-values that follow a well-known pattern or structure which can be automatically verified. For instance, the keys that are intended to be used in some column of some table might be designed to "look differently from" those that are intended to be used in another column or table, thereby simplifying the detection of application errors in which the keys have been misplaced. However, this characteristic of the surrogate keys should never be used to drive any of the logic of the applications themselves, as this would violate the principles of Database normalization.

Disadvantages

Disassociation

The values of generated surrogate keys have no relationship to the real-world meaning of the data held in a row. When inspecting a row holding a foreign key reference to another table using a surrogate key, the meaning of the surrogate key's row cannot be discerned from the key itself. Every foreign key must be joined to see the related data item. This can also make auditing more difficult, as incorrect data is not obvious.

Surrogate keys are unnatural for data that is exported and shared. A particular difficulty is that tables from two otherwise identical schemas (for example, a test schema and a development schema) can hold records that are equivalent in a business sense, but have different keys. This can be mitigated by not exporting surrogate keys, except as transient data (most obviously, in executing applications that have a "live" connection to the database).

When surrogate keys supplant natural keys, then domain specific referential integrity will be compromised.

Query Optimization

Relational databases assume a unique index is applied to a table's primary key. The unique index serves two purposes: (i) to enforce entity integrity, since primary key data must be unique across rows and (ii) to quickly search for rows when queried. Since surrogate keys replace a table's identifying attributes—the natural key—and since the identifying attributes are likely to be those queried, then the query optimizer is forced to perform a full table scan when fulfilling likely queries. The remedy to the full table scan is to apply indexes on the identifying attributes, or sets of them. Where such sets are themselves a candidate key, the index can be a unique index.

These additional indexes, however, will take up disk space and slow down inserts and deletes.

Normalization

Surrogate keys can result in duplicate values in any natural keys. It is part of the implementation to ensure that such duplicates should not be possible.

Business Process Modeling

Because surrogate keys are unnatural, flaws can appear when modeling the business requirements. Business requirements, relying on the natural key, then need to be translated to the surrogate key. A strategy is to draw a clear distinction between the logical model (in which surrogate keys do not appear) and the physical implementation of that model, to ensure that the logical model is correct and reasonably well normalised, and to ensure that the physical model is a correct implementation of the logical model.

Inadvertent Disclosure

Proprietary information can be leaked if sequential key generators are used. By subtracting a previously generated sequential key from a recently generated sequential key, one could learn the number of rows inserted during that time period. This could expose, for example, the number of transactions or new accounts per period. There are a few ways to overcome this problem:

- Increase the sequential number by a random amount.
- Generate a random key such as a UUID.

Inadvertent Assumptions

Sequentially generated surrogate keys can imply that events with a higher key value occurred after events with a lower value. This is not necessarily true, because such values do not guarantee time sequence as it is possible for inserts to fail and leave gaps which may be filled at a later time. If chronology is important then date and time must be separately recorded.

Types of Software for Database Management Systems

Database management system (DBMS) is the software that manages a database. Though with different names (Microsoft, Oracle, MySQL, IBM DB2, Sybase) they help in the organization, storage and retrieval of information.

Oracle 11g

Available in three compatible editions—enterprise, standard and express—Oracle 11g provides database capabilities that run on Windows, Linux and UNIX operating systems. Special features include transaction processing, business intelligence and content management applications. Oracle 11g provides protection from server failure, secures data encryption and total recall of data, and easily manages the largest of databases. The Enterprise edition offers a range of options that include data mining, data warehousing, OLAP, advanced security and management. Other options are real application testing and advanced compression. Oracle promotes database applications by offering a free starter database in Oracle Database 10g Express Edition which users are free to download, distribute, develop and deploy.

Microsoft SQL Server

Microsoft SQL Server 2008 is scalable database management software in four editions: Enterprise and Standard and the R2 editions (Parallel Data Warehouse and Datacenter) designed to meet the needs of large scale Datacenters and Data warehouses. In general the four editions provide management for an organization's database infrastructure while also providing time-critical business intelligence. The Parallel Data Warehouse and Datacenter editions cost much more than the enterprise and standard editions. The standard edition is for small organizations and can save more than 60 percent of the time spent on backups because it has a backup compression feature. Microsoft offers two free editions (compact and express) for students and software developers in addition to a trial version of SQL 2008.

MySQL

MySQL is regarded as the most popular open source database that has ease of use and lowest total cost of ownership compared to other database management systems. Available in four tiers of increasing cost (basic, silver, gold and platinum), it provides high performance and scalable online transaction processing (OLTP) capabilities and multi-terabyte data warehousing applications. The real engine is called MySQL Enterprise Server. Some of the special features of MySQL Enterprise 5.1 server include partitioning that helps manage very large databases and Event Scheduler to help create and schedule jobs. Three other features are Views, which ensures that sensitive information is not compromised, Triggers, which enforces complex business rules at the database level, and Archive Storage Engine for historical and audit data.

Use of DBMS in System Software

Using a general-purpose programming language, user can write a source program in the normal way. However, instead of writing I/O statements of the form provided by the programming language, the programmer writes commands in a data manipulation language (DML) defined for use with the DBMS. Processor may be used to convert the DML commands into programming language statements that call DBMS routines. Using the programming language itself some DMLs are defined as a set of CALL statements. Here given are the two principal methods for user interaction with a DBMS.

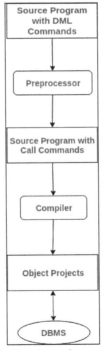

Interaction with a DBMS using a data manipulation language.

Interaction with a DBMS using a query language is the another approach to DBMS. There is no need for the user to write the programs for accessing a database rather user only needs to enter the commands in a special query language defined by DBMS. These commands are processed by a query-language interpreter, which calls DBMS routines to perform the requested operations.

Each and every approach that leads to user interactivity with a DBMS has its own advantages. Results can be obtain much faster with a help of query language, because there is no need to write and debug programs, which becomes very beneficial for the non-programmers to used it efficiently. Allowing the programmer to use all the flexibility and power of a general-purpose programming language is the big advantage of DML however much effort from the user is required by this approach. Most modern database management systems provide both a query language and a DML so that a user can choose the form of interaction that best meets his or her needs.

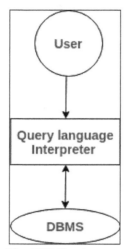

Interaction with a DBMS using a query language.

Here are some steps to show how a typical sequence of actions is being performed by a DBMS:

- Step-1: The sequence of events begins when the DBMS is entered with the help of a call from application program A. We assume this call is a request to read data from the database. There are similar sequences of events for other types of database operations.

- Step-2: The request from program A is stated in terms of the subschema being used by A. To process a request which is being requested from program A and is stated in terms of the subschema which is being used by A, the DBMS must first examine the subschema definition.

- Step-3: Relationship between the subschema and the schema must be considered by the DBMS to interpret the request in terms of the overall logical database structure.

- Step-4: The DBMS examines the data mapping description, after determining the logical database records that must be read in terms of schema. The information regarding the need of locating the required records in the files of the database is given by this operation.

- **Step-5**: At this point, a logical request for a subschema record has been converted into physical requests by DBMS to read data from one or more files. These requests for file I/O are passed to the operating system using the types of service calls.

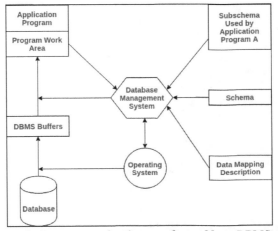

Typical sequence of actions performed by a DBMS.

- Step-6: The operating system then issues channel and device commands to perform the necessary physical I/O operations. These I/O operations read the required records from the database into a DBMS buffer area.

- Step-7: All the data requested by the application program is present in central memory after the physical I/O operations have been completed. The DBMS accomplishes this conversion by again comparing the schema and the subschema.

- Finally, the DBMS returns control to the application program and makes available to the program a variety of status information, including any possible error indications.

References

- Levinthal, Dr David (2009). "Performance Analysis Guide for Intel® Core™ i7 Processor and Intel® Xeon™ 5500 processors" (PDF). Intel. p. 22. Retrieved 2017-11-10

- Types-software-database-management-systems-6804378: itstillworks.com, Retrieved 25 June, 2020

- Charles Babcock (February 21, 2008). "Database Pioneer Rethinks The Best Way To Organize Data". InformationWeek. Retrieved 2018-12-08

- Use-of-dbms-in-system-software: geeksforgeeks.org, Retrieved 08 May, 2020

- Marcin Zukowski; Peter Boncz (May 20, 2012). From x100 to vectorwise: opportunities, challenges and things most researchers do not think about. Proceedings of the 2012 ACM SIGMOD International Conference on Management of Data. ACM. pp. 861–862. doi:10.1145/2213836.2213967. ISBN 978-1-4503-1247-9

Relational Database Management Systems

5

- **Relation**

- **Relational Database**

- **Relational Algebra**

- **Relational Calculus**

- **Relational Data Stream Management System**

- **Candidate Key**

Relational database is a set of a database structured to recognize relations between stored items of information. The program that creates, updates and administers a relational database is termed as relational database management system. This chapter closely examines the related concepts of relational database management system to provide an extensive understanding of the subject.

A relational database management system (RDBMS or just RDB) is a common type of database whose data is stored in tables.

You'll find that most databases used in businesses these days are relational databases, as opposed to a flat file or hierarchical database.

Relational databases have the clout to handle multitudes of data and complex queries, whereas a flat file takes up more space and memory, and is less efficient.

So modern databases use multiple tables as standard. The data is stored in lots and lots of tables, or 'relations'. These tables are divided into rows (records) and columns (fields).

Much like the relationships between data in an entity's relationship diagram, the tables in the relational database can be linked in several ways:

- Characteristics of one table record may be linked to a record in another table.

- A table record could be linked to many records in another table.

- Many table records may be related to many records in another table.

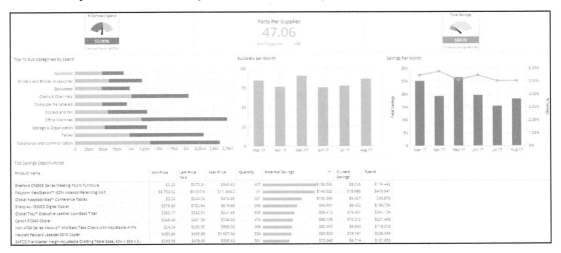

SQL Query

An SQL query is how you access the data. SQL stands for Structured Query Language.

Using an SQL query, you can create and delete, or modify tables, as well as select, insert, and delete data from existing tables.

Benefits of Relational Databases

If you want to design a data storage system that makes it easy to manage lots of information, and is scalable and flexible, the relational database is a good bet.

- Manageability: For starters, an RDB is easy to manipulate. Each table of data can be updated without disrupting the others.

  You can also share certain sets of data with one group, but limit their access to others – such as confidential information about employees.

- Flexibility: If you need to update your data, you only have to do it once – so no more having to change multiple files one at a time.

  And it's pretty simple to extend your database. If your records are growing, a relational database is easily scalable to grow with your data.

- Avoid Errors: There's no room for mistakes in a relational database because it's easy to check for mistakes against the data in other parts of the records. And since each piece of information is stored at a single point, you don't have the problem of old versions of data clouding the picture.

Challenges of Relational Databases

- Scalability: Because relational databases are built on a single server. This means, in order to scale, you'll need to purchase more expensive hardware with more power, storage, and memory.

- Performance: Rapid growth in volume, velocity, variety, and complexity of data creates even more complicated relationships. Relational databases tend to have a hard time keeping up, which can slow down performance.

- Relationships: Relational databases don't actually store relationships between elements, which makes understanding connections between your data reliant on other joins.

The relational model represents the database as a collection of relations. A relation is nothing but a table of values. Every row in the table represents a collection of related data values. These rows in the table denote a real-world entity or relationship.

The table name and column names are helpful to interpret the meaning of values in each row. The data are represented as a set of relations. In the relational model, data are stored as tables. However, the physical storage of the data is independent of the way the data are logically organized.

Some popular Relational Database management systems are:

- DB2 and Informix Dynamic Server – IBM.

- Oracle and RDB – Oracle.

- SQL Server and Access – Microsoft.

Relational Model Concepts

- Attribute: Each column in a Table. Attributes are the properties which define a relation. e.g., Student_Rollno, NAME,etc.

- Tables: In the Relational model the, relations are saved in the table format. It is stored along with its entities. A table has two properties rows and columns. Rows represent records and columns represent attributes.

- Tuple: It is nothing but a single row of a table, which contains a single record.

- Relation Schema: A relation schema represents the name of the relation with its attributes.

- Degree: The total number of attributes which in the relation is called the degree of the relation.

- Cardinality: Total number of rows present in the table.

- Column: The column represents the set of values for a specific attribute.

- Relation instance: Relation instance is a finite set of tuples in the RDBMS system. Relation instances never have duplicate tuples.

- Relation key: Every row has one, two or multiple attributes, which is called relation key.

- Attribute domain: Every attribute has some pre-defined value and scope which is known as attribute domain.

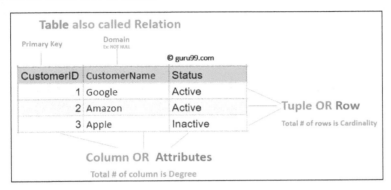

Relational Integrity Constraints

Relational Integrity constraints is referred to conditions which must be present for a valid relation. These integrity constraints are derived from the rules in the mini-world that the database represents.

There are many types of integrity constraints. Constraints on the Relational database management system is mostly divided into three main categories are:

- Domain constraints.

- Key constraints.

- Referential integrity constraints.

Domain Constraints

Domain constraints can be violated if an attribute value is not appearing in the corresponding domain or it is not of the appropriate data type.

Domain constraints specify that within each tuple, and the value of each attribute must be unique. This is specified as data types which include standard data types integers, real numbers, characters, Booleans, variable length strings, etc.

Example:

```
Create DOMAIN CustomerName
```

```
CHECK (value not NULL)
```

The example shown demonstrates creating a domain constraint such that Customer-Name is not NULL.

Key Constraints

An attribute that can uniquely identify a tuple in a relation is called the key of the table. The value of the attribute for different tuples in the relation has to be unique.

Example:

In the given table, CustomerID is a key attribute of Customer Table. It is most likely to have a single key for one customer, CustomerID =1 is only for the CustomerName =" Google".

CustomerID	CustomerName	Status
1	Google	Active
2	Amazon	Active
3	Apple	Inactive

Referential Integrity Constraints

Referential integrity constraints is base on the concept of Foreign Keys. A foreign key is an important attribute of a relation which should be referred to in other relationships. Referential integrity constraint state happens where relation refers to a key attribute of a different or same relation. However, that key element must exist in the table.

CustomerID	CustomerName	Status
1	Google	Active
2	Amazon	Active
3	Apple	Inactive

Customer

Billing

InvoiceNo	CustomerID	Amount
1	1	$100
2	1	$200
3	2	$150

In the above example, we have 2 relations, Customer and Billing.

Tuple for CustomerID =1 is referenced twice in the relation Billing. So we know CustomerName=Google has billing amount $300.

Operations in Relational Model

Four basic update operations performed on relational database model are:

- Insert, update, delete and select.

- Insert is used to insert data into the relation.

- Delete is used to delete tuples from the table.

- Modify allows you to change the values of some attributes in existing tuples.

- Select allows you to choose a specific range of data.

Whenever one of these operations is applied, integrity constraints specified on the relational database schema must never be violated.

Insert Operation

The insert operation gives values of the attribute for a new tuple which should be inserted into a relation.

CustomerID	CustomerName	Status
1	Google	Active
2	Amazon	Active
3	Apple	Inactive

INSERT →

CustomerID	CustomerName	Status
1	Google	Active
2	Amazon	Active
3	Apple	Inactive
4	Alibaba	Active

Update Operation

You can see that in the below-given relation table CustomerName= 'Apple' is updated from Inactive to Active.

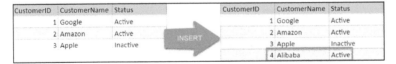

CustomerID	CustomerName	Status
1	Google	Active
2	Amazon	Active
3	Apple	Inactive
4	Alibaba	Active

UPDATE →

CustomerID	CustomerName	Status
1	Google	Active
2	Amazon	Active
3	Apple	Active
4	Alibaba	Active

Delete Operation

To specify deletion, a condition on the attributes of the relation selects the tuple to be deleted.

CustomerID	CustomerName	Status
1	Google	Active
2	Amazon	Active
3	Apple	Active
4	Alibaba	Active

DELETE →

CustomerID	CustomerName	Status
1	Google	Active
2	Amazon	Active
4	Alibaba	Active

In the above-given example, CustomerName= "Apple" is deleted from the table.

The Delete operation could violate referential integrity if the tuple which is deleted is referenced by foreign keys from other tuples in the same database.

Select Operation

In the above-given example, CustomerName="Amazon" is selected.

Best Practices for Creating a Relational Model

- Data need to be represented as a collection of relations.

- Each relation should be depicted clearly in the table.

- Rows should contain data about instances of an entity.

- Columns must contain data about attributes of the entity.

- Cells of the table should hold a single value.

- Each column should be given a unique name.

- No two rows can be identical.

- The values of an attribute should be from the same domain.

Advantages of using Relational Model

- Simplicity: A relational data model is simpler than the hierarchical and network model.

- Structural Independence: The relational database is only concerned with data and not with a structure. This can improve the performance of the model.

- Easy to use: The relational model is easy as tables consisting of rows and columns is quite natural and simple to understand

- Query capability: It makes possible for a high-level query language like SQL to avoid complex database navigation.

- Data independence: The structure of a database can be changed without having to change any application.

- Scalable: Regarding a number of records, or rows, and the number of fields, a database should be enlarged to enhance its usability.

Disadvantages of using Relational Model

- Few relational databases have limits on field lengths which can't be exceeded.

- Relational databases can sometimes become complex as the amount of data grows, and the relations between pieces of data become more complicated.

- Complex relational database systems may lead to isolated databases where the information cannot be shared from one system to another.

Relation

In relational database theory, a relation, as originally defined by E. F. Codd, is a set of tuples $(d_1, d_2,..., d_n)$, where each element d_j is a member of D_j, a data domain. Codd's original definition notwithstanding, and contrary to the usual definition in mathematics, there is no ordering to the elements of the tuples of a relation. Instead, each element is termed an attribute value. An attribute is a name paired with a domain (nowadays more commonly referred to as a type or data type). An attribute value is an attribute name paired with an element of that attribute's domain, and a tuple is a *set* of attribute values in which no two distinct elements have the same name. Thus, in some accounts, a tuple is described as a function, mapping names to values.

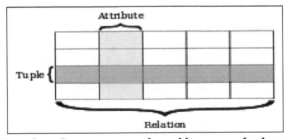

Relation, tuple, and attribute represented as table, row, and column respectively.

A set of attributes in which no two distinct elements have the same name is called a heading. It follows from the above definitions that to every tuple there corresponds a unique heading, being the set of names from the tuple, paired with the domains from which the tuple's domain elements are taken. A set of tuples that all correspond to the same heading is called a body. A relation is thus a heading paired with a body, the heading of the relation being also the heading of each tuple in its body. The number of attributes constituting a heading is called the degree, which term also applies to tuples and relations. The term n-tuple refers to a tuple of degree n $(n \geq 0)$.

E. F. Codd used the term "relation" in its mathematical sense of a finitary relation, a set of tuples on some set of n sets $S_1, S_2,.....,S_n$. Thus, an n-ary relation is interpreted, under the Closed World Assumption, as the extension of some n-adic predicate: all and only those *n*-tuples whose values, substituted for corresponding free variables in the predicate, yield propositions that hold true, appear in the relation.

The term relation schema refers to a heading paired with a set of constraints defined in terms of that heading. A relation can thus be seen as an instantiation of a relation schema if it has the heading of that schema and it satisfies the applicable constraints.

Sometimes a relation schema is taken to include a name. A relational database definition (database schema, sometimes referred to as a relational schema) can thus be thought of as a collection of named relation schemas.

In implementations, the domain of each attribute is effectively a data type and a named relation schema is effectively a relation variable (relvar for short).

In SQL, a database language for relational databases, relations are represented by tables, where each row of a table represents a single tuple, and where the values of each attribute form a column.

Below is an example of a relation having three named attributes: 'ID' from the domain of integers, and 'Name' and 'Address' from the domain of strings:

ID (Integer)	Name (String)	Address (String)
102	Yonezawa Akinori	Naha, Okinawa
202	Nilay Patel	Sendai, Miyagi
104	Murata Makoto	Kumamoto, Kumamoto
152	Matsumoto Yukihiro	Okinawa, Okinawa

A predicate for this relation, using the attribute names to denote free variables, might be "Employee number *ID* is known as *Name* and lives at *Address*". Examination of the relation tells us that there are just four tuples for which the predicate holds true. So, for example, employee 102 is known only by that name, Yonezawa Akinori, and does not live anywhere else but in Naha, Okinawa. Also, apart from the four employees shown, there is no other employee who has both a name and an address.

Under the definition of body, the tuples of a body do not appear in any particular order one cannot say "The tuple of 'Murata Makoto' is above the tuple of 'Matsumoto Yukihiro'", nor can one say "The tuple of 'Yonezawa Akinori' is the first tuple". A similar comment applies to the rows of an SQL table.

Under the definition of heading, the attributes of an element do not appear in any particular order either, nor, therefore do the elements of a tuple. A similar comment does *not* apply here to SQL, which does define an ordering to the columns of a table.

Relation Variables

A relational database consists of named relation variables (relvars) for the purposes of updating the database in response to changes in the real world. An update to a single relvar causes the body of the relation assigned to that variable to be replaced by a different set of tuples. Relvars are classified into two classes: base relation variables and derived relation variables, the latter also known as virtual relvars but usually referred to by the short term view.

A base relation variable is a relation variable which is not derived from any other relation variables. In SQL the term base table equates approximately to base relation variable.

A view can be defined by an expression using the operators of the relational algebra or the relational calculus. Such an expression operates on one or more relations and when evaluated yields another relation. The result is sometimes referred to as a "derived" relation when the operands are relations assigned to database variables. A view is defined by giving a name to such an expression, such that the name can subsequently be used as a variable name. (Note that the expression must then mention at least one base relation variable.)

By using a Data Definition Language (DDL), it is able to define base relation variables. In SQL, CREATE TABLE syntax is used to define base tables. The following is an example.

```
CREATE TABLE List_of_people (

 ID INTEGER,

 Name CHAR(40),

 Address CHAR(200),

 PRIMARY KEY (ID)

)
```

The Data Definition Language (DDL) is also used to define derived relation variables. In SQL, CREATE VIEW syntax is used to define a derived relation variable. The following is an example.

```
CREATE VIEW List_of_Okinawa_people AS (

 SELECT ID, Name, Address

  FROM List_of_people

  WHERE Address LIKE '%, Okinawa'

)
```

Relational Database

A relational database is a digital database based on the relational model of data, as proposed by E. F. Codd in 1970. A software system used to maintain relational databases is a relational database management system (RDBMS). Many relational database systems have an option of using the SQL (Structured Query Language) for querying and maintaining the database.

The term "relational database" was invented by E. F. Codd at IBM in 1970. Codd introduced the term in his research paper "A Relational Model of Data for Large Shared Data Banks". In this paper and later papers, he defined what he meant by "relational". One well-known definition of what constitutes a relational database system is composed of Codd's 12 rules. However, no commercial implementations of the relational model conform to all of Codd's rules, so the term has gradually come to describe a broader class of database systems, which at a minimum:

- Present the data to the user as relations (a presentation in tabular form, i.e. as a collection of tables with each table consisting of a set of rows and columns).

- Provide relational operators to manipulate the data in tabular form.

In 1974, IBM began developing System R, a research project to develop a prototype RDBMS. However, the first commercially available RDBMS was Oracle, released in 1979 by Relational Software, now Oracle Corporation. Other examples of an RDBMS include DB2, SAP Sybase ASE, and Informix. In 1984, the first RDBMS for Macintosh began being developed, code-named Silver Surfer, it was later released in 1987 as 4th Dimension and known today as 4D.

The first systems that were relatively faithful implementations of the relational model were from:

- University of Michigan – Micro DBMS.

- Massachusetts Institute of Technology.

- IBM UK Scientific Centre at Peterlee – IS1. and its successor, PRTV.

The first system sold as an RDBMS was Multics Relational Data Store. Ingres and IBM BS12 followed.

The most common definition of an RDBMS is a product that presents a view of data as a collection of rows and columns, even if it is not based strictly upon relational theory. By this definition, RDBMS products typically implement some but not all of Codd's 12 rules.

A second school of thought argues that if a database does not implement all of Codd's rules (or the current understanding on the relational model, as expressed by Christopher J. Date, Hugh Darwen and others), it is not relational. This view, shared by many theorists and other strict adherents to Codd's principles, would disqualify most DBMSs as not relational. For clarification, they often refer to some RDBMSs as truly-relational database management systems (TRDBMS), naming others pseudo-relational database management systems (PRDBMS).

As of 2009, most commercial relational DBMSs employ SQL as their query language.

Alternative query languages have been proposed and implemented, notably the pre-1996 implementation of Ingres QUEL.

This model organizes data into one or more tables (or "relations") of columns and rows, with a unique key identifying each row. Rows are also called records or tuples. Columns are also called attributes. Generally, each table/relation represents one "entity type" (such as customer or product). The rows represent instances of that type of entity (such as "Lee" or "chair") and the columns representing values attributed to that instance (such as address or price).

Keys

Each row in a table has its own unique key. Rows in a table can be linked to rows in other tables by adding a column for the unique key of the linked row (such columns are known as foreign keys). Codd showed that data relationships of arbitrary complexity can be represented by a simple set of concepts.

Part of this processing involves consistently being able to select or modify one and only one row in a table. Therefore, most physical implementations have a unique primary key (PK) for each row in a table. When a new row is written to the table, a new unique value for the primary key is generated; this is the key that the system uses primarily for accessing the table. System performance is optimized for PKs. Other, more natural keys may also be identified and defined as alternate keys (AK). Often several columns are needed to form an AK (this is one reason why a single integer column is usually made the PK). Both PKs and AKs have the ability to uniquely identify a row within a table. Additional technology may be applied to ensure a unique ID across the world, a globally unique identifier, when there are broader system requirements.

The primary keys within a database are used to define the relationships among the tables. When a PK migrates to another table, it becomes a foreign key in the other table. When each cell can contain only one value and the PK migrates into a regular entity table, this design pattern can represent either a one-to-one or one-to-many relationship. Most relational database designs resolve many-to-many relationships by creating an additional table that contains the PKs from both of the other entity tables—the relationship becomes an entity; the resolution table is then named appropriately and the two FKs are combined to form a PK. The migration of PKs to other tables is the second major reason why system-assigned integers are used normally as PKs; there is usually neither efficiency nor clarity in migrating a bunch of other types of columns.

Relationships

Relationships are a logical connection between different tables, established on the basis of interaction among these tables.

Transactions

In order for a database management system (DBMS) to operate efficiently and accurately, it must use ACID transactions.

Stored Procedures

Most of the programming within a RDBMS is accomplished using stored procedures (SPs). Often procedures can be used to greatly reduce the amount of information transferred within and outside of a system. For increased security, the system design may grant access to only the stored procedures and not directly to the tables. Fundamental stored procedures contain the logic needed to insert new and update existing data. More complex procedures may be written to implement additional rules and logic related to processing or selecting the data.

Relations or Tables

A *relation* is defined as a set of tuples that have the same attributes. A tuple usually represents an object and information about that object. Objects are typically physical objects or concepts. A relation is usually described as a table, which is organized into rows and columns. All the data referenced by an attribute are in the same domain and conform to the same constraints.

The relational model specifies that the tuples of a relation have no specific order and that the tuples, in turn, impose no order on the attributes. Applications access data by specifying queries, which use operations such as *select* to identify tuples, *project* to identify attributes, and *join* to combine relations. Relations can be modified using the *insert*, *delete*, and *update* operators. New tuples can supply explicit values or be derived from a query. Similarly, queries identify tuples for updating or deleting.

Tuples by definition are unique. If the tuple contains a candidate or primary key then obviously it is unique; however, a primary key need not be defined for a row or record to be a tuple. The definition of a tuple requires that it be unique, but does not require a primary key to be defined. Because a tuple is unique, its attributes by definition constitute a superkey.

Base and Derived Relations

In a relational database, all data are stored and accessed via relations. Relations that store data are called "base relations", and in implementations are called "tables". Other relations do not store data, but are computed by applying relational operations to other relations. These relations are sometimes called "derived relations". In implementations these are called "views" or "queries". Derived relations are convenient in that they act as a single relation, even though they may grab information from several relations. Also, derived relations can be used as an abstraction layer.

Domain

A domain describes the set of possible values for a given attribute, and can be considered a constraint on the value of the attribute. Mathematically, attaching a domain to an attribute means that any value for the attribute must be an element of the specified set. The character string *"ABC"*, for instance, is not in the integer domain, but the integer value *123* is. Another example of domain describes the possible values for the field "CoinFace" as ("Heads"",Tails"). So, the field "CoinFace" will not accept input values like (0,1) or (H,T).

Constraints

Constraints make it possible to further restrict the domain of an attribute. For instance, a constraint can restrict a given integer attribute to values between 1 and 10. Constraints provide one method of implementing business rules in the database and support subsequent data use within the application layer. SQL implements constraint functionality in the form of check constraints. Constraints restrict the data that can be stored in relations. These are usually defined using expressions that result in a boolean value, indicating whether or not the data satisfies the constraint. Constraints can apply to single attributes, to a tuple (restricting combinations of attributes) or to an entire relation. Since every attribute has an associated domain, there are constraints (domain constraints). The two principal rules for the relational model are known as entity integrity and referential integrity.

Referential integrity is based on the simple concept of relational vector based analytic algorithms, commonly employed in cloud platforms. This enables multiple interface processing within the referential database, with the additional feature of adding an additional security layer over the dynamically defined virtual environment.

Primary Key

Each relation/table has a primary key, this being a consequence of a relation being a set. A primary key uniquely specifies a tuple within a table. While natural attributes (attributes used to describe the data being entered) are sometimes good primary keys, surrogate keys are often used instead. A surrogate key is an artificial attribute assigned to an object which uniquely identifies it (for instance, in a table of information about students at a school they might all be assigned a student ID in order to differentiate them). The surrogate key has no intrinsic (inherent) meaning, but rather is useful through its ability to uniquely identify a tuple. Another common occurrence, especially in regard to N:M cardinality is the composite key. A composite key is a key made up of two or more attributes within a table that (together) uniquely identify a record.

Foreign Key

A foreign key is a field in a relational table that matches the primary key column of another table. It relates the two keys. Foreign keys need not have unique values in the referencing relation. A foreign key can be used to cross-reference tables, and it effectively uses the values of attributes in the referenced relation to restrict the domain of one or more attributes in the referencing relation. The concept is described formally as: "For all tuples in the referencing relation projected over the referencing attributes, there must exist a tuple in the referenced relation projected over those same attributes such that the values in each of the referencing attributes match the corresponding values in the referenced attributes".

Stored Procedures

A stored procedure is executable code that is associated with, and generally stored in, the database. Stored procedures usually collect and customize common operations, like inserting a tuple into a relation, gathering statistical information about usage patterns, or encapsulating complex business logic and calculations. Frequently they are used as an application programming interface (API) for security or simplicity. Implementations of stored procedures on SQL RDBMS's often allow developers to take advantage of procedural extensions (often vendor-specific) to the standard declarative SQL syntax. Stored procedures are not part of the relational database model, but all commercial implementations include them.

Index

An index is one way of providing quicker access to data. Indexes can be created on any combination of attributes on a relation. Queries that filter using those attributes can find matching tuples randomly using the index, without having to check each tuple in turn. This is analogous to using the index of a book to go directly to the page on which the information you are looking for is found, so that you do not have to read the entire book to find what you are looking for. Relational databases typically supply multiple indexing techniques, each of which is optimal for some combination of data distribution, relation size, and typical access pattern. Indices are usually implemented via B+ trees, R-trees, and bitmaps. Indices are usually not considered part of the database, as they are considered an implementation detail, though indices are usually maintained by the same group that maintains the other parts of the database. The use of efficient indexes on both primary and foreign keys can dramatically improve query performance. This is because B-tree indexes result in query times proportional to log(n) where n is the number of rows in a table and hash indexes result in constant time queries (no size dependency as long as the relevant part of the index fits into memory).

Relational Operations

Queries made against the relational database, and the derived relvars in the database are expressed in a relational calculus or a relational algebra. In his original relational algebra, Codd introduced eight relational operators in two groups of four operators each. The first four operators were based on the traditional mathematical set operations:

- The union operator combines the tuples of two relations and removes all duplicate tuples from the result. The relational union operator is equivalent to the SQL UNION operator.

- The intersection operator produces the set of tuples that two relations share in common. Intersection is implemented in SQL in the form of the INTERSECT operator.

- The difference operator acts on two relations and produces the set of tuples from the first relation that do not exist in the second relation. Difference is implemented in SQL in the form of the EXCEPT or MINUS operator.

- The cartesian product of two relations is a join that is not restricted by any criteria, resulting in every tuple of the first relation being matched with every tuple of the second relation. The cartesian product is implemented in SQL as the Cross join operator.

The remaining operators proposed by Codd involve special operations specific to relational databases:

- The selection, or restriction, operation retrieves tuples from a relation, limiting the results to only those that meet a specific criterion, i.e. a subset in terms of set theory. The SQL equivalent of selection is the SELECT query statement with a WHERE clause.

- The projection operation extracts only the specified attributes from a tuple or set of tuples.

- The join operation defined for relational databases is often referred to as a natural join. In this type of join, two relations are connected by their common attributes. MySQL's approximation of a natural join is the Inner join operator. In SQL, an INNER JOIN prevents a cartesian product from occurring when there are two tables in a query. For each table added to a SQL Query, one additional INNER JOIN is added to prevent a cartesian product. Thus, for N tables in an SQL query, there must be N−1 INNER JOINS to prevent a cartesian product.

- The relational division operation is a slightly more complex operation and essentially involves using the tuples of one relation (the dividend) to partition a second relation (the divisor). The relational division operator is effectively the opposite of the cartesian product operator (hence the name).

Other operators have been introduced or proposed since Codd's introduction of the original eight including relational comparison operators and extensions that offer support for nesting and hierarchical data, among others.

Normalization

Normalization was first proposed by Codd as an integral part of the relational model. It encompasses a set of procedures designed to eliminate non-simple domains (non-atomic values) and the redundancy (duplication) of data, which in turn prevents data manipulation anomalies and loss of data integrity. The most common forms of normalization applied to databases are called the normal forms.

RDBMS

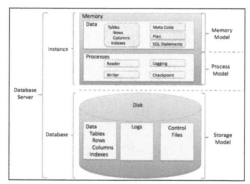

The general structure of a relational database.

Connolly and Begg define Database Management System (DBMS) as a "software system that enables users to define, create, maintain and control access to the database". RDBMS is an extension of that acronym that is sometimes used when the underlying database is relational.

An alternative definition for a *relational database management system* is a database management system (DBMS) based on the relational model. Most databases in widespread use today are based on this model.

RDBMSs have been a common option for the storage of information in databases used for financial records, manufacturing and logistical information, personnel data, and other applications since the 1980s. Relational databases have often replaced legacy hierarchical databases and network databases, because RDBMS were easier to implement and administer. Nonetheless, relational databases received continued, unsuccessful challenges by object database management systems in the 1980s and 1990s, (which were introduced in an attempt to address the so-called object-relational impedance mismatch between relational databases and object-oriented application programs), as well as by XML database management systems in the 1990s. However, due to the expanse of technologies, such as horizontal scaling of computer clusters, NoSQL databases have recently become popular as an alternative to RDBMS databases.

Distributed Relational Databases

Distributed Relational Database Architecture (DRDA) was designed by a workgroup within IBM in the period 1988 to 1994. DRDA enables network connected relational databases to cooperate to fulfill SQL requests. The messages, protocols, and structural components of DRDA are defined by the Distributed Data Management Architecture.

Relational Algebra

Relational algebra, first created by Edgar F. Codd while at IBM, is a family of algebras with a well-founded semantics used for modelling the data stored in relational databases, and defining queries on it.

The main application of relational algebra is providing a theoretical foundation for relational databases, particularly query languages for such databases, chief among which is SQL.

Relational algebra received little attention outside of pure mathematics until the publication of E.F. Codd's relational model of data in 1970. Codd proposed such an algebra as a basis for database query languages.

Five primitive operators of Codd's algebra are the *selection*, the *projection*, the *Cartesian product* (also called the *cross product* or *cross join*), the *set union*, and the *set difference*.

Set Operators

The relational algebra uses set union, set difference, and Cartesian product from set theory, but adds additional constraints to these operators.

For set union and set difference, the two relations involved must be *union-compatible*—that is, the two relations must have the same set of attributes. Because set intersection is defined in terms of set union and set difference, the two relations involved in set intersection must also be union-compatible.

For the Cartesian product to be defined, the two relations involved must have disjoint headers—that is, they must not have a common attribute name.

In addition, the Cartesian product is defined differently from the one in set theory in the sense that tuples are considered to be "shallow" for the purposes of the operation. That is, the Cartesian product of a set of n-tuples with a set of m-tuples yields a set of "flattened" $(n + m)$-tuples (whereas basic set theory would have prescribed a set of 2-tuples, each containing an n-tuple and an m-tuple). More formally, $R \times S$ is defined as follows:

$$R \times S := \{(r_1, r_2, \ldots, r_n, s_1, s_2, \ldots, s_m) \mid (r_1, r_2, \ldots, r_n) \in R, (s_1, s_2, \ldots, s_m) \in S\}$$

The cardinality of the Cartesian product is the product of the cardinalities of its factors, that is, $|R \times S| = |R| \times |S|$.

Projection (Π)

A projection is a unary operation written as $\varPi_{a_1, \ldots, a_n}(R)$ where $a_1, \ldots, a_n$ is a set of attribute names. The result of such projection is defined as the set that is obtained when all tuples in R are restricted to the set $\{a_1, \ldots, a_n\}$.

Note: when implemented in SQL standard the "default projection" returns a multiset instead of a set, and the Π projection to eliminate duplicate data is obtained by the addition of the DISTINCT keyword.

Selection (σ)

A generalized selection is a unary operation written as $\sigma_\varphi(R)$ where φ is a propositional formula that consists of atoms as allowed in the normal selection and the logical operators $\wedge$ (and), $\vee$ (or) and $\neg$ (negation). This selection selects all those tuples in R for which φ holds.

To obtain a listing of all friends or business associates in an address book, the selection might be written as: $\sigma_{isFriend\,=\,true \vee isBusinessContact\,=\,true}(addressBook)$. The result would be a relation containing every attribute of every unique record where isFriend is true or where isBusinessContact is true.

Rename (ρ)

A rename is a unary operation written as $\rho_{a/b}(R)$ where the result is identical to R except that the b attribute in all tuples is renamed to an a attribute. This is simply used to rename the attribute of a relation or the relation itself.

To rename the 'isFriend' attribute to 'isBusinessContact' in a relation, $\rho_{isBusinessContact\,/\,isFriend}$ (*addressBook*) might be used.

Joins and Join-like Operators

Natural Join (⋈)

Natural join (⋈) is a binary operator that is written as (R ⋈ S) where R and S are relations. The result of the natural join is the set of all combinations of tuples in R and S that are equal on their common attribute names. For an example consider the tables *Employee* and *Dept* and their natural join:

Employee		
Name	EmpId	DeptName
Harry	3415	Finance
Sally	2241	Sales
George	3401	Finance
Harriet	2202	Sales
Mary	1257	Human Resources

Dept	
DeptName	Manager
Finance	George
Sales	Harriet
Production	Charles

Employee ⋈ Dept			
Name	EmpId	DeptName	Manager
Harry	3415	Finance	George
Sally	2241	Sales	Harriet
George	3401	Finance	George
Harriet	2202	Sales	Harriet

Note that neither the employee named Mary nor the Production department appear in the result.

This can also be used to define composition of relations. For example, the composition of *Employee* and *Dept* is their join as shown above, projected on all but the common attribute *DeptName*. In category theory, the join is precisely the fiber product.

The natural join is arguably one of the most important operators since it is the relational counterpart of logical AND operator. Note that if the same variable appears in each of two predicates that are connected by AND, then that variable stands for the same thing and both appearances must always be substituted by the same value (this is a consequence of the idempotence of the logical AND). In particular, natural join allows the combination of relations that are associated by a foreign key. For example, in the above example a foreign key probably holds from *Employee.DeptName* to *Dept.DeptName* and then the natural join of *Employee* and *Dept* combines all employees with their departments. This works because the foreign key holds between attributes with the same name. If this is not the case such as in the foreign key from *Dept.Manager* to *Employee.Name* then we have to rename these columns before we take the natural join. Such a join is sometimes also referred to as an equijoin.

More formally the semantics of the natural join are defined as follows:

$$R \bowtie S = \{\, r \cup s \mid r \in R \wedge s \in S \wedge Fun(r \cup s) \,\}$$

where *Fun(t)* is a predicate that is true for a relation *t* (in the mathematical sense) iff *t* is a function. It is usually required that *R* and *S* must have at least one common attribute, but if this constraint is omitted, and *R* and *S* have no common attributes, then the natural join becomes exactly the Cartesian product.

The natural join can be simulated with Codd's primitives as follows. Assume that $c_1,...,c_m$ are the attribute names common to *R* and *S*, $r_1,...,r_n$ are the attribute names unique to *R* and $s_1,...,s_k$ are the attribute names unique to *S*.

Furthermore, assume that the attribute names $x_1,...,x_m$ are neither in *R* nor in *S*. In a first step we can now rename the common attribute names in *S*:

$$T = \rho_{x_1/c_1,...,x_m/c_m}(S) = \rho_{x_1/c_1}(\rho_{x_2/c_2}(...\rho_{x_m/c_m}(S)...))$$

Then we take the Cartesian product and select the tuples that are to be joined:

$$P = \sigma_{c_1=x_1,...,c_m=x_m}(R \times T) = \sigma_{c_1=x_1}(\sigma_{c_2=x_2}(...\sigma_{c_m=x_m}(R \times T)...))$$

Finally we take a projection to get rid of the renamed attributes:

$$U = \pi_{r_1,...,r_n,c_1,...,c_m,s_1,...,s_k}(P)$$

θ-join and Equijoin

Consider tables *Car* and *Boat* which list models of cars and boats and their respective prices. Suppose a customer wants to buy a car and a boat, but she does not want to spend more money for the boat than for the car. The θ-join ($\bowtie_\theta$) on the predicate *CarPrice ≥ BoatPrice* produces the flattened pairs of rows which satisfy the predicate. When using a condition where the attributes are equal, for example Price, then the condition may be specified as *Price=Price* or alternatively (*Price*) itself.

Car	
CarModel	CarPrice
CarA	20,000
CarB	30,000
CarC	50,000

Boat	
BoatModel	BoatPrice
Boat1	10,000
Boat2	40,000
Boat3	60,000

Car ⋈ *Boat*			
CarPrice ≥ BoatPrice			
CarModel	CarPrice	BoatModel	BoatPrice
CarA	20,000	Boat1	10,000
CarB	30,000	Boat1	10,000
CarC	50,000	Boat1	10,000
CarC	50,000	Boat2	40,000

If we want to combine tuples from two relations where the combination condition is not simply the equality of shared attributes then it is convenient to have a more general form of join operator, which is the θ-join (or theta-join). The θ-join is a binary operator that is written as $\underset{a \theta b}{R \bowtie S}$ or $\underset{a \theta v}{R \bowtie S}$ where a and b are attribute names, θ is a binary relational operator in the set $\{<, \leq, =, \neq, >, \geq\}$, v is a value constant, and R and S are relations. The result of this operation consists of all combinations of tuples in R and S that satisfy θ. The result of the θ-join is defined only if the headers of S and R are disjoint, that is, do not contain a common attribute.

The simulation of this operation in the fundamental operations is therefore as follows:

$$R \bowtie_\theta S = \sigma_\theta(R \times S)$$

In case the operator θ is the equality operator (=) then this join is also called an equijoin.

Note, however, that a computer language that supports the natural join and selection operators does not need θ-join as well, as this can be achieved by selection from the result of a natural join (which degenerates to Cartesian product when there are no shared attributes).

In SQL implementations, joining on a predicate is usually called an *inner join*, and the *on* keyword allows one to specify the predicate used to filter the rows. It is important to note: forming the flattened Cartesian product then filtering the rows is conceptually correct, but an implementation would use more sophisticated data structures to speed up the join query.

Semijoin ($\ltimes$)($\rtimes$)

The left semijoin is a joining similar to the natural join and written as $R \ltimes S$ where R and S are relations. The result is the set of all tuples in R for which there is a tuple in S that is equal on their common attribute names. The difference from a natural join is that other columns of S do not appear. For example, consider the tables *Employee* and *Dept* and their semijoin:

Employee		
Name	EmpId	DeptName
Harry	3415	Finance
Sally	2241	Sales
George	3401	Finance
Harriet	2202	Production

Dept	
DeptName	Manager
Sales	Sally
Production	Harriet

Employee $\ltimes$ Dept		
Name	EmpId	DeptName
Sally	2241	Sales
Harriet	2202	Production

More formally the semantics of the semijoin can be defined as follows:

$$R \ltimes S = \{\, t\colon t \in R \wedge \exists s \in S(Fun\,(t \cup s))\,\}$$

where $Fun(r)$ is as in the definition of natural join.

The semijoin can be simulated using the natural join as follows. If $a_1, ..., a_n$ are the attribute names of R, then:

$$R \ltimes S = \pi_{a1,...,an}(R \bowtie S).$$

Since we can simulate the natural join with the basic operators it follows that this also holds for the semijoin.

In Codd's 1970 paper, semijoin is called restriction.

Antijoin (▷)

The antijoin, written as $R \triangleright S$ where R and S are relations, is similar to the semijoin, but the result of an antijoin is only those tuples in R for which there is *no* tuple in S that is equal on their common attribute names.

For an example consider the tables *Employee* and *Dept* and their antijoin:

Employee		
Name	EmpId	DeptName
Harry	3415	Finance
Sally	2241	Sales
George	3401	Finance
Harriet	2202	Production

Dept	
DeptName	Manager
Sales	Sally
Production	Harriet

Employee ▷ Dept		
Name	EmpId	DeptName
Harry	3415	Finance
George	3401	Finance

The antijoin is formally defined as follows:

$$R \triangleright S = \{\, t: t \in R \land \neg \exists s \in S(Fun\,(t \cup s))\,\},$$

or,

$$R \triangleright S = \{\, t: t \in R, \text{ there is no tuple } s \text{ of } S \text{ that satisfies } Fun\,(t \cup s)\,\},$$

where *Fun* $(t \cup s)$ is as in the definition of natural join.

The antijoin can also be defined as the complement of the semijoin, as follows:

$$R \triangleright S = R - R \propto S$$

Given this, the antijoin is sometimes called the anti-semijoin, and the antijoin operator is sometimes written as semijoin symbol with a bar above it, instead of $\triangleright$.

Division (÷)

The division is a binary operation that is written as $R \div S$. Division is not implemented directly in SQL. The result consists of the restrictions of tuples in R to the attribute names unique to R, i.e., in the header of R but not in the header of S, for which it holds that all their combinations with tuples in S are present in R.

Completed	
Student	Task
Fred	Database1
Fred	Database2
Fred	Compiler1
Eugene	Database1
Eugene	Compiler1
Sarah	Database1
Sarah	Database2

DBProject
Task
Database1
Database2

Completed ÷ DBProject
Student
Fred
Sarah

If *DBProject* contains all the tasks of the Database project, then the result of the division above contains exactly the students who have completed both of the tasks in the Database project. More formally the semantics of the division is defined as follows:

$$R \div S = \left\{ t[a_1,...,a_n] : t \in R \land \forall s \in S \left((t[a_1,...,a_n] \cup s) \in R \right) \right\}$$

where $\{a_1,...,a_n\}$ is the set of attribute names unique to R and $t[a_1,...,a_n]$ is the restriction of t to this set. It is usually required that the attribute names in the header of S are a subset of those of R because otherwise the result of the operation will always be empty.

The simulation of the division with the basic operations is as follows. We assume that $a_1,...,a_n$ are the attribute names unique to R and $b_1,...,b_m$ are the attribute names of S. In the first step we project R on its unique attribute names and construct all combinations with tuples in S:

$$T := \pi_{a_1,...,a_n}(R) \times S$$

In the prior example, T would represent a table such that every Student (because Student is the unique key / attribute of the Completed table) is combined with every given

Task. So Eugene, for instance, would have two rows, Eugene → Database1 and Eugene → Database2 in T.

EG: First, let's pretend that "Completed" has a third attribute called "grade". It's unwanted baggage here, so we must project it off always. In fact in this step we can drop 'Task' from R as well; the multiply puts it back on.

$T := \pi_{\text{Student}}(R) \times S$ // This gives us every possible desired combination, including those that don't actually exist in R, and excluding others (eg Fred | compiler1, which is not a desired combination).

T	
Student	Task
Fred	Database1
Fred	Database2
Eugene	Database1
Eugene	Database2
Sarah	Database1
Sarah	Database2

In the next step we subtract R from T.

relation:

$U := T - R$

In U we have the possible combinations that "could have" been in R, but weren't.

EG: Again with projections — T and R need to have identical attribute names/headers.

$U := T - \pi_{\text{Student,Task}}(R)$ // This gives us a "what's missing" list.

T	
Student	Task
Fred	Database1
Fred	Database2
Eugene	Database1
Eugene	Database2
Sarah	Database1
Sarah	Database2

R a.k.a. Completed	
Student	Task
Fred	Database1
Fred	Database2

Fred	Compiler1
Eugene	Database1
Eugene	Compiler1
Sarah	Database1
Sarah	Database2

U aka T − R aka whats missing	
Student	Task
Eugene	Database2

So if we now take the projection on the attribute names unique to R, then we have the restrictions of the tuples in R for which not all combinations with tuples in S were present in R:

$$V := \pi_{a_1,...,a_n}(U),$$

EG: Project U down to just the attributes in question (Student),

$$V := \pi_{Student}(U),$$

V
Student
Eugene

So what remains to be done is take the projection of R on its unique attribute names and subtract those in V:

$$W := \pi_{a_1,...,a_n}(R) - V,$$

EG: $W := \pi_{Student}(R) - V.$

$\pi_{Student}(R)$
Student
Fred
Eugene
Sarah

V
Student
Eugene

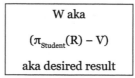

W aka
$(\pi_{Student}(R) - V)$
aka desired result

Student
Fred
Sarah

Common Extensions

In practice the classical relational algebra is extended with various operations such as outer joins, aggregate functions and even transitive closure.

Outer Joins

Whereas the result of a join (or inner join) consists of tuples formed by combining matching tuples in the two operands, an outer join contains those tuples and additionally some tuples formed by extending an unmatched tuple in one of the operands by "fill" values for each of the attributes of the other operand.

The operators defined assume the existence of a *null* value, ω, which we do not define, to be used for the fill values; in practice this corresponds to the NULL in SQL. In order to make subsequent selection operations on the resulting table meaningful, a semantic meaning needs to be assigned to nulls; in Codd's approach the propositional logic used by the selection is extended to a three-valued logic.

Three outer join operators are defined: left outer join, right outer join, and full outer join. (The word "outer" is sometimes omitted.)

Left Outer Join (⋈)

The left outer join is written as $R \bowtie S$ where R and S are relations. The result of the left outer join is the set of all combinations of tuples in R and S that are equal on their common attribute names, in addition (loosely speaking) to tuples in R that have no matching tuples in S.

For an example consider the tables *Employee* and *Dept* and their left outer join:

Employee		
Name	EmpId	DeptName
Harry	3415	Finance
Sally	2241	Sales
George	3401	Finance
Harriet	2202	Sales
Tim	1123	Executive

Dept	
DeptName	Manager

Sales	Harriet
Production	Charles

Employee ⋈ Dept			
Name	EmpId	DeptName	Manager
Harry	3415	Finance	ω
Sally	2241	Sales	Harriet
George	3401	Finance	ω
Harriet	2202	Sales	Harriet
Tim	1123	Executive	ω

In the resulting relation, tuples in S which have no common values in common attribute names with tuples in R take a *null* value, ω.

Since there are no tuples in *Dept* with a *DeptName* of *Finance* or *Executive*, ωs occur in the resulting relation where tuples in *Employee* have a *DeptName* of *Finance* or *Executive*.

Let r_1, r_2,..., r_n be the attributes of the relation R and let $\{(\omega,..., \omega)\}$ be the singleton relation on the attributes that are *unique* to the relation S (those that are not attributes of R). Then the left outer join can be described in terms of the natural join (and hence using basic operators) as follows:

$$(R \bowtie S) \cup ((R - \pi_{r_1,r_2,...,r_n}(R \bowtie S)) \times \{(\omega,...\omega)\})$$

Right Outer Join (⋈)

The right outer join behaves almost identically to the left outer join, but the roles of the tables are switched.

The right outer join of relations R and S is written as $R \bowtie S$. The result of the right outer join is the set of all combinations of tuples in R and S that are equal on their common attribute names, in addition to tuples in S that have no matching tuples in R.

For example, consider the tables *Employee* and *Dept* and their right outer join:

Employee		
Name	EmpId	DeptName
Harry	3415	Finance
Sally	2241	Sales
George	3401	Finance
Harriet	2202	Sales
Tim	1123	Executie

Dept	
DeptName	Manager
Sales	Harriet
Production	Charles

Employee ⋈ Dept			
Name	EmpId	DeptName	Manager
Sally	2241	Sales	Harriet
Harriet	2202	Sales	Harriet
ω	ω	Production	Charles

In the resulting relation, tuples in R which have no common values in common attribute names with tuples in S take a *null* value, ω.

Since there are no tuples in *Employee* with a *DeptName* of *Production*, ωs occur in the Name and EmpId attributes of the resulting relation where tuples in *Dept* had *DeptName* of *Production*.

Let s_1, s_2,..., s_n be the attributes of the relation S and let $\{(\omega, ...,\omega)\}$ be the singleton relation on the attributes that are *unique* to the relation R (those that are not attributes of S). Then, as with the left outer join, the right outer join can be simulated using the natural join as follows:

$$(R \bowtie S)\cup(\{(\omega,...,\omega)\}\times(S - \pi_{s_1,s_2,...,s_n} (R \bowtie S)))$$

Full Outer Join (⋈)

⋈ The outer join or full outer join in effect combines the results of the left and right outer joins.

The full outer join is written as $R \bowtie S$ where R and S are relations. The result of the full outer join is the set of all combinations of tuples in R and S that are equal on their common attribute names, in addition to tuples in S that have no matching tuples in R and tuples in R that have no matching tuples in S in their common attribute names.

For an example considers the tables *Employee* and *Dept* and their full outer join:

Employee		
Name	EmpId	DeptName
Harry	3415	Finance
Sally	2241	Sales
George	3401	Finance
Harriet	2202	Sales
Tim	1123	Executive

Dept	
DeptName	Manager
Sales	Harriet
Production	Charles

Employee ⋈ Dept			
Name	EmpId	DeptName	Manager
Harry	3415	Finance	ω
Sally	2241	Sales	Harriet
George	3401	Finance	ω
Harriet	2202	Sales	Harriet
Tim	1123	Executive	ω
ω	ω	Production	Charles

In the resulting relation, tuples in R which have no common values in common attribute names with tuples in S take a *null* value, ω. Tuples in S which have no common values in common attribute names with tuples in R also take a *null* value, ω.

The full outer join can be simulated using the left and right outer joins (and hence the natural join and set union) as follows:

$$R \bowtie S = (R \bowtie S) \cup (R \bowtie S)$$

Operations for Domain Computations

There is nothing in relational algebra introduced so far that would allow computations on the data domains (other than evaluation of propositional expressions involving equality). For example, it is not possible using only the algebra introduced so far to write an expression that would multiply the numbers from two columns, e.g. a unit price with a quantity to obtain a total price. Practical query languages have such facilities, e.g. the SQL SELECT allows arithmetic operations to define new columns in the result SELECT unit_price * quantity AS total_price FROM t, and a similar facility is provided more explicitly by Tutorial D's EXTEND keyword. In database theory, this is called extended projection.

Aggregation

Furthermore, computing various functions on a column, like the summing up of its elements, is also not possible using the relational algebra introduced so far. There are five aggregate functions that are included with most relational database systems. These operations are Sum, Count, Average, Maximum and Minimum. In relational algebra the aggregation operation over a schema $(A_1, A_2, ... A_n)$ is written as follows:

$$G_1, G_2, ..., G_m \, g_{f_1(A_1'), f_2(A_2'), ..., f_k(A_k')} \, (r)$$

where each A_j', $1 \le j \le k$, is one of the original attributes A_i, $1 \le i \le n$.

The attributes preceding the g are grouping attributes, which function like a "group by" clause in SQL. Then there are an arbitrary number of aggregation functions applied to individual attributes. The operation is applied to an arbitrary relation r. The grouping attributes are optional, and if they are not supplied, the aggregation functions are applied across the entire relation to which the operation is applied.

We have a table named Account with three columns, namely Account_Number, Branch_Name and Balance. We wish to find the maximum balance of each branch. This is accomplished by $_{\text{Branch\_Name}}G_{\text{Max(Balance)}}(\text{Account})$. To find the highest balance of all accounts regardless of branch, we could simply write $G_{\text{Max(Balance)}}(\text{Account})$.

Transitive Closure

Although relational algebra seems powerful enough for most practical purposes, there are some simple and natural operators on relations that cannot be expressed by relational algebra. One of them is the transitive closure of a binary relation. Given a domain D, let binary relation R be a subset of $D \times D$. The transitive closure R^+ of R is the smallest subset of $D \times D$ that contains R and satisfies the following condition:

$$\forall x \forall y \forall z \big((x,y) \in R^+ \wedge (y,z) \in R^+ \Rightarrow (x,z) \in R^+\big)$$

There is no relational algebra expression $E(R)$ taking R as a variable argument that produces R^+. This can be proved using the fact that, given a relational expression E for which it is claimed that $E(R) = R^+$, where R is a variable, we can always find an instance r of R (and a corresponding domain d) such that $E(r) \ne r^+$.

SQL however officially supports such fixpoint queries since 1999, and it had vendor-specific extensions in this direction well before that.

Use of Algebraic Properties for Query Optimization

Queries can be represented as a tree, where:

- The internal nodes are operators.

- Leaves are relations.

- Subtrees are subexpressions.

Our primary goal is to transform expression trees into equivalent expression trees, where the average size of the relations yielded by subexpressions in the tree is smaller than it was before the optimization. Our secondary goal is to try to form common subexpressions within a single query, or if there is more than one query being evaluated at the same time, in all of those queries. The rationale behind the second goal is that it is enough to compute common subexpressions once, and the results can be used in all queries that contain that subexpression.

Selection

Rules about selection operators play the most important role in query optimization. Selection is an operator that very effectively decreases the number of rows in its operand, so if we manage to move the selections in an expression tree towards the leaves, the internal relations (yielded by subexpressions) will likely shrink.

Basic Selection Properties

Selection is idempotent (multiple applications of the same selection have no additional effect beyond the first one), and commutative (the order selections are applied in has no effect on the eventual result).

- $\sigma_A(R) = \sigma_A\sigma_A(R)$
- $\sigma_A\sigma_B(R) = \sigma_B\sigma_A(R)$

Breaking up Selections with Complex Conditions

A selection whose condition is a conjunction of simpler conditions is equivalent to a sequence of selections with those same individual conditions, and selection whose condition is a disjunction is equivalent to a union of selections. These identities can be used to merge selections so that fewer selections need to be evaluated, or to split them so that the component selections may be moved or optimized separately.

- $\sigma_{A \wedge B}(R) = \sigma_A(\sigma_B(R)) = \sigma_B(\sigma_A(R))$
- $\sigma_{A \vee B}(R) = \sigma_A(R) \cup \sigma_B(R)$

Selection and Cross Product

Cross product is the costliest operator to evaluate. If the input relations have N and M rows, the result will contain NM rows. Therefore, it is very important to do our best to decrease the size of both operands before applying the cross product operator.

This can be effectively done if the cross product is followed by a selection operator, e.g. $\sigma_A(R \times P)$. Considering the definition of join, this is the most likely case. If the cross product is not followed by a selection operator, we can try to push down a selection from higher levels of the expression tree using the other selection rules.

In the above case we break up condition A into conditions B, C and D using the split rules about complex selection conditions, so that $A = B \wedge C \wedge D$ and B contains attributes only from R, C contains attributes only from P, and D contains the part of A that contains attributes from both R and P. Note, that B, C or D are possibly empty. Then the following holds:

$$\sigma_A(R \times P) = \sigma_{B \wedge C \wedge D}(R \times P) = \sigma_D(\sigma_B(R) \times \sigma_C(P))$$

Selection and Set Operators

Selection is distributive over the set difference, intersection, and union operators. The following three rules are used to push selection below set operations in the expression tree. For the set difference and the intersection operators, it is possible to apply the selection operator to just one of the operands following the transformation. This can be beneficial where one of the operands is small, and the overhead of evaluating the selection operator outweighs the benefits of using a smaller relation as an operand.

- $\sigma_A(R \setminus P) = \sigma_A(R) \setminus \sigma_A(P) = \sigma_A(R) \setminus P$
- $\sigma_A(R \cup P) = \sigma_A(R) \cup \sigma_A(P)$
- $\sigma_A(R \cap P) = \sigma_A(R) \cap \sigma_A(P) = \sigma_A(R) \cap P = R \cap \sigma_A(P)$

Selection and Projection

Selection commutes with projection if and only if the fields referenced in the selection condition are a subset of the fields in the projection. Performing selection before projection may be useful if the operand is a cross product or join. In other cases, if the selection condition is relatively expensive to compute, moving selection outside the projection may reduce the number of tuples which must be tested (since projection may produce fewer tuples due to the elimination of duplicates resulting from omitted fields).

$$\pi_{a_1,\ldots,a_n}(\sigma_A(R)) = \sigma_A(\pi_{a_1,\ldots,a_n}(R)) \text{ where fields in } A \subseteq \{a_1,\ldots,a_n\}$$

Projection

Basic Projection Properties

Projection is idempotent, so that a series of (valid) projections is equivalent to the outermost projection.

$$\pi_{a_1,\ldots,a_n}(\pi_{b_1,\ldots,b_m}(R)) = \pi_{a_1,\ldots,a_n}(R) \text{ where } \{a_1,\ldots,a_n\} \subseteq \{b_1,\ldots,b_m\}$$

Projection and Set Operators

Projection is distributive over set union.

$$\pi_{a_1,\ldots,a_n}(R \cup P) = \pi_{a_1,\ldots,a_n}(R) \cup \pi_{a_1,\ldots,a_n}(P).$$

Projection does not distribute over intersection and set difference. Counterexamples are given by:

$$\pi_A(\{\langle A=a,B=b\rangle\}\cap\{\langle A=a,B=b'\rangle\})=\varnothing$$
$$\pi_A(\{\langle A=a,B=b\rangle\})\cap\pi_A(\{\langle A=a,B=b'\rangle\})=\{\langle A=a\rangle\}$$

and,

$$\pi_A(\{\langle A=a,B=b\rangle\}\setminus\{\langle A=a,B=b'\rangle\})=\{\langle A=a\rangle\}$$
$$\pi_A(\{\langle A=a,B=b\rangle\})\setminus\pi_A(\{\langle A=a,B=b'\rangle\})=\varnothing,$$

where b is assumed to be distinct from b'.

Rename

Basic Rename Properties

Successive renames of a variable can be collapsed into a single rename. Rename operations which have no variables in common can be arbitrarily reordered with respect to one another, which can be exploited to make successive renames adjacent so that they can be collapsed.

- $\rho_{a/b}(\rho_{b/c}(R))=\rho_{a/c}(R)$
- $\rho_{a/b}(\rho_{c/d}(R))=\rho_{c/d}(\rho_{a/b}(R))$

Rename and Set Operators

Rename is distributive over set difference, union and intersection.

- $\rho_{a/b}(R\setminus P)=\rho_{a/b}(R)\setminus\rho_{a/b}(P)$
- $\rho_{a/b}(R\cup P)=\rho_{a/b}(R)\cup\rho_{a/b}(P)$
- $\rho_{a/b}(R\cap P)=\rho_{a/b}(R)\cap\rho_{a/b}(P)$

Product and Union

Cartesian product is distributive over union.

- $(A\times B)\cup(A\times C)=A\times(B\cup C)$

Implementations

The first query language to be based on Codd's algebra was Alpha, developed by Dr. Codd himself. Subsequently, ISBL was created, and this pioneering work has been acclaimed by many authorities as having shown the way to make Codd's idea into a useful language. Business System 12 was a short-lived industry-strength relational DBMS that followed the ISBL example.

In 1998 Chris Date and Hugh Darwen proposed a language called Tutorial D intended for use in teaching relational database theory, and its query language also draws on ISBL's ideas. Rel is an implementation of Tutorial D.

Even the query language of SQL is loosely based on a relational algebra, though the operands in SQL (tables) are not exactly relations and several useful theorems about the relational algebra do not hold in the SQL counterpart (arguably to the detriment of optimisers and/or users). The SQL table model is a bag (multiset), rather than a set. For example, the expression $(R \cup S) \setminus T = (R \setminus T) \cup (S \setminus T)$ is a theorem for relational algebra on sets, but not for relational algebra on bags.

Relational Calculus

The Relational calculus consists of two calculi, the tuple relational calculus and the domain relational calculus, that are part of the relational model for databases and provide a declarative way to specify database queries.

The relational calculus is similar to the relational algebra, which is also part of the relational model: While the relational calculus is meant as a declarative language which prescribes no execution order on the subexpressions of a relational calculus expression, the relational algebra is meant as an imperative language: the sub-expressions of a relational algebraic expressions are meant to be executed from left-to-right and inside-out following their nesting.

A relational algebra expression might prescribe the following steps to retrieve the phone numbers and names of book stores that supply *Some Sample Book*:

- Join book stores and titles over the BookstoreID.
- Restrict the result of that join to tuples for the book *Some Sample Book*.
- Project the result of that restriction over StoreName and StorePhone.

A relational calculus expression would formulate this query in the following descriptive or declarative manner:

Get StoreName and StorePhone for book stores such that there exists a title BK with the same BookstoreID value and with a BookTitle value of *Some Sample Book*.

The relational algebra and the relational calculus are logically equivalent: for any algebraic expression, there is an equivalent expression in the calculus, and vice versa. This result is known as Codd's theorem.

The raison d'être of the relational calculus is the formalization of query optimization. Query optimization consists in determining from a query the most efficient manner (or manners) to execute it. Query optimization can be formalized as translating a relational calculus expression delivering an answer A into efficient relational algebraic expressions delivering the same answer A.

Relational Data Stream Management System

A relational data stream management system (RDSMS) is a distributed, in-memory data stream management system (DSMS) that is designed to use standards-compliant SQL queries to process unstructured and structured data streams in real-time. Unlike SQL queries executed in a traditional RDBMS, which return a result and exit, SQL queries executed in a RDSMS do not exit, generating results continuously as new data become available. Continuous SQL queries in a RDSMS use the SQL Window function to analyze, join and aggregate data streams over fixed or sliding windows. Windows can be specified as time-based or row-based.

RDSMS SQL Query Examples

Continuous SQL queries in a RDSMS conform to the ANSI SQL standards. The most common RDSMS SQL query is performed with the declarative SELECT statement. A continuous SQL SELECT operates on data across one or more data streams, with optional keywords and clauses that include FROM with an optional JOIN subclause to specify the rules for joining multiple data streams, the WHERE clause and comparison predicate to restrict the records returned by the query, GROUP BY to project streams with common values into a smaller set, HAVING to filter records resulting from a GROUP BY, and ORDER BY to sort the results.

The following is an example of a continuous data stream aggregation using a SELECT query that aggregates a sensor stream from a weather monitoring station. The SELECT query aggregates the minimum, maximum and average temperature values over a one-second time period, returning a continuous stream of aggregated results at one second intervals.

```
SELECT STREAM

    FLOOR(WEATHERSTREAM.ROWTIME to SECOND) AS FLOOR_SECOND,

    MIN(TEMP) AS MIN_TEMP,

    MAX(TEMP) AS MAX_TEMP,

    AVG(TEMP) AS AVG_TEMP
```

```
FROM WEATHERSTREAM

GROUP BY FLOOR(WEATHERSTREAM.ROWTIME TO SECOND);
```

RDSMS SQL queries also operate on data streams over time or row-based windows. The following example shows a second continuous SQL query using the WINDOW clause with a one-second duration. The WINDOW clause changes the behavior of the query, to output a result for each new record as it arrives. Hence the output is a stream of incrementally updated results with zero result latency.

```
SELECT STREAM

    ROWTIME,

    MIN(TEMP) OVER W1 AS WMIN_TEMP,

    MAX(TEMP) OVER W1 AS WMAX_TEMP,

    AVG(TEMP) OVER W1 AS WAVG_TEMP

FROM WEATHERSTREAM

WINDOW W1 AS (RANGE INTERVAL '1' SECOND PRECEDING);
```

Candidate Key

In the relational model of databases, a candidate key of a relation is a minimal superkey for that relation; that is, a set of attributes such that:

- The relation does not have two distinct tuples (i.e. rows or records in common database language) with the same values for these attributes (which means that the set of attributes is a superkey).

- There is no proper subset of these attributes for which (1) holds (which means that the set is minimal).

Candidate keys are also variously referred to as primary keys, secondary keys or alternate keys.

The constituent attributes are called prime attributes. Conversely, an attribute that does not occur in ANY candidate key is called a non-prime attribute.

Since a relation contains no duplicate tuples, the set of all its attributes is a superkey if NULL values are not used. It follows that every relation will have at least one candidate key.

The candidate keys of a relation tell us all the possible ways we can identify its tuples. As such they are an important concept for the design of database schema.

Example:

The definition of candidate keys can be illustrated with the following (abstract) example. Consider a relation variable (relvar) R with attributes (A, B, C, D) that has only the following two legal values $r1$ and $r2$:

r1			
A	B	C	D
a1	b1	c1	d1
a1	b2	c2	d1
a2	b1	c2	d1

r2			
A	B	C	D
a1	b1	c1	d1
a1	b2	c2	d1
a1	b1	c2	d2

Here $r2$ differs from $r1$ only in the A and D values of the last tuple.

For $r1$ the following sets have the uniqueness property, i.e., there are no two distinct tuples in the instance with the same attribute values in the set:

$$\{A,B\}, \{A,C\}, \{B,C\}, \{A,B,C\}, \{A,B,D\}, \{A,C,D\}, \{B,C,D\}, \{A,B,C,D\}$$

For $r2$ the uniqueness property holds for the following sets;

$$\{B,C\}, \{B,D\}, \{C,D\}, \{A,B,C\}, \{A,B,D\}, \{A,C,D\}, \{B,C,D\}, \{A,B,C,D\}$$

Since superkeys of a relvar are those sets of attributes that have the uniqueness property for *all* legal values of that relvar and because we assume that $r1$ and $r2$ are all the legal values that R can take, we can determine the set of superkeys of R by taking the intersection of the two lists:

$$\{B,C\}, \{A,B,C\}, \{A,B,D\}, \{A,C,D\}, \{B,C,D\}, \{A,B,C,D\}$$

Finally we need to select those sets for which there are no proper subset in the list, which are in this case:

$$\{B,C\}, \{A,B,D\}, \{A,C,D\}$$

These are indeed the candidate keys of relvar R.

We have to consider *all* the relations that might be assigned to a relvar to determine whether a certain set of attributes is a candidate key. For example, if we had considered only *r1* then we would have concluded that {A, B} is a candidate key, which is incorrect. However, we *might* be able to conclude from such a relation that a certain set is *not* a candidate key, because that set does not have the uniqueness property (example {A, D} for *r1*). Note that the existence of a proper subset of a set that has the uniqueness property *cannot* in general be used as evidence that the superset is not a candidate key. In particular, note that in the case of an empty relation, every subset of the heading has the uniqueness property, including the empty set.

Determining Candidate Keys

The set of all candidate keys can be computed e.g. from the set of functional dependencies. To this end we need to define the attribute closure $\alpha+$ for an attribute set α. The set α^+ contains all attributes that are functionally implied by α.

It is quite simple to find a single candidate key. We start with a set α of attributes and try to remove successively each attribute. If after removing an attribute the attribute closure stays the same, then this attribute is not necessary and we can remove it permanently. We call the result $minimize(\alpha)$. If α is the set of all attributes, then $minimize(\alpha)$ is a candidate key.

Actually we can detect every candidate key with this procedure by simply trying every possible order of removing attributes. However there are many more permutations of attributes $(n!)$ than subsets (2^n) That is, many attribute orders will lead to the same candidate key.

There is a fundamental difficulty for efficient algorithms for candidate key computation: Certain sets of functional dependencies lead to exponentially many candidate keys. Consider the $2 \cdot n$ functional dependencies $\{A_i \to B_i : i \in \{1,...,n\}\} \cup \{B_i \to A_i : i \in \{1,...,n\}\}$ which yields 2^n candidate keys: $\{A_1, B_1\} \times ... \times \{A_n, B_n\}..$ That is, the best we can expect is an algorithm that is efficient with respect to the number of candidate keys.

The following algorithm actually runs in polynomial time in the number of candidate keys and functional dependencies:

```
function find_candidate_keys(A, F)

    /* A is the set of all attributes and F is the set of functional
dependencies */

    K[0] := minimize(A);

    n := 1; /* Number of Keys known so far */

    i := 0; /* Currently processed key */

    while i < n do
```

```
foreach α → β ∈ F do

    /* Build a new potential key from the previous known key and the
current FD */

    S:= α ∪ (K[i] - β);

    /* Search whether the new potential key is part of the already
known keys */

    found:= false;

    for j:= 0 to n-1 do

        if K[j] ⊆ S then found:= true;

    /* If not, add if

    if not found then

        K[n]:= minimize(S);

        n:= n + 1;

    i:= i + 1

return K
```

The idea behind the algorithm is that given a candidate key K_i and a functional dependency $\alpha \to \beta$, the reverse application of the functional dependency yields the set $\alpha \cup (K_i \setminus \beta)$, which is a key, too. It may however be covered by other already known candidate keys. (The algorithm checks this case using the 'found' variable.) If not, then minimizing the new key yields a new candidate key. The key insight is that all candidate keys can be created this way.

References

- Dennis Elliott Shasha; Philippe Bonnet (2003). Database Tuning: Principles, Experiments, and Troubleshooting Techniques. Morgan Kaufmann. p. 124. ISBN 978-1-55860-753-8

- Relational-data-model-dbms: guru99.com, Retrieved 14 July, 2020

- T. A. Halpin; Antony J. Morgan (2008). Information Modeling and Relational Databases. Morgan Kaufmann. pp. 772–. ISBN 978-0-12-373568-3. Retrieved 28 November 2012

- Relational-database, glossary: sisense.com, Retrieved 12 May, 2020

- Hector Garcia-Molina; Jeffrey D. Ullman; Jennifer Widom (2009). Database systems: the complete book (2nd ed.). Pearson Prentice Hall. ISBN 978-0-13-187325-4

- Beeri, C.; Dowd, M.; Fagin, R.; Statman, R. (1984). "On the Structure of Armstrong Relations for Functional Dependencies" (PDF). Journal of the ACM. 31: 30–46. CiteSeerX 10.1.1.68.9320. doi:10.1145/2422.322414

PERMISSIONS

INDEX